STARTUP WEALTH

HOW THE BEST ANGEL INVESTORS MAKE MONEY IN STARTUPS

JOSH MAHER

Booktrope Editions
Seattle, WA 2015

Cover Design by Greg Simanson
Edited by Elizabeth Flynn

PRINT ISBN 978-1-5137-0332-9
EPUB ISBN 978-1-5137-0383-1
Library of Congress Control Number: 2015915468

SPECIAL THANKS

Special thanks to all of the angel investors who accepted my outreach. You have all provided an incredible learning experience for me as an individual and I hope that your insights can inspire and educate thousands of angel investors all over the world. My interviews with angel investors are ongoing. All interviews are either here in this book or are being released online. If you see a name in the list and the interview isn't available online, feel free to reach out. If you want to be interviewed or want to recommend someone to be interviewed, I'd love to hear from you.

In no particular order: Jeffrey Carter, Greg Neufeld, Jon Staenberg, Dan Rosen, Bril Flint, David Bangs, Boris Wertz, Howard Lindzon, Gary Ritner, Mike Crill, Rui Ma, Warren Katz, Semyon Dukach, Chris DeVore, Bart Lorang, John Ives, David Tisch, Andy Liu, Michael Dornbrook, David Cohen, Joanne Wilson, Chris Sheehan, Lars Johansson, Christopher Porter, Bill Warner, Will Herman, Jim Deters, Peter Weiss, Chuck Porter, Nicholas Wyman, Christopher Mirabile, Rudy Gadre, Brad Feld, Michael Eckert, Jim Connor, David Verrill, Geoff Entress, Bob Bozeman, Michael Greeley, Manny Fernandez, Kirk Coburn, Dave McClure, Charlie O'Donnell, Catherine Mott, Susan Preston, Tim Berry, Gil Penchina, Matt Dunbar, Rob Tucci, Semil Shah, and Will Herman.

Thanks to all the supporters, early readers, and people providing feedback. I can't list everyone as there've been so many valuable people helping, including Marc Brown, Brad Carpenter, Alex Modelski, Keith Laepple, Geoff Harris, John Sechrest, Janis Machala, Dave Schappell, Ari Newman, Laura Bastian, Lizabeth Flynn, Greg Simanson, Martin Jones, Randy Williams, Naval Ravikant, Barry Ritholtz, Marc Andreesen, Danielle Morrill, and Erik Berg.

Also a special thanks to Brad Feld for your support, Michael de la Maza for your generous contribution of your mentorship manifesto and to my lovely wife Robin Maher for your countless hours reading early drafts.

This book is dedicated to the giants
who let me stand on their shoulders.
Thank you for the support along the way.
I couldn't have done it with you.

INTRODUCTION

THE VALUE HAD DOUBLED in just under a year; this was definitely the best investment in my portfolio. This single stock made up for the losers in my portfolio. Half of my investments had lost value, a few had gained a bit, but this one had doubled, making my entire portfolio a winner in just a year's time. It amazes me that investing creates situations like this. I was able to construct a portfolio with a pool of risky bets and create value, all because I picked at least one that got lucky. Understanding market demand and positioning was obviously one of the most important parts of being an investor, but that wasn't all there was to it. Understanding what else it took to be a great investor, pick great companies, and build a great portfolio needed more work.

At the time this was happening, my portfolio was small and the activities of the stocks recorded safely in the back of a spiral notebook left over from the school year before. I was ten at the time when I began my paper investing experiment, and I was not one to read the newspaper when I could have been reading about the adventures of the Hardy Boys instead. The Gulf War was being fought at the time, and my father was making a point of giving me the Sunday edition of the *Everett Herald* newspaper every week so that we could discuss what was going on in the war at dinner.

The *real* reason I didn't complain, though, was that by the time I finished reading the articles about the war, the people, the politicians, and the companies involved, I was ready to dig into the stock prices in the back of the business section. I'd get out my notebook and copy down the current prices of the stocks in my portfolio.

One of the stocks that I followed was Lockheed Martin. At the time, the stock was trading at around four bucks at the beginning of the war and had doubled to nearly eight bucks a share by the end, not to mention the dividends along the way. I'll never forget the success I had in that stock as a child fascinated by the markets and the businesses that allowed anyone to be an owner. That allowed me to be an imaginary owner of both mediocre and successful companies and it was entirely up to me which ones I wanted to be an owner of. No one had to invite me, I didn't need special privileges, and I could just open an account and be an owner.

I wanted to own some of those companies for real so badly at that age. We weren't poor, but we weren't rich either. Smack in the middle like most of the people in America at the time, I wanted to own some of these businesses that would pull me into the upper echelon of society. I wanted to take all the money I'd earned on my paper route and be a partial owner in some of these companies that clearly had better business operators at the helm than I was at the time.

More than once halfway through the war, I asked my father if he could open an account for me for real and more than once he turned me down with a small grin. I kept asking as the war progressed and my investment in Lockheed Martin skyrocketed. The cost was always too high or the headache for him too burdensome. Undaunted, I kept watching my portfolio's performance. I knew my mother wouldn't know how to open an account, and I felt trapped with my little spiral notebook of stocks that had doubled and no way to go out and actually buy shares in these companies.

Eventually, the war ended and my father stopped giving me the newspapers. I don't know if he unsubscribed or just kept them at his office, but I couldn't find them anywhere around the house. I'd hunt in his big desk drawers before he got home from work in search of an old edition, but I only found old electricity bills and business cards of his colleagues.

Without the weekly feed of the prices in the newspaper or the ability to actually become an owner of the companies I followed, I eventually lost interest. We didn't have a television at home yet and I was almost embarrassed by the fact that I had this secret fascination of investing in companies. Then puberty took over, and that was it. I was distracted by girls, distracted by friends, and eventually I had many other sources of constant distraction.

Through middle school and high school, I pursued an amazing array of businesses and financial transactions that weren't exactly above board. They were always profitable, but not very sustainable. Running dice games in the middle-school boys' restroom paled in comparison to what followed. Nonetheless, those businesses were a teaching ground that would help me understand the basic concepts of adding value for paying customers and customer service. They also drew me to computers in the 1990s as the Internet was coming of age.

I graduated high school without ever owning a share of a company. If I would have actually purchased a share or two of Lockheed with my $100 back in 1990, I would have had a seven-time return in eight years by the time I graduated from high school (plus dividends/splits)!

Seeing the momentum and excitement in the market in the late 1990s, I immediately went after and landed a contract job at Microsoft. There I saw the aftermath of the meteoric rise in wealth around the company. I'd race through traffic in my beat up Oldsmobile with the speedometer that permanently read zero and weave through the exotic car lot that everyone called the parking lot. Hummer, Jaguar, my jalopy, and a new Lamborghini was a common parking arrangement at the time. It was obvious wealth had been created before I arrived. Along the way I followed my father's investment ideals and focused on acquiring real estate in the late 1990s and early 2000s. That would turn out to be an advantage later on, but for the time being I was enamored with the wealth creation I'd seen.

I'd missed the wealth creation at Microsoft, so eventually I found my way to working for my first startup, SafeHarbor Technology Corp., a couple years later. Their tag line was "Get online, or get in-line," a way to convince businesses that they could move more phone support to the web using their amazing technology. The first day on the job we were celebrating our latest round of financing; the whole company stayed late playing casino games in a Monte Carlo–themed party, with new TVs being handed out as prizes thanks to our new venture capitalist board members. I had stock coming to me, and our revenues and headcount was growing. What could go wrong?

When the tech bubble burst, the world crashed around us and I watched as more than half the company was let go. Some of the few staffers who remained had already been through similar horrors at local dropouts like NetZero. This side of the momentum bubble bursting scared me, with my growing family at home and heavy real estate payments.

Not every company failed from this era. I heard about a local startup called Amazon starting, and as I looked to leave what I saw as a failing business, I had some choices to make. Should I consider joining this young online book company competing against Barnes and Noble, where I might witness meteoric wealth creation, or would I find myself on the wrong side of the bubble bursting yet again? I was unsure about how to pick the right companies to work for. How could I tell which would be the safer, surer bet, a company building software that "eats" phone support technology, in Marc Andreesen's words, or a company building software that "eats" bookstores?

I wanted more stability, so I moved on to larger companies like Washington Mutual Bank and EMC Corp. to pay the bills for my growing family. As it turned out, the run-up from 2001 to 2007 was an incredible time to be a real estate investor *and* a tough time to build amazing startup companies. I clearly had missed the boat on Amazon, but I was happy with the bit of real estate I owned and the family I'd built.

During this time I was a student of the markets again, and I was finally in the position to buy shares of companies that I wanted to own. I studied the lifecycles of companies and markets. The more I researched, the more I found an appreciation for the "growth at a reasonable price" approach of Berkshire Hathaway.

My investing followed a similar path, which led to a desire to invest at the earliest of stages. That meant focusing on how I could invest in the earliest-stage companies without destroying my own net worth along the way, since I'd seen the devastation before.

This led me to angel investing and thinking through how I could design a portfolio with reduced risk to my overall net worth. I discovered that a lot of people were interested in this space as well and a diverse pool of thought about how to invest in startups with less risk.

As I invested more and more in startups, I continued to meet interesting people taking unique approaches to investing. Some were focusing on investing for impact or focusing on niches. The more I looked at my own investing, the more these alternatives to investing seemed out of reach. I pulled back to a core methodical approach that aligned nicely with my value investing preferences.

As you read through the profiles in the book, think about how you can learn from each of the investors' approaches. You'll find investors who would have been able to see the difference between software that eats phone support and software that eats the bookstore. You'll find other investors who also can't tell the difference and use other risk mitigation techniques to make it easier. You'll also find a group of investors taking new and unique approaches to investing in startups.

All three groups of investors can be successful as the investors represented in each section demonstrate. It's also easy to be unsuccessful with any of the techniques used by the investors in this book. I hope you can learn to be successful from the investors here in this book as well as from the additional profiles on http://startupwealth.com. All the interviews were conducted in 2014 and 2015.

If you're new to early-stage investing, you will find a lot of terms that are somewhat unique to the practice. There is a lot of industry jargon used, a lot of specific legal terms referred to off-hand, and a few places where they are described in more depth within the individual chapter. In all cases, every word that's used often in early-stage investing is reviewed in the glossary at the end.

THE MOMENTUM INVESTORS

MORE THAN 100% WITH MIKE CRILL

"Mr. Morgan buys his partners; I grow my own."

—ANDREW CARNEGIE

"... if you can really work with them [entrepreneurs] side by side where they don't see you as an investor, where they see you as a real business partner, you can learn so much more about the team and the company."

—MIKE CRILL

I WAS INTRODUCED TO MIKE through a mutual friend, Yi-Jian. Yi-Jian is the director at one of the most active angel groups in the country, the Alliance of Angels in Seattle. When I asked Yi-Jian who I should be interviewing for this book, Mike was at the top of his list and he volunteered to introduce me.

Mike invited me to his gorgeous home overlooking Kirkland's Yarrow Bay to chat about his approach to angel investing. He was an incredibly gracious host and invited me in, where his blue Great Dane puppy greeted me just as excitedly. I was excited to learn what made him tick, why he was so good at investing, and what could others learn from his experience.

Mike Crill started out as the chief financial officer (CFO) of two different startups in the late 1990s that had $1 billion initial public offerings (IPOs). With such huge exits to the investments, Mike was set up well, and many of his colleagues at the time were retiring, while others were becoming venture capitalists (VCs) or starting new companies. Mike's personality was better suited for angel investing, and he took that path as a full-time endeavor. He was incredibly active in as much as eight angel groups at once (Alliance of Angels, Tech Coast Angels, Band of Angels, and all the other groups locally in the Seattle area). He found companies through these groups as well as through his network.

He was excited to share his experiences in investing with me. His angel investing includes 168 investments over 17 years, including 39 positive exits as of November 2013. That is 39 exits where he made or at least didn't lose money. That is a huge number and is why he has an internal rate of return (IRR) of 47%. Now he's winding down his portfolio aiming for retirement. His approach has a lot to offer a new investor looking for alpha (or outperformance from the norm) in angel investing.

Mike's approach boils down to actively engaging with companies and going as far as paying the salaries for supplemental team members out of pocket. The more value he added, the more equity he'd obtain, and the more equity he had, the larger the payoff would be for him. Mike's work for equity approach was unique at the time, although it is common now. At one time he had 35 people working for him, investing up to $2 million per year in companies.

What's your process for finding deals and filtering them to the right companies to work with?

To start off, when I find a possible deal, I invest a small amount of money and time to see if there is a real opportunity. Most angels follow a conventional approach to diligence, spending weeks checking references and such. I'd rather spend a week actually trying to sell their product. If you work *with* someone and actually build out their financial plan, if you can really work with them side by side where they don't see you as an investor, where they see you as a real business partner, you can learn so much more about the team and the company. This approach allows a much deeper level of diligence. I call this "diligence from within."

As the companies grow, I continue to work more and more with the best ones and continue to place the right resources with the company. After that I bring in other angel investors who would be good partners for the company. By bringing in other angel investors later in the process, I can minimize their downside along with mine.

What about downside risk?

There's always downside risk. I've written off about 75 investments, though, thankfully, all under $20k except one. I had a half a million dollar loss last year. Several angel investors and venture capitalists also lost their capital when the company struggled to find a successful exit.

What was wrong with that company? What did you learn from that investment not working out?

It was the wrong mix of market, product, and timing. Although the founder also turned out to be the wrong person in the role.

What do you look for in a founder?

I look for the un-fundable CEO, who may not be the tall, good-looking, well-spoken, well-educated man who can sell anything. I look for the founder who's driven and welcoming of help from the right team even if he doesn't seem to fit the mold that most investors like. There are a lot of great opportunities left untouched because the founder isn't a great fundraiser. Sure, I'll follow the formula, like when we invested in Henry Albrecht of Limeade, but having an open mind has been very worthwhile.

A good example is Bob Mustacich of RVM Scientific. He holds a doctorate in physical chemistry from Harvard and invented the first portable gas chromatograph, a highly specialized device with highly technical sales to a finite set of buyers. While Bob clearly understood the product and the market, he didn't fit the mold of the fundable CEO. Bob was too geeky for most people.

I had a hard time getting other angels excited about the deal simply because of how un-fundable the CEO appeared to be. Eventually, I was able to bring in additional angels and keep Bob as the CEO through the life of the company and the eventual sale to Agilent. Bob was the right kind of person for that business and he didn't fit the mold at all. He was, in fact, one of the brightest and most diligent people I've ever known and was exactly what that company needed.

What are the top things you avoid?

I've always avoided super-hot deals in super-hot spaces. Back in the late 1990s, everybody was doing dotcom deals. It didn't matter what these guys were selling; they could be selling red socks online. There were so many investments made. I don't actually know the statistics, but I think if you go back and see how many of those dotcoms actually made money, you would find rather few. Other than Amazon and eBay I don't know how many, but not a lot. There were thousands of them funded. We probably looked at a deal a week that was a classic dotcom e-tailer. Out of some 30 investments during that time frame, we did two in that space. One we turned into B2B and the other one failed. We could've easily done tons because that's what everyone was doing.

Later in the mid-2000s it was social networking. The word *viral* was in every business plan. It was once a week we would have an opportunity to invest in one of these companies with a viral or social aspect. Again, through that time frame we invested in two. Again, there were thousands and how many of them made money?

Sure, there were a couple of superstars that made a crap-load of money - you could have done Facebook – but, as a class, social networking deals had far too many losses for angels.

And there were probably a bunch of others that sold at the right time. But the denominator was massive, so given the choice of picking a dozen social networking deals and doing some random dozen material science deals, you would do better on the material science deals because the space and valuations just got so overheated and there was too much money chasing what turned out to be too small of an opportunity.

How hard did you look at the competition?

We seriously look at the competition and how well funded the competition is. We've had opportunities where there's a great CEO, a great product, everyone is excited—but they are going into direct competition with three venture-backed companies. Are we going to cobble together $1 million from angels in Seattle and go after a market where we are fighting competitors with $20 million? It is just hard to do.

We look for something where it is hard to define who the competitors are and hard to understand the market because the company has something truly innovative. We like thinking about replacements, not a new offering with direct competitors. We learned the hard way that incremental improvements just don't get it done.

We had this one deal. It was a small quick failure for us. We invested in this guy who had invented a better fake diamond. There is a high-end fake diamond on the market called Moissanite. A one-karat fake might sell for $500 in a setting and it is a really nice fake diamond. This guy had developed a technology that produced a better one. We had jewelers and appraisers involved and it was a harder, better, clearer diamond. If you tried to quantify it, it would be something like 20% better.

We thought that we could sell it for a little less money; after all it was a better diamond. That was one where the first thing we did was put a sales guy on it and in two months the sales guy came back with absolutely nothing. He was telling us that no one cared enough about this small change. They do care about the price savings, but it wasn't worth it to buy from an unknown name at a small savings.

How do you differentiate investments to find great teams?

Everybody always wants to get the guy who just had a big exit, the speaker everyone wants at their angel or entrepreneur events. It scares the hell out of me when my CEOs go to hear these guys speak. You're going to go hear some things from a person who's going to come from a position of credibility who's going to tell you how to make it work. Now this is a guy who did it one time, in one time frame, in one business, in one industry. But it's not your time frame, your business, or your industry, and it's not going to work for you. It's not bad for you to hear what these people have to say, but it is bad for you to sit in the pews like this is the truth and take notes on it. That can be very dangerous. The guy who's done it once doesn't necessarily have something that's going to be applicable to you.

We have our own story around this problem. We successfully sold the Coffee Equipment Company that makes the Clover machines to Starbucks. As you can imagine, that's an unusual deal and an unusual company. We had the world's most expensive automated French press. It was a nice exit for everybody, and when we sold, everyone wanted to hear the CEO talk. He was a decent speaker as well, so it made him all the more alluring.

I went the first time to hear him speak and give advice to people. I just kept thinking time after time that it was such bad advice for the audience. In reality he had a hardware product that, in the end, had one buyer who really wanted it. It was very well positioned as a cult product, and that was intentional. It was in an industry that accepted that; baristas and independent coffee shops are very accepting of that. They are hipsters and cultish, so all of that worked.... If your market's not like that, and it probably isn't, then the core premise that worked for them isn't going to work for you.

The same problem applies to angels trying to value their investments.

The same goes for pricing deals. If you're going to get into valuation and pricing a deal and you're getting advice from someone, the first thing you want to ask is, "How many checks have you written?" Everybody seems to have an opinion on how these companies should be priced. I often have CEOs come back to me and say, "My lawyer says that instead of a \$3 million pre we should be at \$6 million," to which I say, "Then at \$3 million your lawyer is going to write a pretty big check, right?"

How do you think about valuation?

If you want to understand what's happening, it's not about the companies that are presenting. It's about the companies that are getting funded. So if you want to understand what market terms are, you need to look at the funding. You might see 20 companies shopping their deal at $5 million pre, but you might find out that the only companies that got funded at that same stage and in that same time frame actually raised money at $2 million pre. Looking just at people's desires or wants doesn't really tell you where the market is. It can be harder to do because you have to be a little more plugged in. You can't do without that information.

How do you get that information with some of the new tools like AngelList available?

To be clear, I might be a dinosaur when it comes to this. Back in the day, in the late 1990s there were prior iterations of those. Garage.com had something like this and I invested in one of their deals. It was a crazy time and I'd like to think that we learned from that. Most of those businesses as far as I know don't provide their numbers in terms of how many deals get funded and to what extent, so I'm skeptical that most such sites are actually seeing much activity outside of the local market. When it got started, there were scads of these matchmaker websites. I think that if someone really wants to make angel investments they will find all that they want in their own backyard.

Angel investing is generally a local activity. There are very strong correlations between success and collaboration with other angels. I think that's better and more effective because you're invested with people you know versus invested with people [off] a website. I just don't know if those sites are necessary. If they're not necessary they may not last long. They all went away after the dotcom bubble. In fact, everything went away, the incubators went away.

What's interesting is that there were other business models that didn't go away during the dotcom [meltdown] and the recession. CFO rentals, marketing, PR firms—they didn't disappear. They may have been impacted, but they didn't go away. Incubators disappeared and these matchmaker websites disappeared. It's possible that when times get bad the weakness of these businesses cause them to dissolve. So many things are different now, though, so it is possible that some of the market dynamics have changed. Like I said, I'm a bit of a dinosaur.

How do you work with other angel investors?

I got to a point where it was impossible for me to support all the investments I'd made. Because of that, I got comfortable with a handful of other investors. As we started to make bigger investments, I would stay very active with some investments and rely on some of these other angels to be active in other investments. Once we got to a point where a big investment was being made, I would often look to another angel and say, you take the board seat. That actually worked. So now with this portfolio that I have, there are half a dozen investments like this. Greg [Bennet] is on the board of two and I'm on the board of others, and that's very effective for us.

How do you know who you can trust that much?

It's easy to tell who you can count on. Really, what you're looking for is people who're going to do the work. In this case, that means making phone calls and running models. Those two things separate the men from the boys on diligence. Anyone can go to meetings and have conversations with the team. For some reason there's a break when it comes to where someone is actually going to pick up the phone and call customers, partners, and the like. Or not just look at what the company is providing, but actually produce your own models for how this thing is going to work. In total, for a diligence lead, they are averaging 20 to 60 hours of work.

Do you only work with other angels who do that much work?

We made a relatively small investment in a company and a well-known angel investor went into the deal after me. I was helping out with all the administrative stuff so anything regarding this investor on diligence would have been through me. The investor never asked me what I thought of the deal. The only diligence he did was look at stuff the CEO gave him, like the financials, the annual report, that sort of thing. Never did anything else. That's fine if that's how you want to invest. But because he invested, three other guys did. I learned about this after the fact and I was shocked, thinking, "Gosh, they probably figure that the lead looked at a lot of stuff." I mean, he negotiated the valuation, I know that, but that's it. We've had this happen before where there's the "who did the diligence" thing, which you've just got to ask.

What about investment structure? How do the terms and that valuation that's negotiated come into play for you?

On the equity side, there are many different terms, but assume you're getting preferred stock; most everybody does. The two preferred terms that matter are your liquidation preference and anti-dilution. Everyone seems to do the same anti-dilution (weighted average). I see differences in liquidation preference. I'm a big fan of just a 1x participating, which is about the norm. For a while it was 2x non-participating; I never liked that. I think we're back to 1x participating. That's a totally reasonable way to do it and it aligns investors' and founders' interests. Otherwise, of course valuation matters. Valuation is directly related to the option pool. That's another way to push the valuation down so that's a factor.

Then there's third-tier stuff, which doesn't necessarily matter that much because it's just not used that much, like registration rights. Still, your term sheet should have all those things. On one hand, those things are always vanilla so you think there's never going to be an impasse. They generally end up not mattering.

Convertible notes are different. They're more complex and there are more terms that do matter and they are somewhat more situational. Have you talked to Eric Michelman? Eric and I have done, I don't know, six, eight deals together. We've done a bunch of notes and a bunch of debt deals together, probably four or five loans in addition to the convertible notes.

Eric is a very thorough investor and we had both spoken to angel groups about convertible notes, and one of the points in a paper I wrote on the subject was something a lot of people have overlooked, which is who can change the terms of the note. Notes often state that a majority of holders can elect to change the note terms and bind all holders. In the paper, I cautioned investors that it's easy to have the majority of the note holders with economic interests divergent from your own. The other investors might be prior investors in the company where you're not. They might be option holders in the company. They might be friends or family. They might be investors who're strategic investors like distributors or suppliers.

There are a lot of different ways where they would somehow have a different set of interests. Sure enough, Eric was getting ready to speak on the topic of notes, and a week before he was speaking, he had that happen. A majority of the note holders elected to forgo all their note consideration, and basically forced a pay-to-play on the note. It was a negative outcome for him. That's just one example of how notes are situational and can be more subtle.

It still sounds like you don't necessarily have a preference on equity or debt and look at it per deal.

It's important to realize that when you invest in a convertible note, you're pretty much buying equity. I've done a lot of notes. I've always been comfortable with them. In the late 1990s we did notes like crazy. In the late 1990s, the pitch was you do the note and you can end up being in the venture round without ever having to pay the fees associated with being an LP in the venture fund. At the time that was somewhat true because angels generally expected to be followed by venture money. Then we found that angels couldn't rely on VCs following us and interest in notes waned. Then it came back when people started putting caps on their notes.

Personally, I'm not crazy about caps. I understand how they're effective in theory. But there are two problems with that. One, if you work a cap that makes sense for the investor, the cap should be "What's the company worth today," right? The only reason we're doing notes is because we don't want to have a tiny preferred round out there or we don't want to spend the legal fees or we want to keep this flexible. We should then give the investor the value the company is today.

That doesn't happen for the most part. Caps are generally inflated, and as such, those follow-on rounds—and again I don't know the statistics, but I think this is probably right—I would bet most of those follow-on rounds end up getting done at the cap. Which means you were a sucker for writing the check when you did.

Why not just leave your money in the stock market or wherever you want to and then come in on the follow-on round because you would have gotten the same thing? Interest rates alone are never worth it given the risk you're taking. It just doesn't make sense.

If we do rely on a cap, then I try to get the entrepreneur to agree that the cap should be set at what the company is worth today. That rarely happens, even after the effect of interest or warrant coverage. Usually, what we'll do is just throw the cap right out and I'll put in a big discount. I think that's a better solution and it only carries the small risk of a runaway valuation in the priced round.

The average angel wants to see 50% IRR on his successful investments. So you want to get a 50% discount (or discount combined with interest), which you're not going to get. But yeah, but you could do 30%. Plus interest, you know. Maybe get 30% plus interest, so 38%. And maybe that's good enough for you. We often do our notes and get 2% or 3% per month that the note sits out there. So 2% or 3% per month the note sits out there about a year, plus interest, so you're then in the 30% to 40% range. And then just discount off whatever the hell deal is done. And at that point, we haven't screwed up the company by putting a cap figure in the note, which the new investor is probably going to use as a benchmark and say, well, that should be the valuation.

So maybe that company does even better on the priced round, or maybe not. But no matter what, if I had to look at my choice of either going in that next round or the convertible note I went in so I got 30 or 40 points off, that's not a bad deal. I can do that. You have to trust that the next deal is going to be okay.

How much of your net worth is invested in early-stage companies?

It's changed. Probably in all of the decade from 2000 to 2010 it was about 95%, up to a little bit over 100% because when the recession started we lived off of credit cards for a while because we ran out of cash. Since around 2010, I've been working really hard at getting it down. Even now it's probably at 60%. I gambled everything on the success of our startups. When I would be sitting there with these entrepreneurs and sitting with another angel investor, I'd be telling them that I really believed in it. I'm betting on this thing - not fooling around. If those deals didn't work out, I'd be living in a very different house.

What about the other angels you're bringing in? Were they more willing to follow you because you had such conviction?

You'd have to ask them. As time went on, I would say I built some really good solid trust in the relationships. I feel great about it to this day. Where you got to a point when you look at deals and I would tell somebody, "This is the new thing that I'm doing, I'm going in big, I think you'd like this," and I had people say, "Well, if you're doing it, okay." That made me feel really good, not because they thought I was smart or a good stock picker, but because they knew the integrity was there, my commitment was there. These guys all have more money than I did and they were taking way more risk. That creates a lot of credibility. I never invited others to join me in a deal unless I was in for at least $50,000 and committed to invest more. Until the big loss last summer [2013], only one co-investor lost one $25,000 check in a deal I advocated.

I built some pretty close friendships and good relationships, even when those deals don't work out. I have a couple of these good friends who lost out big. I'll explain to them, here's what happened. It's just one of those things. All I hear back is "Hey, you lost more than I did and it's harder for you to lose it. No hard feelings at all, I'm sure you did your best." All of that makes me feel good. It just says a lot. If you look at angel investors and people who invest together, they've been working through a lot of deals over protracted periods. They're either good friends or they hate each other.

If I've created a good relationship, it's not because we got lucky and that takes you full circle. The other point I wanted to make is that we talked about the rock star CEO. Remember, [the one] who everyone wants to talk to, that rock star VC who invested in a company that did so well. Don't ever listen to any angel investor who tells you how we did that because he works so hard or we're so good. I've had a couple of bigger wins and I could tell you it was not because I was good. It's not because the CEO was good. The difference between a good outcome and a fantastic one is being at the right place at the right time and a couple of other things. Granted, someone could screw that up and not have it materialize. As investors, our goal ought not to be "How do I find the 100x opportunity?", because you don't. It's "How do I not lose money?" My goal has always been to avoid value loss in the portfolio. If you think about it, when we have wins as angel investors, we talk about a 3x, a 5x. We don't even talk about percentages because that doesn't matter. If you're in the stock market and you talked about a 20% gain, you'd be talking about great returns, right? We talk about 3x and 5x. All you need to do to boost your proposed return is just don't lose.

If your gains are going to be that big, just don't have too many losses. That's what my focus has always been on. Sure, I might try to make the good ones great, but I manage my portfolio to make sure I don't lose the bad ones. The great ones? It will happen. I can't force that. I can maybe stop a loss.

What do you do to try to stop a loss?

Probably the best example we had of that is that we made a big investment. Over a million-dollar investment in a local company called Escapia and I got brought in by the VCs. They completely changed the business model. I was a big believer. One of the best CEOs I've ever worked with. A terrific, hard-working, great guy. We had a good close relationship. I was the CFO there.

As time went on we executed on a new model, and things were looking pretty good. It was early 2008, and we had just raised our last funding round. Very tired investor base. None of the old investors from the prior business model came into this at all. A lot of my friends put in new money. Greg [Bennett] was in the deal.

Then the recession hit. That was the fall of 2008 and our business dropped more than 60%. We had to go raise money again. Nobody was going to touch us at this point. So we went from a business that was looking pretty interesting to, oh crap! How are we going to make this thing go? By then the company had gotten kind of big—40 people.

What did you do?

I did a couple of things. One, I worked my tail off to try and cut a deal that I thought was fundable. I got the terms done, worked with all the existing investors to try to get whoever I could to come in. I brought in new capital. Invested a lot more myself. We couldn't afford a lot of things; we had to let a sales guy go. We had to let the whole marketing group go. I had some ideas for ancillary products and marketing things. I just started doing those on my own. Anyway, in the end we sold the company. Everybody who came in with us doubled their money. The guys who did the last round got up to a 3x return. Except for the fact that those investors before us didn't get anything, I'd say that was lemonade out of lemons. I put all my effort into making sure that people weren't losing money. We had a positive return. Everybody who came in with us and after us had a positive return.

Unfortunately, we couldn't do anything for the folks who had invested in the old business model and there were some sour grapes on that end. But I was begging these guys to write another check. That's just an example of focusing on not having a loss. It absolutely would have been a loss. That year, I think I did three quarters of a million dollars myself in that company. And it was risky.

* * *

I learned a lot from Mike and I left his house thinking about the feasibility of putting together a structure like his, as well as why doing so wasn't more common. At the end of the day, his ability to make great investments stemmed from his operational role, and that definitely takes skill outside of just putting cash on the table.

GIVE FIRST WITH BRAD FELD

"The purpose of life is not to be happy. It is to be useful, to be honorable, to be compassionate, to have it make some difference that you have lived and lived well."

—RALPH WALDO EMERSON

"Your job is to help the entrepreneur be successful. Don't come with this endless sort of cynical view about their success; instead, come with 'How can I help?'"

—BRAD FELD

I REACHED OUT TO BRAD to ask if he wanted to be interviewed for my book and found he was one of the most approachable people out of all the people I solicited for the book. He immediately understood what the book was about and put me in touch with about twenty other angels around the country whom he'd worked with over the years, and I had the pleasure of profiling some of the best investors in the country as a result.

When I interviewed Brad for the book, we spent some calendar tag and finally found a time that worked for both of us. I spent weeks re-reading all the relevant blog posts before the interview and wasn't sure he'd have much else to add to the conversation. Of course, it turned out that he had a lot more to add. I encourage you to go read his blog posts as supplemental material to this chapter and this book as a whole, as there's a wealth of information there. You can find out all about him at http://about.me/bfeld.

Brad is a venture capitalist by profession and an angel investor by passion. He started out as many do, as an entrepreneur, and developed an amazing talent for identifying great investments to make along the way. As a venture capitalist he focuses on technology and as an angel investor he focuses on an area of personal interest for him, natural foods. The interview with Brad went as most do, smooth and insightful. We started in the usual place and I learned a lot by the end.

How did you get started angel investing?

I sold my first company in the fall of 1993 to a public company. That company was based in Boston and was started in 1987. It was self-funded; we never raised any outside money. When we sold it, I continued to work for the acquirer for the next eighteen months, and starting in early 1994, I began making angel investments in tech companies.

I would say that between 1994 and 1996, I made about 40 angel investments. Most of them were $25,000 checks. A few were $50,000. I occasionally would make a second investment so I'd end up investing a total of $50,000 in a company that I'd put $25,000 in initially.

That angel experience was very successful. I ended up investing in a handful of companies that became public companies down the road, including a company called Net Genesis, which was one of the very first Internet software companies. It went public in 1999 and was worth about a billion dollars in the IPO. I was also an investor in a company called Critical Path, which was a San Francisco–based hosting company. They went public and I think their peak market cap was about $5.5 billion.

I had a handful of those and I had a bunch of companies that got acquired. A few got acquired for a lot, and one of them was Harmonix, which got acquired in 2007, and they were the Guitar Hero/Rock Band guys.

They got bought out for $175 million plus an earnout, and when the earnout finally got resolved through a bunch of litigations, it ended up being about an $800 million deal, and I was one of the seed investors there. I had a series of very successful investments and a bunch of zeroes as well.

I co-founded a venture firm in 1997 called Mobius Venture Capital. It was originally called SoftBank Technology Ventures. That firm raised three funds, and invested through 2005 in companies, so I didn't make any angel investments between 1997 and 2005 because of my agreement with my existing limited partners (LPs).

In 2005 we decided not to raise another fund for Mobius, and so I made another 30 or 40 angel investments in tech companies. This time, I was typically writing $50,000 to $100,000 checks, sometimes $25,000, and sometimes doubling down. A handful of those companies have been very successful. A bunch of them are still operating and growing, but a number of them have failed.

In 2007, my partners and I started a new firm called Foundry Group. We've raised a couple of funds since then, so I stopped making angel investments in tech, but I started making angel investments in non-tech things, mostly food - natural foods. I'm in Boulder, and there's a huge amount of natural food activity here. I was kind of fascinated by it and made some angel investments into the space. I have a couple of friends who started companies that were not tech-related companies and made some angel investments there as well. I have probably made another 30 or 40 investments since 2007 in addition to cofounding Techstars with David Cohen in 2006.

There were four of us who co-founded Techstars, and we funded the first two programs ourselves. We each invested in 10 companies, which meant I essentially had angel investments in another 20 companies through the first two years of Techstars. In year 3, my partners at Foundry and I started doing those investments together. I also have invested in probably about 30 venture capital funds, including a whole bunch of them that are seed investors.

I have a lot of investments in other companies that are at the seed level through those venture funds. Then in the fall of last year [2013], my partners and I started FG Angels to use the AngelList syndicate program—we created the first syndicate that was a fund. We're doing 50 angel investments through AngelList. Foundry Group invests $50,000 in each of the companies and syndicates are anywhere from $150,000 to $450,000.

That's the history. Overall, I have no idea what the total number of angel investments I've made are, but the ones that I made directly probably is closing in on 200. If you include all the indirect ones that

I've been involved in, not including the venture funds, it'll probably get up to 500. Then if you include all the venture funds I'm an investor in, it's thousands.

Were you looking for different things during the different time frames?

In 1994–96 and 2006–07, I was mostly focused on tech. All of my venture investment has always been tech. When I say tech, I really mean software and Internet, but it extends some beyond just software and Internet because I'm very comfortable with investing in consumer electronics product connected to the Internet. I'm invested now in companies like MakerBot, Fitbit, and Orbotix. It's not just limited to raw software. The angel investments I made most recently are all in natural foods. I've always done a few natural foods things along the way, but I've really sort of accelerated that ramp recently. It's been stuff I know and the natural foods was stuff I'm interested in and I'm starting to learn a lot about.

I decided I wanted to continue to make a lot of angel investments. I like to make angel investments, I like to help at the very early seed stage, and I like to be involved in this ever-expanding network. While I get to do plenty of that through the venture vehicle, there's something about writing small checks out of your own bank account at the seed level that's always been satisfying to me. I thought about an area that I knew well enough and had some kind of affinity for. That I felt like wasn't going to interfere with my venture capital activity, so I could just sort of do it, but without it being a time-consuming thing. Natural foods was the obvious one because of the number of companies with a proximity to Boulder and the expanding network. There's a lot of history and a heritage of network of that here and I'm already involved in that network because I've been living in Boulder.

The economics of the companies were very easy for me to understand quickly because they had a lot of characteristics that are shared with some parts of the tech industry. There are some things that were different but I was able to really lock down and pretty quickly. That ended up being a very good constructive thing for me. When I thought about it, I think about other things and I see lots of stuff in energy and solar and natural power and aerospace and biotech. I don't know anything about those industries or the economics and how they work. I'd just be passing money at random shit if I were to do that. I don't really want to do that.

Is understanding the economics as important as understanding what the business is and the market?

When I said "economics," it should be broader than just that. Understanding how the business works is what I mean. Do I understand the stages of the business, from the very beginning through getting your first product out, through getting local distribution? Understanding how the business works from local direct sales versus product distribution through retail channel, whether it's Trader Joe's or Whole Foods or wherever you're going, privately more products versus branded products. Then understanding how you go from a single stock keeping unit (SKU) or a single SKU family to a multi-SKU family, and how those things work.

In a lot of ways, the distribution dynamics for a natural foods company like Justin's Nut Butter, where I'm an investor, is no different than distribution dynamics for a company like Fitbit. If you actually look at the economics, you look at the revenue, the gross margin, and the amount that you have to give to the retail channel, the way distribution works, your whole supply chain dynamics from raw material through finished product, a lot of that stuff is the same.

The percentages and numbers might be different but that's okay, that's category-specific dynamics. Then you get into marketing, promotion, and branding. How does that work? If you look at the marketing, promotion, and branding for many of these companies, it's similar again to physical product company companies. There are many things that are different along the way. There are valuations, what the cash flow characteristics of the companies are long term, what the risk dynamics are, the things that slow you down, competitive forces—all that stuff is different.

At an angel level, you're not experiencing that. You're mostly on an awareness and understanding of how that's going to unfold as the company scales. You hope that the company scales and that you have to do all that shit.

What about the teams of people who're running the company? Are you looking at the same kinds of things in the entrepreneurs themselves?

Pretty similar. My primary selection criteria for making any investment, not just angel investments, but any investment, is to first focus on the entrepreneur. Is the entrepreneur completely obsessed about their product? Not passionate—but obsessed. There's a meaningful difference between passion and obsession. A lot of people can get fired up about promoting a product. It's a whole different thing to be obsessed about a product and the product quality, making sure the product customer experience is the best that's possible.

First, assuming yes to obsession, do I have any affinity for the product? If the answer is I don't care about the product, then that's an easy place to stop. Those are my first two places. Then assuming yes to those, I go deep on the people through the lens of "Do I want to be a long-term investor or partner with these entrepreneurs?" I'm not looking for what's on their resume. I'm not looking for what their experience is. I'm not looking for how successful or unsuccessful they've been in the past on different things. I really am making a broader judgment about whether I want to be a business partner with them, as an investor, even if I'm a tiny investor. I'm using that lens.

I use that lens, not just for my angel investments but for my venture capital investments as well. We have a different set of priorities on our venture capital investments that allows us to filter stuff like amount of money they've raised already and a set of themes that we invest in. If they're not within a theme, we say no.

The angel side is more relaxed, but similar characteristics to start with. I can say no to something on the venture side in less than a minute 99% of the time, because it's not in a theme; they've raised too much money, it's too late-stage. Assuming that it gets through that, then I focus on "Are the entrepreneurs obsessed about their product? Do I have affinity for the product?" If yes to both of those, then do I want to work with these people long term?

I've learned on the venture side and especially on the angel side that I think people overanalyze the uncertainty, overanalyze what you have no knowledge of because it hasn't happened to you. You try to figure out what the potential of the business is based on a whole bunch of factors that probably are wrong, because they're hypotheses.

The only way you're going to know which ones matter is to actually get out there and test them. That comes back to the people and the quality and the nature of the people that you're getting on with. "

As a well-known investor, you bring a lot to the table when you make an investment. Do you look at that as reducing your risk?

I hope so. Part of my evaluation of the people is not just "Do I want to work with them?" but "Do they want to work with *me*?" I don't want to be an investor in a company with somebody who doesn't want me as an investor.

That's an important part of it. I think I help at the angel level in different ways. If you took a survey of the 200-plus companies where I have been an angel investor and asked them, "Of all your angel investors, was Brad the most helpful of your angels? Was Brad helpful at all? Was Brad hurtful?" I think you would get a lot of answers that I was very helpful to the most helpful, and I don't think you'd get many or any that would say I was hurtful. If you tried to get qualitative and understand exactly what I did, you wouldn't see any patterns.

It's a whole bunch of different things. It covers the spectrum across the company in different stages. For a lot of people probably what you get is, "He was just really responsive and empathetic. Whenever I had an issue, I could call him and he'd work though it with me. He was just very supportive." You'd get a lot of soft stuff, but you'd also get, "When we were selling the company, we'd never sold a company before and Brad was deeply involved with us, helping negotiate the transaction even though he didn't have any other economics other than his investment in the company." Or network, business deals, feedback on product strategy—you'll get all of that in the mix, just depending on the company and what the founders need and what they reached out to me about.

Do you look for investing opportunities in companies alongside other people who can complement some of those things or offer similar things to what you offer?

I would categorize myself as a small and promiscuous angel investor rather than an investor who tries to make a relatively small number of investments of larger dollar amounts, as an angel. As a VC investor, I have a somewhat different strategy. I have three categories of investments as an angel investor.

The first category is where I write a $25,000 or $50,000 check and I help them to gather half a million to a million-dollar syndicate with my friends following me into the deal. I don't take any other economics for that, it's just that I've got a bunch of people who like to invest in stuff I like. If they want to invest, great, if they don't, that's fine too.

The second category is where I'm one of the people on that list, so I have a bunch of friends who make angel investments and there's a number who'll put in $25,000, $50,000, or $100,000 and they'll ask around to their friends, "Anybody else want to play?" Sometimes I will and sometimes I won't, depending on whether I like it.

The third category is just kind of random, where I run into something, I'm interested in it, and I just toss them money. Those three categories are different, but in all three of those categories there's generally some syndicate dynamics at different levels. I'm not sure I'm being terribly precise and take the approach of, "Okay, we need to go get the following four other people in the round because that's going to help you build your company." We're exposing it to a quality set of people who can help if they want. The minimum thing the entrepreneur is going to get is some cash and everything beyond that cash is going to be upside.

What about as a percentage of your net worth? Do you have a percentage dedicated to early stage?

Not really. I would say I'm reasonably undisciplined about that. Some of it is a function of having made plenty of bucks. When I started my first company, we were very profitable, so even younger in life I had more money than I needed. While my lifestyle has expanded as I've gotten older and I have more shit, a bigger house, and that sort of thing, I don't have an excess need for money. We don't have any kids. My wife and I plan to give all our money away while we're alive. We're very philanthropic. We give away a lot of money each year. I'm much less on a net worth optimization strategy and much more on an amount that feels very comfortable for me on an annual basis.

An example of the fact that I'm not disciplined particularly is that, after taxes, I made about a million and a half bucks after the sale of my first company. I had somewhere between a million and two million bucks, I don't remember what it was, let's say somewhere between the two. I turned around and other than putting $160,000 as a down payment on a house, I invested almost all of the rest in startups. At that time I was making some money through consulting projects, so my net cash flow was probably close to zero on a month-to-month basis.

Neither of us were stressed about it. It wasn't "Oh my gosh, we only have $97,000 of savings anymore," because I think we both had a lot of confidence that the investments were good investments, and that we could have some returns. Worst case, I could make more money. It didn't matter that much.

Of course, across my whole angel portfolio, I probably had, of all the money I've invested on a realized basis, probably 10x. On an unrealized basis of what's remaining, I don't know what the number is exactly, it's more than 1x but probably 2x on an unrealized basis. Probably about half the money I've invested is still at play. Very good return on invested capital from that perspective.

Then the venture fund investments have also been interesting because I definitely had a few clunkers in there, but for the most part, on a diversified basis, it's been a relatively safe asset. I think our overall return across all the venture funds I've invested in on a realized base was probably about 2x. Unrealized, probably another 1x in there somewhere, which is about what you would expect. A good performance on a venture fund is a 3x return, so that's some that didn't do well. I've got some venture funds I've been in that have been 10x the money or 15x the money and there's one that's 20x the money or so.

The point is that, over this 20-year period, I haven't been disciplined about it from a spreadsheet perspective. I'm qualitatively disciplined. My tempo's about the same every year. It's not a surprise that in the first two and a half, three years that I did this, I did about 40 investments and the next time I did it, I had two years and I did about 30 investments. About the same tempo. On the food side, for example, I'm doing about one a month, right? So I'm doing another a dozen a year, that's a good pace. It's not like I don't have the capacity to do one a week, but I just don't feel like it. I'd rather roll through it that way.

For the ones that failed, did they give you any kind of feedback on things you should be avoiding?

Sure, the biggest cause of failure of these companies generally is a people issue. So you have to evaluate the people. There are a lot of companies that almost by definition, even though they have lots of promise, ultimately fail at some point because of market conditions or scale. Or they hit something that changes on them. Long, long list of things.

But with the early fail, like the fail out of the gate or the fail in that seed level, the dominant reason is people issues. So I think my focus is on the people, who they are, and what their character is. Getting their level of obsession around the product. I think those things have continued to be the most important part of the cycle for me, on the evaluation part of the curve.

How do you go about judging the people you're investing in?

It's of course a spectrum, right? Some are first-time entrepreneurs, so you have no track record. You have to use your instincts based on your interactions with the people. Some are people who have a lot of history, and you understand where they are in their life. You're trying to evaluate what they've done.

For me, listening to how people describe what they've done, both the successes and the failures are often very instructive. I think there's not a right way to describe them. You can tell whether people have internalized the lessons of their past experiences. You can tell whether they own what happened. Whether they were the ones who caused the problem or not. Were they participants in the problem where things were failures.

If they're comfortable with failure, and the lessons they've learned from failure, versus being defensive or trying to ignore it, all of those things come across. There should be no surprises. The more somebody owns experiences, the clearer somebody is about what works and what doesn't work. Why something happened. Their participation in it. That makes such an enormous difference to me in terms of my evaluation of the person.

It's relatively easy to get sucked into highly charismatic people and then get turned off by people who aren't highly charismatic. It's the case of the extrovert who's a good salesman versus the introvert who's just really smart but awkward in that interaction. Or the experienced person who's pitched a line and is very comfortable versus the first-time entrepreneur who's very nervous and doesn't know the best way. Trying to figure out how to remove the bias of what you're experiencing and actually try to deal with the substance of the information is part of that evaluation.

It's qualitative. I don't have a checkbox. I'm not asking a series of 15 questions. I'm not doing a bunch of reference calls. I might send out some emails to people I know, where I'm looking for quick qualitative feedback. You know people are very quick with positive. It's very easy to know the difference between positive and negative. When somebody who's blowing off the response, which is always meaning negative but they don't want to respond, occasionally, somebody will say, "You should call me." Whenever somebody says something like that, that means I'm going to get a good story. I'm going to have to process the story, but it's going to be a story.

Do you do that with everyone, or only some people?

I do that with most angel investments. When I do a reference check on somebody, it's not 20 people. It's a couple of highly trusted people I know who are engaged. I never ask for references. I'm not interested in knowing who you want me to talk to. Instead, I look for people you're going to have been connected to through other resources.

Not surprisingly, a lot of the people I engage with on the angel side are people who were referred to me by somebody I trust already. They come in with somebody else endorsing them.

What are the top three things angel investors should avoid?

Number one, avoid not having a strategy. Figure out what you're going to do and how you're going to do it. When I talked about not necessarily having an allocation of my net worth, that was a deliberate decision. I didn't do it that way, but instead I said I feel comfortable investing $25,000 a year in 10 companies, which is a quarter-million dollars a year. I'll reserve one to one for some of those companies and I'll invest another $25,000, while for others I won't.

My plan is to do it at a steady pace, so I'm essentially investing in about a company a month for the foreseeable future. If you look at the way that worked out in the past, it sort of looked like that. What happened was I invested a bit more. I didn't do five investments in one month or write one investment of $250,000.

I decided I was going to do primarily tech, and the stuff outside of tech would be things supporting a friend who was trying a business outside of tech. Things that were outside tech I generally didn't bother with because I didn't know anything about them. Some of them were successful businesses, but I didn't know about them.

I like to use this phrase—I think angel investors should be promiscuous. You should do more rather than less investments. You should do more that are smaller. You should be focused on building your network of other people who are angel investors to bring them into deals and have them bring you into deals. If you just show up and are just making investments, that's a problem.

The second thing you shouldn't do is hold back, like if you're going to be an angel investor, start writing checks. If it takes you 12 months to write your first $25,000, you're making a mistake. You're going to get better deal flow by making investments and getting known as somebody who actually writes checks.

Then the third is don't ever lose sight of what your role in the process is. When you're a $25,000 or $50,000 investor in a company where you now own half a percent or one percent of the company, don't torture the entrepreneur. Your job is to help the entrepreneur be successful. Don't come with this endless sort of cynical view about their success; instead, come with "How can I help?" Constantly try to help the entrepreneur and know that the entrepreneur's world is complex, it's uncertain, all kinds of things aren't working all the time. As entrepreneurs, they may not be communicating well with you because they don't know how to communicate with the investors yet or they may not be focused on it. Give them a pass on that stuff. Engage.

Engage not from a "Tell me how you're doing? Give me a report," but from "Is there an introduction I can make? Is there anything I can help you with on the product side? You need to access the so-and-so, I can help you get access. Oh, you never negotiated a reseller agreement? I'll send you over the reseller agreement we use in my company."

* * *

It was a great conversation with Brad and I must say I learned a lot. Afterward, I started to reflect on the fact that Brad truly lived the way that he described himself. He is a give-first type of person, as was evidenced by his openness to everything I am working on. He had a lot of things going on and was interrupted a few times while we were talking, but he never let that get in the way of his focus on our conversation and the value he was trying to add to the readers of this book.

TRANSPARENT INTEGRITY WITH JOANNE WILSON

"I want to put a ding in the universe."

—STEVE JOBS

"Sometimes I feel like I'm creating community, I'm creating jobs, I'm creating success, I'm creating a new industry, and I like the feeling of that."

—JOANNE WILSON

I WAS INTRODUCED TO JOANNE through Brad Feld and was pretty excited to get to know the famed angel investor from New York. Joanne is a prolific investor and with her husband, Fred Wilson, she is half of a power couple in early-stage finance. Fred does the venture capital with Union Square Ventures and blogs at avc.com, while Joanne does the angel investing and blogs at gothamgal.com. You should follow both blogs if you want to learn how to be a better angel investor. Joanne offers insights into how she goes about engaging with entrepreneurs in her community, and you'll see in the interview why she finds this important.

Joanne and I had a great conversation and I felt incredibly motivated to go work with more entrepreneurs as a result. We talked about a few things that have been discussed in other places like convertible notes, side letters, and pro-rata rights. We also talked a lot about the importance of connection with entrepreneurs and how critical it is to put in the work and add real value as an angel investor. This is the part that inspired me the most. I had similar conversations with other angel investors, but there's something about Joanne's infectious and raw East Coast style that really made it provoking for me. I hope you find the same.

Why don't you tell me about how you got started angel investing?

I've been involved in the tech industry since the mid-1990s. The reality is that I've been involved in investing through osmosis for over 25 years. When the entire industry imploded or exploded – you could call it one or the other – in the 1990s, I got off the bandwagon and started to blog. I started blogging with the thought that I didn't want to lose my connection to the industry and I didn't want to lose my credibility. On the other hand, I really didn't want to start a business and I wondered, "What's next?" Over time, I realized that people reading my blog were not the people in the tech industry who were waiting for something new because many of them left and never returned to the industry. Entrepreneurial perhaps in spirit, but they didn't stay to see the next iteration. Some stayed, but not everyone. So I started really building this new audience of people, and many of them were women. I'd been watching what was happening in the technology industry in regards to the next generation of the web and how the Internet was going to be used as a platform to build businesses. I was watching one particular company, Curbed Media, and met Lockhart Steele.

I was obsessed with Curbed Media. My husband came home one day and I said, "Curbed media is at the beginning of how people are going to take in their content on a daily basis. This is where we're going," and he said, "Lockhart Steele is looking for money. They're going to raise some cash." Then he said, "You should invest, you would be awesome at this." He had to confirm with his LP's that it would be okay. There wasn't a conflict in the companies that he was investing in. My husband's partnership has a certain thesis and that's what they follow. He came back the next day and he said, "Do it."

You can talk to people who've known me for a long, long time, good or bad. There's nothing that I haven't touched that I haven't ended up growing. If I opened a lemonade stand on Monday, I'd want a chain by Friday. So now all of a sudden I'm in one investment and almost a decade later, I'm in over 85 investments. I was slow at the beginning because I was definitely learning and getting my feet wet. My advice to every new angel investor is to ask yourself at the end of 12 months, "Do I like everything still?"

What were you learning as you started slow and ramped up over time?

I think I've gotten better. I believe that's what happens to anybody in any job. You get better at figuring it out. I've always been a generalist, one of the people who reads 25 magazines a month. Taking all the information in and looking at the big picture. That's something I've always been interested in. Through that knowledge I think I've gotten better at picking the right jockey.

Do you think it's because you've seen so many businesses at this point that it's just easier to figure out which ones really have it?

Yeah. I've met with plenty of people now that I think, "Well, that's a great idea, but this person is certainly not capable of making that happen." At the end of the day it's such hard work. Even the greatest ideas with bad salespeople won't get off the ground or bad ideas with fabulous salespeople can explode. In many ways there's no reason for the success and failure of many of these businesses. At the end of the day, it's all about execution.

How do you filter for that? How do you figure out if they can execute?

That's a tough one. I'm not in it at that level where I am working directly on execution. I don't jump in when they are a $15 million business and think, "This person has been a fantastic entrepreneur. They built something really interesting or they're holding the company back because they're incapable or a micro-manager. They're incapable of letting people do the right thing. They're not taking the company in the direction that we want them to." That is a whole different ball game that's way outside of the angel investing world.

You're not necessarily as engaged with the company by the time they hit those inflection points. Is it harder to see those things?

Yeah. It's much more difficult. I'm at the point where I talk to all the founders that I have backed all day long. I've led several deals. I'm on many boards. This Thursday I'm having breakfast with one of my original investments. They were just valued at over $100M. I still see [the founder] and have breakfast with her. She still reaches out occasionally with questions. I'm involved in all of them and have my fingers in those pies in different ways, but the early ones, you can't tell someone who just raised a million and a half dollars, "Wow! You aren't the person to run this business, you have to help them build a foundation for growth."

I think it's usually a question of "How can we make you better at running this business?" I'm a big believer in getting help and I've said to many entrepreneurs, "Listen, you've got a great idea. You actually have the skill sets. These are your issues. You're never going to see success unless you speak to a CEO coach every week. They're going to get to know you, how you run your business, and how you manage your people. They'll help you become a better leader. It's this dirty little secret, but all of the top founders-turned-CEOs all talk to someone.

How much time would you estimate you spend with the companies that you've invested in?

At this point, it's a full-time job. I'm investing our capital back into entrepreneurs. I'm not passive. I'm very involved.

How much of that time is connecting with new entrepreneurs?

A lot. There's a lot of people I invest with, there's a bunch of people I talk to who send me stuff that might be too early for them [but I find] interesting. I get messages from them, saying, "This might be something you're interested in," and I get a lot of cold calls too. In fact, if the business interests me through an email introduction or just a random email where I read the deck and say, "Wow! I like that idea" or "That's interesting. I'd like to learn more about that," I'll engage and then eventually meet or not meet, but I won't just see someone. If I saw everyone who emails me, I'd never get time to do anything else.

How did you go about building this network of people who send you interesting companies that fit into your view?

The first investment I made was in a technology business. It was a content business, but technology was the platform to provide their content. The second business was in food, a consumer products business. At the end of the day, when you've got money to spend, everybody knows it. I also blog every day, so there's a whole audience from that. I've been in New York for a long time and am connected. It just sort of snowballed.

One woman emailed me and said she loved what I do, wanted to talk to me, so we got together. Another one introduced me to someone else and a relationship developed. I've always been a fantastic networker and I think that to really get great deal flow as an angel, you have to spend a lot of time networking. There are a lot of great avenues for people to start to angel invest and learn about it, like New York Angels. There are great communities for people to go and talk to each other about deals and see pitches from founders. They network within each other. I'm not part of those groups, I'm more of a loner, but do see the value in every one of them.

When you engage with a company that sounds interesting, how do you go about due diligence?

I don't torture these people. That's one of the things that's really important about being an angel. A lot of angel groups put these people through the ringer. I want to see that the entrepreneur obviously has a path, a road map, and can do finances. I want to see that they understand that if they do this, this is what's going to happen. They need to know what jobs need to be filled early on. They need a clear understanding of what type of foundation needs to be built to move the company forward.

I do want to see some traction and I want to see a built product. I want to see people engaged in a course they believe in but are nimble and flexible when it comes to molding their business. It could all fall part tomorrow or it could take off like wildflowers. I'm pretty quick in decision making and I also bring in other people to look at things differently than I do, which is the real bonus. Each business is different, but the foundation of doing the business is pretty much consistent throughout.

Is the business savvy more important than the entrepreneur/market fit?

There are times that these companies are having growth issues and they call me. One of the people I invested in called me the other day, and he asked about a couple of directions they were thinking about and I said, "No, don't do that one. I've seen that before and it has yet to work. I know someone you can create a fabulous partnership with and you should talk to them first." He was happy and because they're young, small, and open to guidance. Other times, the phone call is incredibly different when they call and say, "I haven't taken a salary for a year and a half, we just closed a round and I would actually like to pay myself some money." Silly as that is to have someone to say to you, I hear it. I told her, "Yes it's okay, give yourself a raise."

Sounds like you're in a mentoring role as an angel.

It's absolutely true. I would definitely consider myself a mentor to everyone I'm involved with.

How do you try to structure the deals you close?

I'm really entrepreneur-friendly. The documents should be simple and not onerous but also with some depth. For me, the important thing is I own 1%. I want to be able to own one percent for life, and I want to own it in preferred stock.

So whatever the easiest way is to make that happen without too much complexity?

I received these documents the other day on a deal we were working on. It was literally four inches of paperwork and I thought, "Why would they send this to me?" I think the quicker the better. Simple terms but not too simple. At the beginning I really hated convertible notes, but then I realized it really doesn't make any difference. If you're going to succeed, you convert. You know what I mean? If you're not going to succeed, it doesn't make any difference. These notes are always changing which is frustrating upon conversion, but you learn to make sure you're legally covered on the dollar amount you expect to convert at.

Do you always follow-on, on all future rounds?

I make everyone sign a side letter that says I can follow on, I'm pro rata for life. I won't screw with their documents or their deals, but I don't want to get pushed out by a VC who comes in and says they're taking all of it. I took the risk, I got involved at the beginning. I didn't just give money. I really got involved and I want to ensure that I get the letter so I can continue my ownership.

Do you always put the money in on every future round?

Mostly. I had one recently that was really, really expensive. I passed and even the entrepreneur said, "Yeah, I would pass if I were you too." I had another one where I didn't take the full amount. At some point it becomes too expensive. Once I have a certain amount of capital in the company I usually call it a day because I have enough exposure. At that point I will end up being diluted but that is okay. My mind shifts from the 1% ownership to "What returns will I see for the capital I have put in the company?"

Do you double down on down rounds?

I've been very lucky, and I haven't been in the down round. I've only been in up rounds.

How many winners and losers would you have that have exited?

I've had two that have exited and they've both been winners. I had two that went out of business, which was very upsetting but many lessons learned. All the rest are still in business.

Were there things you learned or changed as a result of having one of the businesses that you invested in fail?

I'm kind of glad in the end that I lost that one in a big emotional way because you sort of have to lose something to understand early red flags. It's interesting, because at the very end as I tried with my superpowers to prop this thing up, one of the investors, who's a major, major investor, called me up and said they weren't going to put any more money in to save this thing. I said okay. Then he says, "Listen, what you've done for this guy is beyond the call of duty, particularly for the amount of money involved, but it's over." I thought, "Oh my God." I've thought about that conversation several times, and you know what? It really was an eye-opener to the reality between the investors and the angels.

How do you think about company valuations?

It's a very good question. I don't want to put in too much because I have a number in my head, and that number is not going to put money into $12 million valuations. I have seen companies that have been way too high and I thought to myself, "You know what? I'm going to pass." I had one that actually came back and he had to do a down-round in order to get other people to give him this bridge loan. I said, "You were too high to begin with, but I like your business," so I came into that round.

It's important at the beginning to be real about your valuation. You have some people who say, "They shouldn't be valued at more than $2 million if they've never done a deal." But it's very simple. You don't want to sell someone more than 20% of your business from the very beginning. If you raise enough money for the first time that covers you for the first nine to 12 months, the second time it should be 18 months and the third time it's two years. If you need to raise $3 million on the last round, your valuation should be at $12 million. I'm a big believer in that, unless you really fucked up and you need the money to get over that hump and you have to take a hit. Hard goods and CPG companies are different because it costs more money to really get them built.

The other point is that I've seen people say, "Well, I think the valuation should be much lower." Do you really want to cram down an entrepreneur at this level? If it's three or if it's five, does it really make a damn bit of a difference? Truly. If we all believe that this is all going to be great and there's going to be upside, my biggest concern is there's going to be no upside.

Some people come to me for the first round and say, "I'll be at an $8 million valuation." I have to tell them, "You're out of your mind, let's try three or four." You don't want to be in a position where you can't raise money because you're not worth eight at the next round. You started something, you built something. You can feel it, you can taste it, it's going up, but it's still young, it's you and one other person. I get it, but know your next valuation. I'm looking at it and thinking, "Hmm, something's really happening here. Let's make it five or six." Eight? Where are you going from that? I think that's more in Silicon Valley than in New York where there's no issues with price inflation. Maybe just because there's more money flowing, maybe because there's so many more deals going on. I don't know why, but I do know that as an angel, someone who really cares passionately about entrepreneurs, and having them succeed is my number one. Sometimes I feel like I'm creating community, I'm creating jobs, I'm creating success, I'm creating a new industry, and I like the feeling of that. I also don't like the feeling of ever losing any money, but who does? I don't look at it and say to myself, I'm going to have 100 companies and if one is the killer, fuck the other 99. That's probably why I have only lost one business so far. I will do almost anything to help them survive.

Is that equally important to not losing your money?

I think it is. Of course I care about the money, I'm not a philanthropist when I invest in founders. I like to make money with my money, and that comes in all different sizes and shapes. For instance, I invest in restaurants as well. I invested in a couple restaurants starting a chain. I'm invested in one restauranteur where we've invested in all of his restaurants. A few we've gotten our money back, a few not yet, but we can see it happening. I'll never have the kind of returns in that business over ten years that I'll have from a successful technology business, but it's okay, because it's a different investment and I get different things from it.

Does such a broad portfolio allow you to allocate more money to angel investing?

The reality is that we invest in two things, real estate and entrepreneurship, and that's it. One more risk taking, one less risk taking. The difference with angel investing is it begins at zero. Real estate, you can actually do the numbers and see does this make sense, am I getting the right cap on my investment, and what kind of a return am I going to get on an annual basis? It's much more like late stage investment.

What's your view on early-stage funds or a venture fund?

It all depends on who's running the fund. Who's running the fund and what's their track record? We're seeing a lot of people on AngelList and other places, which is like this Internet angel group, but they're not groups because everyone isn't making their own decisions. It's basically I'm going to put money behind this person, because I think they're going to invest well for me. I see some of the top people on AngelList who have raised a lot of money from other angels with the belief that they have a big name and they're very connected to the communities, so they get great deal flow. Just because you have great deal flow doesn't mean you're good at decision making in regards to investments. Are they rolling up their sleeves? Are they just shooting money into the wind? I'm not so sure, but certainly time will tell.

I guess it's easy to be on AngelList and offer yourself as being someone to follow.

It's built for early participants who are in a very small group of people, a bunch of men essentially in Silicon Valley. I logged in and looked at how it worked, I saw I could share my deals with other people, send them the deck, and let them follow me. They are essentially my LP and that makes me really uncomfortable because I want investors to make their own decisions. I see a lot of people getting funded on those things who are the investors and I really wonder if they have a track record.

I would certainly like to see a lot more women who've had financial successes invest in other women and help them grow their businesses, because there's a tremendous value in that. Not only to help people grow their businesses, though that's a good feeling, but to share their knowledge with founders. I've had a bunch of women who follow me in deals who've never done angel investing before and they ask a lot of questions at the beginning, which I think is really important; it's how you learn. There are these two women who were trying to invest $10,000 each for this one investment and they couldn't get there. These two women have had tremendous success in their own careers, and even though they kept saying, "We don't understand these businesses," I had to tell them, "Let's have a conversation because, actually, you do understand the business. You've done so many different things that you're discounting in regards to your 30-year career. You have a lot to offer and a lot of thought process." I said, "I want you to think about your $10,000 each that you're struggling to make a decision over - how much did you spend at your Christmas vacation last year?" That was the ah-ha moment. They thought, "Oh yeah." This is something long term where we can make a difference and hopefully see our capital grow.

Where do you prefer to invest?

I prefer to be in my 'hood, but I am going to start spending a lot of time in Los Angeles; I actually have a deal or two there. I have a couple in San Francisco, but the majority of my investments are in New York and I actually have four in Europe. They may totally be outliers, but it's not like I didn't talk to them all at the very beginning. This one particular woman came to me and all the stars aligned. I skyped with her once a month and I knew the person who put the biggest check into this round personally.

You said you had two positive outcomes? You want to tell me a little about one of those?

Yeah, one of them sold to a privately held company. It was great. She's happy as can be, we all did well, and there's upsides going forward over the next three years; if she hits each milestone, we all get more cash, which I think is great. There's not even a question that she's going to hit those milestones, so I'm really happy with that. The other one was sold to another company that's also venture backed. It was great and it was 80% cash and 20% stock, which I really like, because we all made four or five times our money in cash and now there's more upside coming down the pike. The cultures were similar, which is so important, and each of the founders have really taken on a major role in that company now. I think they got us for a bargain, but it was a great outcome for everybody, and am really happy with that.

Is there was anything that you wish you would have known starting out in angel investing?

I wish I could say, "Yes, here it is," but there really isn't. The one thing I could equate this business to is real estate, in that even if you build a hundred homes or a hundred offices or a hundred buildings, every single one takes on a life of its own. You can learn from the past experiences, "Oh, we went through that before," or "We did this, and this is how we figured out the option pool," or "We found this really helpful or don't spend money on this." The reality is that every company has its own issues, its own assets, and no matter how many times you do it, it's always different for each individual organization. The key is who you're working with. Once you put money in, you're essentially married to that company if you're an involved investor. You should be willing to help those companies. As an early-stage investor you really got to trust your gut and instincts, in regards to, "Are these people or person someone I think has the ability to execute in scale?" I want to invest in someone who understands when it's not working and starts to think, "We're going to pivot right or we're going to evolve left, but we're not going to keep doing what we're doing, because it's just not working."

What things do you wish you would have known to avoid?

When you see a red flag, you know it. I think that when you see documents that are disastrous, you should walk. Especially if they keep telling you, "No, this is standard stuff." That's a huge red flag. Nothing's standard in this business. When people are continuing to go through new hires because they can't keep them under their roof, that's a red flag. I think there are others. When someone says, "I love this, but I sure don't want to be doing this in three years because I'm just going to grow this thing and sell it." That's a red flag. When someone sends me a deck that already tells me the exit strategy in the last phase, that's a red flag. I always say, "Really? It could take you 10 years." It's a ride and it's a really fucking hard ride and to think otherwise, you're fooling yourself.

Those are some of the lessons I've learned. When you say to someone, "So this is what we're going to do the first year and what are you thinking the second year," and they say, "I haven't thought that far" or "This is what I'm thinking and I think it's going to take at least three years to get there." You think to yourself, "Okay, that's a good sign." Versus someone who says, "Oh this will be quick." It's a long, long road. Every year there's one of those freaks like Snapchat or Instagram. That's the few actors who become stars, or the kids who all want to be NBA players. There are always one-offs, but most take time.

There are businesses my husband has been sitting on the board for almost 18 years and now they are huge and I'm sure they will eventually go public, but it took a long time to get there.

* * *

I learned a lot through my conversation with Joanne. I was impressed by her candor and openness. I'm sure any entrepreneur she works with appreciates that. I'm sure some find it abrasive as well, but I can appreciate that she's upfront with what she's asking and consistent with her needs. I also think her simple terms, side letter for pro-rata rights, and down-to-earth valuations are incredibly useful to think about.

MOMENTUM, NOT FOMO WITH DAVID COHEN

"Beginning is easy — continuing hard."

—JAPANESE PROVERB

"...entrepreneurs do stuff. They don't just talk about stuff, but they actually do stuff. We look for progress."

—DAVID COHEN

I FIRST MET DAVID at Howard Lindzon's Stocktoberfest down in San Diego. David came by to talk about Techstars and what he was building. I later connected again with David through Brad Feld. Most people who are angel investing today know what Techstars is. Techstars was founded by David Cohen, Brad Feld, David Brown, and Jared Polis in 2006. Today, Techstars runs a three-month-long program in Austin, Berlin, Boston, Boulder, Chicago, London, New York City, Seattle, and Techstars Cloud. Each of the ten companies that get into a program in one of these cities receives $18,000 in seed funding and are offered a $118,000 convertible debt note by a group of prominent VCs immediately upon acceptance into Techstars. Participants raise an average of more than $2.5 million in outside capital after the program. Today [July 2015], Techstars has invested in over 556 companies over nine years, 75 of which have had successful exits, 62 failed, and the remaining 419 are still in operation. In total, the companies that have been through Techstars have raised more than $1.7 billion in capital from investors. Techstars has also partnered with corporate partners such as Qualcomm, Disney, Ford, Barclays, Nike, Sprint, Verizon, Magna, McDonalds, Honda, R/GA, DAMA, and Kaplan to run a number of vertical programs.

David shared a lot with me about how he views entrepreneurs, what he looks for, and how he thinks about investing in the team. Not many of the interviewees were able to easily articulate what about the team makes them want to check that box, but he was able to explain his views in a way that any investor can learn from.

How did you get started angel investing?

I was an entrepreneur and worked at startups, and after some success decided I was interested in angel investing. I dipped into different things. I joined a local angel group and discovered for myself the market value of angel groups. Sometimes they are very good and sometimes they aren't. I made a little money and wanted to get some mental exercise. I wanted to help, to give back, and to make money while giving back.

How long have you been angel investing?

I started around 2005. I attended meetings with one angel group to try to find some deals but this particular angel group was mostly people who weren't really investing. I quickly learned that wasn't the best way to find your deals. The first investment I ever made was in a company called SolidWare. I invested $50,000 as I was just learning, but I learned a lot, and I really like the entrepreneur. Just a few weeks ago it actually paid off too—I made 2x on that. I never expected to make anything on that first investment. That's angel investing, though; sometimes it takes a long time. That was nine years to make 2x. I was investing with other bright people, some of whom I would get to know better later. Brad Feld was one. He was investing in that deal.

That's how I got into it and I just started finding deals locally, meeting people who were doing things. I started blogging about angel investing and that attracted a bunch of people to submit ideas to me. I did 10 or so investments before realizing I didn't like the fundamental model.

What didn't you like about it?

I don't like the idea of meeting somebody once, writing a check, and then not hearing from them much. It's the reason I started Techstars. Techstars is much more hands-on. You actually get to live with the company for three months and learn a lot about what they are made of before you actually invest. So rather than writing a check and hoping it works, you experience the company and *then* you write a check and you actually have an impact on the company and their ability to build a network.

Do you only invest then at this point in companies that go through Techstars?

We primarily invest in Techstars companies, but I'm also a first-round investor in companies like Uber and Twilio, which were founded or run by Techstars mentors. I've been through an evolution. My first 12 or so investments were personal, investments with just my own money. Then I started Techstars and have made in the order of 400 investments that way.

I did a few separate angel investments through about 2008. Then in 2009 I raised a venture fund. Now I'm investing other people's money, and that's not compatible with angel investing. Generally, you don't want to mix those. If you're investing other people's money, they don't want you investing your own money beside it. Obviously, a big chunk of my own money is in that venture fund as a result. The fund became my full focus after 2009, and then in 2012 I raised the second fund. We'll have to see what happens next.

Why move so quickly from angel to venture fund manager?

Mostly that was inbound. People saw that we'd built this thing called Techstars, and it had a real interesting deal flow. Suddenly, they were like, "Hey, you know, why don't I just give you some money to invest?" I never set out to become a venture capitalist. I just had that opportunity; people liked what I was doing, so I did it. It's nice to be risking your money along with other people's money. Then you really get disproportionate upside when it works. I was able to get scale, because there wasn't another way that I could support all of the investments that were available to me.

Do you support your portfolio differently as a VC than as an angel?

As we put money into a company, me or somebody on my team usually ends up on the board. When I was an angel investor, I rarely did that. I think people misunderstand the motivation of angel investors a lot. They think of it as purely financially driven, and usually, that's just one dimension of it. Of angel investors, 80% lose money so financial returns can't be the primary motivation. While I was an angel investor, my motivations were financial, giving back, and to get a good mental exercise. With that combination, I didn't feel like I had to be on the board or have control of any kind.

Once you invest a lot of money as a venture capitalist, you have a fiduciary responsibility for other people's money and you start to act differently as a result.

Do you start to look for different qualities in the companies that you're investing in?

Yeah, I think you do. There are plenty of deals that I would have done as an angel that I wouldn't have done through the venture funds. The reason is because you don't necessarily see the product being huge. It's not enough anymore to just like the people and believe in what the people are trying to do. You also have to understand the potential for a financial outcome for the people you're investing on behalf of. As an angel investor, I can invest in the people and the mission.

How do you pick between huge products and great teams?

You need both. The right people is clearly the first thing that we look at, though. We believe the right people will build the right company over time. Maybe they'll pivot and explore the market. For the venture funds, we're really looking at great teams that also have an idea in the market we're interested in. They are sort of equal, but we always need more teams.

If they are equal, how do you get to a fair valuation?

I think the valuation and the market are macro driven. A company in San Francisco is going to be worth more as a seed investment valuation-wise than a company in Portland, OR. That's just the way it is. Geography actually ends up having more to do with it than experience. That's a really weird thing sometimes and we're disciplined about not overpaying because somebody is somewhere. That also means that we're mostly investing outside of the Bay Area.

So you aren't willing to pay the Bay Area premium?

No, in the first round I would never pay for that. We will invest in the Bay Area, but we won't invest $10 million pre-money for a company with an idea and a prototype. That is just a bad investment.

What are you looking for in the people and teams?

I have this theory that I talk about a lot that entrepreneurs do stuff. They don't just talk about stuff, but they actually do stuff. We look for progress. That's a leading indicator. It doesn't mean you're done; it just means you're actually out there building a product, getting customers to use it, getting feedback and learning.

We also look for raw technical talent. We're looking for great horsepower on the tech side and some balance. We don't like teams that are completely technical. We like some balance, someone who can talk to customers and work with investors. We do like tech heavy and we look for the source of their passion. We want to know where they're coming from. If it's all coming from the head and not also the heart, it tends to not be a great fit for us.

Finding the source of their passion must be incredibly difficult, right?

Yes, but if I don't believe that it's coming from your heart on some level, I'm not going to invest. You have to be trying to solve a problem that you care about. It doesn't have to be your problem, it could be just a problem you associate yourself with. My first company was an ambulance dispatch software company. Pretty easy to get passionate about picking people up in ambulances when you ride around on them and see what's happening out there. Other people get passion from solving their own problem.

We had a company called Scriptpad that I always use as an example. The entrepreneur's dad was almost killed by a written prescription and he was pissed off. He was like, "Why are we still writing prescriptions?" You could tell that was coming from a place of passion in him.

What structure do you prefer to invest with?

Given the choice, I'm always more interested in simple preferred equity structures; 1x preferred, I think, is more aligning and everybody has the same goals. That said, I do plenty of convertible note investing, so I'm not religious about it. If the round is coming together and it's relatively small, say under a million and a half dollars, I'm fine with convertible notes.

When it gets into the multi-millions of convertible notes and giant party rounds, generally I'll stay away from that. You're always going to invest in the company that you care about the most, regardless of structure. Equity is just much more aligning, though, and when we're leading a round, that's what we go for.

How much time do you spend on those deals that you're leading?

We don't do a ton of due diligence, we're pretty light on it, we're only $100,000 investors. We're generally in rounds of half-million to a million and a half dollars so we'll do background on the people and talk to people they know. Too much due diligence can leave you not investing because you end up talking yourself out of the best opportunities. Good deals happen every week, they turn out great and are usually coming together quickly. You do what you can to make sure you believe in the people. You check their references. You look at the product and then you make a quick decision. We optimize ourselves to make decisions in a couple days.

Are all the good deals being done quickly and the bad deals being done over longer periods of time?

I don't find that there's a correlation. It tends to take longer for deals that are in locations without vibrant early-stage investment communities. The ones that are oversubscribed that people are super-excited about, those happen really quickly.

Sometimes it can be three or four months, even if I'm leading a deal. That's even when I have a lot of investors who want in. We get halfway there and once in a while it doesn't even come together. There's just not enough interest. Usually, if it's in a good startup location like New York, Boston, Boulder, Seattle, or the Bay Area, they come together pretty quickly.

Do you wind up investing because of a fear of missing out (FOMO)?

We have no FOMO, we're never going to do a deal because it's moving quicker than we're comfortable with. We know there's plenty of stuff we'll miss out on. We want to try to make quick decisions, especially in good deals. Sometimes they're done in a week. With Uber, if I had said I needed a couple of weeks, I wouldn't have been in it!

I bet you're glad you made that decision quickly!

Yeah, I'd be kicking myself! When you love it, you just got to go and you don't worry about all these other things. You just get in it.

What were you thinking when you made that decision?

Well, you love all your children the first day, right? Was it one I loved more than any other? No, but it was very compelling. It was reasonably priced. I really liked Ryan Graves, whom I consider to be the original operator and a founder of the company. I loved the business concept, even though the sharing economy was nascent back then.

It was literally a 20-minute conversation. I said, "Hey Ryan, I'd like to be in." It was over a beer and he said, "I think I can get you in if you're committed." I said, "All I have to do is a little bit of checking on you, but I could do that today or tomorrow." He said, "Great!" That was it. He held it for me for a day or two while I checked on him and that was it, we were in. The round happened in a couple of weeks and I committed midway.

Jumping in that quickly can lead to losing a lot of money quickly, no?

Due diligence is helpful, but gut reactions are often better than due diligence. You should do your basic due diligence. Looking at spreadsheets and reading business plans can get in the way when it's mostly about the people, their integrity, and what they're trying to accomplish.

I'm sure not all are Uber, though.

Yeah, we've had zeroes, 1x, and so on.

How are you transferring those things that you learn from one investment to the next?

You really begin pattern matching. I'm invested in over 400 companies now and you start to pattern match for people who are just good salespersons and don't necessarily execute. They've got to prove that they can actually get stuff done, they've got to actually have something. Just this week, we passed on a company because the founder had a great vision, but we weren't confident on their ability to execute on the scale. Most of the companies I've been involved in have failed with good effort. They haven't been squandering or anything, the business just wasn't working, so we decided to not keep investing or they just sold it.

I've been involved in somewhere around 60 acquisitions now of companies that I've invested in. I'd say that 15 to 20 of them have been acqui-hires. Sometimes it makes sense to sell a company just for the talent to get your money back. In fact, I'm an investor in a company called ExitRound and that's one of the things they do—help those transactions happen.

Looking back at 400 investments, what are the key patterns that a newer investor may not recognize?

A couple things come to mind, and Fred Wilson actually wrote an awesome post on this several years ago. I think it's called "Difficult CEOs." As an individual investor, you think about the fact that this is my money, I want to invest in people I really like, and I think that's a good high level filter. You're going to be spending time with these people and you want to support people that you really like—kind of a "no-assholes rule," if you will. I've actually learned that you need to like them, respect them, and they can't be evil. There are some who are kind of assholes that—and no, I'm not going to name any names—in the business context, they are perfectly good people but they sometimes piss other people off in business. Not by doing things immoral or unethical or illegal but by being super-aggressive. I've learned that sometimes you don't get along with those people like they're your best friends, but they build awesome businesses. So you have to balance that a little. When I first started investing, there were some entrepreneurs I didn't like and I didn't even want to talk to. It really is so much about people and their talent. If they just have an idea, as much as you believe in their excitement about that idea, if they're not doing something about it, they're not really entrepreneurs. Don't let them say, "Well, we need the money to make progress." That's the ultimate BS line. "How can we build software without the capital to build software?" Well, you know, good entrepreneurs do that.

The other thing I noticed is that the best entrepreneurs consistently surround themselves with the best networks. They're constantly building their network. They realize the value of having somebody in their corner to make introductions to customers. They're not lone wolves; they don't say, "I don't need any help. I know exactly what I'm doing." They question themselves. They have the imposter fear. "Am I really good? How can I mitigate the mistakes I might make?" I think that's a good trait that I've seen.

What should new angel investors avoid?

I think everybody ends up with their spaces that they really like and don't like. It's specific to the investor so I, for example, generally avoid Adtech. I don't understand it well enough and I really don't care about it. I have no energy for it. So I think you avoid things that don't excite you personally because you just won't put any energy into it and you'll write it off sooner. You have to care about what you're investing in, so just avoid investing in something that doesn't sound like a good business opportunity. If you don't care about it, don't do it.

* * *

David focuses on investing in people who're actively building products and making progress, the more upward momentum the better. What surprised me most is that he's happy to invest in entrepreneurs he doesn't like. This is incredibly different to some of the other investors in this book who would make likeability a prerequisite to investment.

UNDERSTAND THE INDUSTRY WITH BOB BOZEMAN

"If no mistake have you made, yet losing you are ... a different game you should play."

—YODA

"Focus on quality. Then make sure the fit is good. If you try to wear a pair of shoes that don't fit, then you've got blisters on your foot."

—BOB BOZEMAN

BOB WAS ACTUALLY a cold call for me. I wasn't really familiar with Bob's background and history before I saw him associated with the SV Angels group. As I dug a little deeper into the SV Angels group and some of Bob's background, I became excited to try and get connected to him. Finding very few connections to him in my network, I attempted a multipronged approach: I started establishing relationships with some of the other folks in his network who were bigger connectors and I sent him an email through LinkedIn. Always amazed at the power of LinkedIn's emails! Bob responded and let me have one shot at explaining myself over email. Apparently I did okay, and he agreed to have a bit of a phone conversation that quickly turned into a full interview.

Bob and I talked about several interesting aspects of investing in early stage. He had an early fund with Ron Conway, who's a well-renowned startup investor. He also talked about learning from Don Valentine, the founder of Sequoia Capital. Now Bob works mostly on his angel deals in Northern California and has raised two small funds (Northern California Investment Funds I and II) which he also manages for backing worthwhile ventures.

We talked a lot about Bob's investing style and started the conversation getting into some of the differences between venture capitalists and angels. Bob had a lot of interesting insights to share in this regard. He said, "I think you'll see that with the venture capitalists, the fundamental difference is that their eye for quality is much better."

I found this intriguing and before we dug into any of the standard stuff I discussed with the other angels, I wanted to understand this more. I asked him to expand the differences, and he replied: "The fundamental difference between venture capital and angel investing is that VCs have that eye for success, can keep track of that, and the vetting process is a really important factor in how they process companies and deal flow. A lot of the angels are busy, but they're not necessarily working on the best quality. The regimentation of how VCs have learned to be VCs is much different than how angels have learned to be angels. Even with VCs you'll find that it's really only the top 5% that really make the big bucks. The big winners. It isn't even the VCs in general, it's got to be the top VCs. That's the thing about it—I'll call it the Las Vegas effect. When you walk into Vegas you hear all the bells going off for people who are winning. But the reality is, there are 20 times more people who are losing. You just don't hear *that*, right?

"Then you talk with people in the parlor and ask them whether they're happy playing the game. They're generally happy or they would be leaving, right? But they may not be winning. Some people just don't see whether they're winning or losing, so the way to get at that is really important, because that's what you've got to weigh in terms of learning what's working and what's not," he concluded.

Before we began the interview in earnest, I was curious about how my own angel investing experiences in Seattle measured up against other areas and wanted to learn what Bob's thoughts were about Seattle. Bob's response gave me hope for the Seattle ecosystem and my odds for success investing in early-stage companies. Bob replied: "I think Seattle's a good area for early-stage investing, and they do have a thirst for knowledge. You get a sense of that, and essentially, when you go anywhere outside Silicon Valley, you really see a difference of challenges for early-stage investors. It's different in Silicon Valley just because there's so much formal venture money there, angel, and super-angel money."

It is a good sign for investors all over the country who are investing in their own backyards. Finding great companies in overlooked markets is easier; however, helping them grow with the amount of capital they need is another story. With that out of the way, I wanted to start the interview.

How did you get into angel investing?

I'm an old-timer. In the days that I grew up, venture capital was sort of the cat's meow and I actually came to Silicon Valley when it was just orchards. The early venture capitalists in those days were like me. They were operators of businesses who had become successful and they were young enough that they still wanted to stay active. Their mentorship really became the principle behind the money. In those days, even the best VCs were relatively small and had very little money. They were forced to aggregate their money. They really couldn't build decent-sized businesses. The goal those days was to build substantial businesses. It wasn't like it is today—going for opportunity.

I basically learned from a guy named Don Valentine, whom I consider to be the best VC who ever walked on earth. I watched how he developed his business. Then how venture capital sort of did their business. The guy I worked with at Altos Computer Systems was a guy named Ron Conway, who's well known in the angel community. He and I partnered with two funds back to back with Casey McGinn. Casey was the third partner. We did a lot of investing early on, but it was before there really were a lot of angel investors. We actually called our fund Angel Investors LP.

It was called angels, but it was really a formal venture capital fund. We had to do what all angels have to do and watch what the requirements are for the money behind you, so that when we invested in an opportunity, we'd immediately try to go to the best venture capitalists and get them to back us up. Fortunately, we were very successful doing that. But that's probably the biggest risk that most angels worry about, who's going to take on the company. Once they have their money, it's sort of on their shoulders.

Did you mostly go back to the venture folks you'd worked with in the past, and work to partner with them?

We did with about half of the hundreds of companies we funded. Out of those, half of the companies we got funded through Sequoia and about a third through Kleiner Perkins. In those days Kleiner Perkins was the number two fund. Then maybe about 20% with Accel, which was very good and is even better now. We were able to get very good quality. The last, the bottom 10% of the companies, we end up going to 50 different VCs to get them funded. We knew how hard it was to go out and scrape your money off Silicon Valley.

Did you find the companies Kleiner Perkins wasn't excited about were just as successful as the ones they were excited about?

No, our big one was Google. That was obviously one of the best that's ever happened. We never had any doubt about Google. But when we really tried to get funding for Google, we actually had a lot of challenges. People thought search was really soft. They really felt search was done, because we'd done Ask Jeeves previously and there had been all kinds of adequate search engines, so the niche was cluttered.

It seemed like forever, just because you're in such agony, but the reality was, it didn't take that long. I can't remember what it took, but maybe three weeks or something. In those days everything was hot. We thought it was going to be something that people would be fighting over, so for us to spend three weeks on it was actually grueling.

What did you see in Google at the time that was hard for others to see?

There were many paths that led us to Google, but when we finally sat down with Larry and Sergey, they had a lot of dedication for the search problem. We really liked that. Just to get a couple of guys who really felt that their life's work was going to be on all the problems that search entails, you really see the devotion to the problem. That's important to have people with the devotion for really solving the problem. We really believed in them.

They didn't have a business background, so it was all technology and opportunity?

They had a good cluster of talent around them. One of the people who got us involved with them was the computer science head at Stanford University. He was just an outstanding guy. He was an example of many others like that. They had always the best talent around them. That goes back to the heart of early-stage investing, in that it's not just the money, it really is the mentorship.

One of the things about Silicon Valley that most people don't realize is, it's developed as an amazing machination of throughput. Just the idea of having a round A, round B, and round C doesn't exist throughout the country. When you go out in other parts of the country, they'll think in terms of the differences between an A, a B, and a C. Silicon Valley views it as the requirements to financing. Venture capitalists require it to synchronize the way everybody winds up, and mass produces companies.

If you don't get enough money on your round A, and you're basically not ready for a round B, you're what they call a tweener. If you're a tweener, you're in trouble. Basically, you're going to get a fourth round of dilution, and the model works for three rounds; it doesn't work well with four rounds.

Did the Google investment change your investment style?

You have to think of it this way. We were really betting on the Internet. Our model was really what Don Valentine once said where you look for what's going to be the next big wave. In our mind, clearly the Internet was going to be the big wave, but nobody felt as strongly as we did, so we had a lot of running field to get out there first with a lot of the best deals.

Then the smaller guys started showing up. They'd pick up the deals where they saw a vision. One of the things I learned from just the exercise is that vision investors are very different from metrics investors. If you look throughout the country, most angel investors really don't feel comfortable with vision investing. They like to see the metrics. The obligation of your first money into an investment is to establish the metrics for the company. If you can't do that, you put at risk your follow-on investment.

There are just more who are metrics investors. You're putting a risk on the table that you won't find with somebody who maxes up your vision. Whereas if you start giving metrics, you know that people will react to metrics.

If you're investing mostly on vision and working to get those companies to a place where they can take a next round, do you care about how you're making that investment in terms of structure, or how much percentage?

Not as much. I remember Ron came over to me one day. I was looking at a business deal. He said, "What are you looking at?" I said, "I'm looking at all these numbers." He basically picked up the plan, tore the numbers off the back, threw them in garbage can, and said, "I never waste time with numbers." I don't know if it was that dramatic, but it seemed that way to me at the time, because he was right. He eventually said, the numbers are always wrong. What you have to get right is the dynamics of the market you're serving and what's the selling proposition. Most people who run a business learn that the P&L is sort of where you've been, and not where you're going.

If you're an investor and you require a P&L to really determine whether you're doing well, you're just late to the game. You should start thinking about where the bow of the boat is pointed rather than looking at the wave in the back.

Did you spend more time getting to know the market you were interested in?

We were going after anything that we thought would be the best play in the Internet space. It was long before anything really was there. You were redoing everything, right? What we really learned to do was to vet deals. We would get about 150 deals a weekend, and go through those and try to get 10 deals that we would get pitched on Tuesdays. Out of 10 deals maybe we would get one that we could then spend a lot of time on and decide whether it was going to be worth our investment.

Every week. That's why I got tired of pitching. After you did that with 500 companies like that, you were very tired. Early-stage investing people really like it, because it's exciting, but it's a lot of work to do it right.

How did you stay engaged with the companies you were investing in?

That was part of the obligation. We knew we were going to do a lot of companies, so the obligation was get the best VC behind us so we didn't have the burden of taking them all the way. That's a big difference between an angel investor and a formal venture capitalist; the venture capitalist has to stay with them all the way. The angel investor basically is passing to the VC who doesn't like to have a lot of angels, or a lot of noise around. They actually want you gone.

You will still get the call from the entrepreneur, because the entrepreneur doesn't necessarily always agree with that process, right? It doesn't mean you have lost your commitment to working with entrepreneurs, but there's no way you can do the volume of companies we did once we took that attitude. That's one reason why now when I work on investments, I really do what I call one-of-a-kind deals where I can really work with the companies. I always have half a dozen companies I'm working on, but that's about the max you can work on at one time.

If you really want to stay with the vision and help see the vision through, that's a much different process than what angel investing is fundamentally.

Do you see angel investing as trying to help them tidy up the package to move to the next stage?

The vision had to be there first. What you find is, some deals just aren't going to be packaged to the extent that there's a buyer out there. As much as you may believe in it, unless you have a buyer it doesn't matter. There's no transaction. You've got to make sure that they're marketable properties. That's number one.

Even though we may get all excited about a particular deal, there are a lot of things to do. We would watch our queue. If we built up more than a dozen companies, we'd have to stop until we got those companies funded.

One of the reasons why we saw the bubble coming before anybody else was that we stopped seeing the number of companies getting funded in the next round. Two-thirds of the way through our second fund, we closed it down, sold the fund to Crédit Suisse, and gave about a third of the money back to the investors.

This was well before the bubble popped?

I would say six months. Not so much before that a lot of people weren't worried about it, but definitely it was good timing. Most people sat on their cards, whereas we saw that companies would be more successful if they had deep-pocket people who picked up the funds and were able to then serve the purpose of following our investing, and keeping those companies alive.

Sitting at the start of the machine, was it more important to have those relationships with the VCs or entrepreneurs?

You needed to get the best deal flow. They work together. In other words, you wouldn't be able to work with the top VCs if they didn't respect your deal flow.

If you're doing what I am doing now, where you're looking for relatively few things to work on, you don't need to put the massive amount of energy we did. You're really working the quality of the network. At some point, the quality of the network works stronger for you than you really need. Sequoia will always get the strongest kind of deals, because their reputation is the best. They can maintain some of that volume by not having to do much. As long as they're successful, they'll maintain the majority of that pipeline process.

How do you think a newer angel without those connections fits into the process?

They have to do one of a few things. There's a whole mess of menus of things you can pick from. One menu would be to go to places that aren't well-served. For example, most universities are well-served. I went and interviewed every post-graduate candidate at Stanford before anybody else was doing that. That's another way we spotted Google.

There are schools that aren't like that. If I looked at Chico, for example—nobody really cares about Chico, right? I went to Chico and started going through all the best profs and said, "Who are the best students who stick out?" You just find underserved areas. If you just stick a sign up that says "Money," you'd think you have deal flow because everybody'd run in your door. The reality is, you've got to find people who aren't really distracted by signs that say money. You've got to find the people who have something unique.

So mimicking what works in the Valley in underserved areas?

They may think they get good deal flow because they get people passing deals around, but everybody looks at those deals. The best deals are the ones that you discover, frankly. You've got to really say, "Hey, I know people in this industry who want to start businesses. I've got to go out and start chatting with them and find out which of them is hottest to trot on a good, decent, constructive idea." Only the best angels work that way. They don't just get involved in deal flow because the deals that flow all around everybody have the same shot from everyone. They're going to be average deals. They're not going to be the best deals.

What do you think about mentors finding deal flow in accelerators like YC and Techstars?

There's a phrase that beauty is in the eye of the beholder. You really find that even really good deals get overlooked. I think there's an empathy that's required by the angel to look at the business and say, "I really buy into that." When you get into the analytics that a lot of metrics investors get into, you lose all that empathy.

I would say creating a bond with an entrepreneur that says, "Hey, we are both teaming up and this is important." The accelerators are pretty good because they're really the modern mentorship model. The original days of accelerators were really too expensive. They weren't fundamentally practical for the entrepreneur. Today, because the entrepreneurs are younger and have less experience, they really require more metrics. You see a change in that sense.

What's really key is the guys who are mentoring aren't just going through the mechanics of passing on knowledge. They're really trying to find out where can they really find a bond and become a partner in the business in the true spirit or sense.

How do you see the somewhat similar things like AngelList, and all of the online investing activity?

Number one, it's hard thinking about money in the early stages. That's where all the risk is. It's also where all the raw diamonds are. In the mining days, look how much of the mountains were just washed down the river. There was a huge amount of searching necessary to find the good nuggets. That's what the goal is. It's motivational for people who want to go do the hard work of doing that.

It's hard right now when you're moving away from Silicon Valley for early-stage companies to get funded. Crowdsourcing and all the other forms of doing that are good, because they help people who are really going through too much hardship. They really shouldn't have that much pain to be an entrepreneur.

I'm a big fan of crowdsourcing. I think they're going to be challenged for a while, because they're learning how to do it well. Just like anything, they need to learn how to do it well. You're going get a lot of crap, and you're going to see some things that stand out. One of the things that's very good is they're starting to get specialized. You get, for example, a crowdfunding site in health care, separate from crowdfunding in another space. You get people who start learning how to eyeball deals with quality better than just going through a lottery. That's the key to really good investing, to really focus on quality.

I was reading today Steve Case was quoted as saying he thinks all early-stage companies should be forced to crowdsource. We have a company we invested in called RevoLights. RevoLights did crowdfunding to get their first product out. It was good for them. It was good to do all that kind of stuff. Not everybody can pull that off. It took a lot of talent.

What you see with things like AngelList is the companies that are good at getting backing. For example, where you see Google's got another way to back a certain deal, then the momentum picks up and everybody jumps on the moving train. When the momentum's not there, they've got to build the momentum from nothing, you see it just lie there and just die publicly. That's not good for them.

I think there are going to be tricks. It's like anything, successful companies really learn fast. There's not going to be anything given. Everything has to be earned.

Google was obviously a success. What happens with failures?

I would say one would be, you get behind a vision and nobody else sees it. That's pretty depressing. It's depressing for the entrepreneur, it's depressing for the backer. That's part of what you have to learn how to deal with. That's why one of the tricks is seeing whether the timing's right or not.

It's why some people are better at picking companies. Ron Conway's very, very good at fashion. He has a nose for fads. I have no nose for fads at all, so I always look for deals that I think are longstanding opportunities that are stable and could surge. What Larry and Sergey talked about to me was great, because you can do more. Warren Buffett talks about building a moat around an area that's important and that's going to be a valuable property. That's why I always looked for market geography, market space where there's white space. You find white space you can get into first and then build a moat around it to protect it. Most people today are quick-flipping and looking at features rather than market opportunities. To me those are fundamentally different.

Ron's very good at that. If you know that you're good at doing that, and you can make money doing that, it's good. If you're like me and know you can't be good at it, then don't do it. You're just going to lose your shirt.

There are some people who are just good at the timing. It's a bit like stock picking. I'm a much better stock picker and would rather do that than do the balanced portfolio type approach. Different people just have different approaches. That's what you'll find with angel investing; they've got to look at what they're good at. I would meet with three VCs a week to develop our deep queue. We asked what kind of companies they wanted to see and they would tell us this and this, and this and this. We would serve them a company just like that and get nothing from them.

Then I'd look at what the companies were they were actually investing in and serve them something like that. That they would knock out of the park. A lot of times what they say was one thing but they really mean another. That's where I come back to the idea of beauty is in the eye of the beholder. You have to look at it from their point of view. If they like blondes, then you have to deliver a blonde.

Were there times that you were bringing them blondes, and it still wasn't working?

I would say, what do you want to see? They'd say, I want to see a strawberry blonde, so I'd give them a strawberry blonde, and nothing. Then I'd look and see that they *really* liked redheads. Throw them a redhead and they would pick that one up. That's how you find their comfort zone. It doesn't move around as much as people think. It's important to read comfort zones.

When you look at stretching comfort zones, you're challenging everybody. The best businesses really do stretch those comfort zones, but you have to recognize that situation. For example, in the music industry, the whole mindset was not like the IT industry where they were used to disruptive technologies coming in left and right. You'd have to realize if you were moving from something that you were used to like the IT industry and tried and apply that technology into the music industry, you're probably going to get killed.

Just like the automotive aftermarket. It is a horrible market and unless you're experienced with it you won't realize how bad it is. If you're experienced with it you can say, "I know how to deal with it," so you'll run circles around other people who don't understand why it's not a rational opportunity.

When you were interviewing students at Stanford, what were you looking for?

There are probably a series of things. Number one, you find out who's got an idea. Some just don't have an idea. The first thing you want to do is find out who's got what ideas and then you rate how good the idea is. You look for people who match the idea. You find that there are a lot of ideas that are pretty interesting, but the people aren't right for it. Or you might find the ideas are pretty weak, but the people are good. Then you struggle. You say, why are such good people working on such a weak idea?

If you find you're spending a lot of time upgrading the deal, you're doing what the entrepreneur should do. One of the hard things for me as an investor and a previous operating guy is that I was used to working hard on companies. The worst kind of an investor is the operator who really picks the specs because the investor is not really supposed to do that. They're supposed to bet on the operator, and let the operator do it right.

I'm exaggerating a little because there's overlap there, but it gives you the idea of why these seeds are so careful about taking on deals that have hair on them. If they have to fix a lot of things, all of a sudden they find themselves not just working on the exposed hair, but the underarm hair. It gets worse.

You want to be careful and make sure you're looking for deals that are just going to knock you on the side of the head and make you say, "Wow! That's really fantastic and you're fantastic as an entrepreneur." What you see are a lot of people trying to kind of upgrade the team, or upgrade this, or upgrade that. What they're finding is that the chemistry of getting a team together is not something they can do. The entrepreneur has to do it.

Should angels avoid feedback altogether?

You want to give feedback. One of the disappointments of the venture capital community is they're not quick to give feedback, because they want to keep their options open. If all of a sudden something becomes a hot deal, they want to get in on it. If the opinion they had just told everyone about the entrepreneur suddenly changed, the likelihood of them establishing a rapport with that entrepreneur would be less.

A lot of times you give them the feedback, and they just don't agree with you. That's fine. You've got multiple viewpoints. If you don't give them the feedback, they don't learn. One of the important aspects of venture capitalship is to provide good experience and viewpoints on problems that are challenging. Building businesses is really all those things.

For an angel who has some investments under their belt, how do they get better at being an angel, or picking companies, and building that engine?

Just because you're an investor doesn't mean you have any different problem than anybody else. Everybody has to learn, and expand their comfort zone, and figure out how to deal with things that are new. The thing about investing in new businesses is that there's a lot of unknowns. You're really trying to say, "I've got to deal with risks. Can I manage the risks the right way?"

Usually, one of the biggest things that investors do first is they don't look for quality. Once they learn that quality makes all the difference, then they usually put too much money into the good quality rather than using the money they've got to run the risk out by slowly growing into the deal.

What you find is that when you're working a deal over a long period of time, you're actually more effective. The earliest part of the business is the slowest part because of that. You've got to make all your changes on the least amount of money. Running out your biggest risks with the least amount of money is your number one job.

That's a challenge. A lot of people don't think that way, especially when you've got the entrepreneur saying, give me money, give me money, I'm ready, I'm ready, I'm ready. They want to get out into the field and work. You don't want to hurt them with that attitude, but you also want them to understand that it's your money that they're burning, and they've got to start thinking about it as their money, too. Because it's their equity that you're really buying with that money.

There's a little bit of a development process. That's why most Seeds are pretty much weighting people who have done it before more than people who are naïve about the process.

It's easier when they know how the game works?

Right. Getting experience along the way on all sides of the bench is really valuable. The company that requires a lot of mentoring is just a higher-risk deal, because you don't know whether they're going to accept it. If they're living off your experience, or they're not. If they're not living off your experience, then it's risky, because you're there because of the money only. That's one of the things you learn early on. What is your value-add on this deal? If it's money, you throw it over the wall and then you walk away. That's usually not what angel investing's all about.

You've got to make sure you're emotionally and in all other ways connecting with the entrepreneurs and his team, so you get the spirit of learning out of the way at a dime, rather than a dollar.

Do you prefer to invest multiple times into the company, as they progress before they really take off and go with the VC?

When I was basically a venture capitalist, I had a fund and our goal was to get money out of the deal. Then we made sure that we got strong people behind us to take on the deal. Money was really the tool to get positioned and established. You weren't looking for weaknesses that had to be covered. You were really betting to the strengths. That was the perfect game.

As an angel you find these guys aren't really ready for venture capital, so you're having to use your money to get them to a certain point. I learned through that process that there were really two buckets that companies ended up going into. They were the ones that were using me, because it was the money, or they were using me because of the experience. I shouldn't even have put the money in. I should have said, "Don't look at me and the money. Let me help you with experience," and kept the money as a separate angle.

A lot of times you give an entrepreneur guidance and mentorship and you're going to be there for the long haul to develop them to the sweet spot that everybody's defined as success. If all he's looking at is the money, sometimes your advice gets viewed at as "That's what's good from the money viewpoint, but that might not be the best for the company." You start getting a divergence of viewpoints. I found a lot of angels are actually better when they don't put money in, but they put advice in, and they put time in.

Ron's a good example. He will combine a lot of people's money and syndicate them. His name will carry a lot of weight, so they'll get other people's money behind his. He's getting a lot of clout but putting in a small amount. It's syndication that allows you to put very little of your own money in and get the clout of big syndication. That's why you see angel groups. They will basically get behind somebody who'll take the lead on a deal and throw in their money behind that guy.

Would these folks blindly follow Ron in or do their own work?

You look at track records. If you're working on a health-care deal and you're not very good at health care, but you liked certain aspects about the deal, a lot of times people will think that the deal is clean. A lot of times you'll see the details, but you really understand 80% of that, and it's so compelling, you don't want to ignore that other 20%, but it's all foreign stuff. That's where you've got to structure your comfort zone.

Understanding that you're stretching your comfort zone versus getting into dangerous territory is one of the things you have to learn how to eyeball. Early on I would only do tech deals, because that's all I knew. When I stopped doing just tech, once I started doing a whole mess of industries, I started realizing you can spot where the risks are even better, because you're more objective. You're standing away from the problem and able to see it with more visibility.

Are there other lessons that you've learned along the way?

Just focus on quality, quality, quality. Then make sure the fit is good. If you try to wear a pair of shoes that don't fit, then you've got blisters on your foot. It's bad when you're investing in a business that you find over time that everything is moving away from where your comfort zone is. You just don't stay with the business. I think getting a long-term view, and staying with that view, even though you're an early investor, is probably the hardest thing to come to grips with, but it's one of the most important things.

The last thing is, with this idea of vision investing versus metrics investing, if you're more comfortable with metrics investing, then don't do angel investing. The early stage isn't going to be good for you and you're going to be driving the entrepreneurs for all the wrong reasons. They don't have metrics until they're well into their business. A pure metrics investor should try to participate more in A rounds, or something like that, or syndicate behind people who are vision investors.

Anything investors should avoid?

People could look at it like a get-rich-quick scheme. I don't have any emotional reaction going to Las Vegas, even though I pull the handle on a bunch of things; it doesn't really change my life. You have to think about investing as that way. It's not a get-rich scheme. It's a way of building opportunities out there in these markets that will have value over time. You put a lot of energy into that. It's a lot easier to make money just in public stocks, because you don't have any liquidity issues. You don't have any delays in selling, all those kinds of things. You should understand what you're getting involved in, and have the patience for it, and have the appetite for the disciplines that you need to really be successful.

* * *

The insights from Bob on investing as a fad/vision or momentum investor or a metrics or value investor were something I found with most angel investors I interviewed. In fact, all fit into either those two categories or a third that Bob didn't discuss, which is the alternative investor where investors are trying to make investments that have a social impact or who're trying to invest in startups like an index fund. Bob clarified my view of what a vision investor should be looking for. Often, I found fad investors confusing vision investing with fad investing and Bob's subtle clarification was helpful.

Bob also offered some very actionable advice on the venture funding machine and how to find great opportunities and how to think about the next phase for those great opportunities. Having someone else to fund the business is important, and not thinking about that from the start can make seeing those investments through to the end a difficult task. We all know what happened to some of his early investments such as Google. RevoLights, one of his newer investments, isn't doing too badly, either; they just raised a $1 million Series A in May of 2014.

FIND YOUR PET ROCK WITH HOWARD LINDZON

"Good jockeys will do well on good horses, but not on broken-down nags."

—WARREN BUFFETT

"Good jockeys continue to win races on different horses. To me, the unicorns are the entrepreneurs."

—HOWARD LINDZON

I MET HOWARD through the usual channels—online, social media, and discussions about investing. But our introduction to each other wasn't initially related to startups and angel investing. Howard is a serial entrepreneur building companies related to public market investing. I found him through my own passions and research into public market investing, and only later did we connect on angel investing.

When I started the research for this book, I interviewed other professional stock market investors who are active angels such as Jeffrey Carter and included Howard here to represent the rest you can find online at my website. Our interview was one of the few where we recorded video, and the whole video episode is available online. Included here is the edited version.

How did you get started angel investing?

I think it always starts by accident because I'm not a professional. It started in college. I had an MBA, and I was looking for a job in Arizona. I took a job as a broker in 1991, but obviously that's a sales job, so it's easy to qualify directly. I got hooked on angel investing when I was reading the local business journals to find clients. I cold-called this young guy, a local kid, with a product called the Gripp. I called him to invest in the company. I ended up writing him a check that I really couldn't afford to write. That product became like the Pet Rock of the 1980s.

I kind of hit a jackpot right off my first angel investment. I think I was doing it based on the fact that I hate regular work and was willing to risk money I don't have on a person I hardly knew to start a company. No skill at it, no real due diligence, even though I had an MBA and just pure product instinct. A lot of hard work later—I think 40 million sales later, with huge margins—I thought he was a pretty smart guy.

Looking back now, how much skill do you think is really involved in angel investing?

What has gotten really popular is Internet angel investing, because that's where all the new money is. People are going to plow their money back into what they know or think they know. When I got my first hit, I became addicted. It's easy to get a product on QVC. Show me your plastic mold, we could do that in China and will cost blah, blah, blah, even though I wasn't an expert but I did have an understanding of margins on distribution. The next 10 products we backed were idiotic failures, even though we understood distribution margin.

Even though we were supposed to have learned all this from one successful product, in the end I didn't really learn anything until ten failed consumer products later, which kind of got boring and tiring. So I left angel investing in the late 1990s because I realized how hard it was to catch a unicorn. Basically, my first company was a unicorn. There were no outside investors, amazing distribution, and it made families wealthy. I mean, it was like a real unicorn.

It wasn't a billion-dollar type of unicorn, but it was a unicorn in a sense that it had everything that creates bad habits. Unicorns are the mystical things for VCs. Their job is to make money and return it to the limited partners, and hence they came up with this term *unicorn*. I don't call them unicorns when the entrepreneur can't do it again. To me, a unicorn is an entrepreneur who can do this multiple times, not the fact that a company got there. There's nothing to learn from a company that just got there. That's what the whole tech industry is trying to solve now, how to do this one thing or that one thing.

I think it's all people oriented. It's the entrepreneur who learns that's important. Good jockeys continue to win races on different horses. To me, the unicorns are the entrepreneurs.

Do you try to follow more entrepreneurs into other products or other companies that they build?

Yeah, that's key. The best investors write blank checks in their mind to great entrepreneurs. That's what makes unicorns—you can't forget them and even if you see one, it doesn't mean you can do anything with it. Unfortunately, the tech industry is all upside down, but it's the farthest along in terms of discussion and interest and passion and the drama. The entertainment-type drama, with real stuff on the line.

Look at Silicon Valley right now. Supposedly, people are throwing rocks at the corporate buses filled with Google employees who are settling into the area and pushing out the old timers, but everybody still wants to hang with all the people on the buses.

You are outside of Silicon Valley. Does that allow you to be more contrarian to what happens in the valley?

I think you get this too, because you invest in stocks. I think everybody needs to invest in stocks. That's why I'm so excited about companies like StockTwits, RobinHood, and all these lightweight products that can help people. If I told you StockTwits was going to teach you how to learn Chinese and that could help you raise a hundred million dollars, people would clamber over it. Yet, all it does is help you learn to invest and learn the language of the markets, so it has zero interest to any company in the world. Now, I'm not mad about that, because I understand the playing field in which we live.

Chinese, Spanish language learning companies are worth gazillions. Why should I learn Spanish to go get a job that makes me $150,000 a year? I could learn the language of the markets and make money from my desk or from my iPhone doing five trades a year for the rest of my life. Now, that doesn't sound altruistic. You say that kind of shit on Twitter and people will take your head off, but they're not thinking through what that really means, because the markets are this incredible freedom machine, an incredible opportunity machine.

Now you can take the job that you want because you understand that you know what to do with the money once you make it. If you look at what Silicon Valley is trying to do to Wall Street with Wealthfront and with all of the others, they think that just by taking the fees out of the system that you're going to be a better investor. That's the wrong way to look at it. I mean that's true, but that's the only statement at the top of every new company—"take fees out of the system." I'm with you. That's not the same for everyone in Silicon Valley. Thinking that's the only business Silicon Valley could do is to squeeze the fees out of the system is bullshit.

That's not an education. That's not teaching people anything. You better give them the fishing rod and then let them go and do everything else in life they were going to do, but who know how to manage their money themselves. Fundamentally, people are teaching this stuff right from the beginning. You have to separate the company from the ticker symbol and you have to understand behavioral economics. That's the opportunity.

Thinking about angel investing is no different. I thank the 1990s and 2000s for the technology and for how broken the ethics system has become. The 1990s and 2000s rigged the system. The system is now so repulsive, broken, and unpunished you think it should be out of style. Now standing away from all that is what makes all the difference.

These Wall Street firms are doing everything they can to stand next to their pipe. Guess what, Netflix is up 400% over the last year. What machine helps you do that? What millisecond machine helps you do that? That's instinct, and that's understanding how trends work. All that real-time information has only led to the returns getting better for people standing farther away from the machine.

That's where I think we've come. You gave your price. You get close to the system. Then the machines take over and it's like oh my God. Stocks are doing crazy wild things because the machines are all grinding for nickels and fractions of a penny. Once they break beyond that, nobody owns stocks anymore.

No human beings own stocks, if you understand the catalyst and you understand patterns and you understand how markets work, if tons of money will be made away from the line of scrimmage, that's how I think about it. I try not to get myself down about all the cheating and fraud because I'm thinking of things with five- and seven-year patterns.

Do you think you miss out on opportunities being so far away from the line of scrimmage?

The hardest part for beginners is that you can't have it all. You have to pick your spot. Again using a sports analogy, whether you're a fat golfer or skinny golfer, sometimes you hit it long, but in the end you only have to do one part of the game really well to stand out. The stock market is just an opportunity machine. You don't have to trade airline stocks if you have no edge and don't understand the catalyst. Anyone can go read Y Combinator's Hacker News or TechCrunch and follow people who really love tech instead of following the tech stock gossip all day. The entertainment of tech stocks is talking about signals that nobody at the line of scrimmage is looking at. That's why trends work. I can't explain it perfectly, but that's obviously what's happening.

That was the point of WallStrip back in 2006. I was living in Phoenix when I talked to Fred Wilson and I told him, "I am going to do a three-minute video show about nothing." It was inspired by Larry David, the guy who created the *Seinfeld* show with Jerry Seinfeld. I told him, "I am going to do a show about nothing. We are going to pick the dumbest things. Stocks that are at all-time highs and I am going to prove to people that people are wrong, the stocks that are doing well continue to do well." It's a long-understood philosophy, a momentum of things in motion tends to stay in motion and that applies to stocks.

It didn't have anything to do with information. We talked about the products and goofball skits and it was a hit. That was the proof that CNBC doesn't need to be in New York. Even CNBC knows that. They're in New Jersey, for God sakes. The problem is nobody there really cares about the market. It's so obvious. From the very top down we have Comcast, this gigantic bulwark, they are the new Standard Oil, and they own CNBC, so think about how evil this is. They don't even care what goes on at CNBC.

Comcast is so big that their business channel runs unchecked because Comcast is making so much money from cable deals that it has nothing to do with the content. Right now they cut this deal with Netflix. Netflix can worry about the content. Comcast only needs to worry about the government and distribution and everything else. He who has the most profits gets the most attention from Comcast. Why worry about it? Because you can still make money with the corporations cheating and with the analysts issuing strong vibes right before they announce a banking PO. We are at all-time highs and there are shenanigans both at the corporate level and the government level, yet you can still make money.

I live in San Diego. I am at peace with the lifestyle that I have. I don't want to become a billionaire by luck or accident and not by hard work and good ethics. I think we have to give people the tools to live with so they are happier living on $150,000 a year because I think anybody can make $150,000 a year.

What do you think about the gap between making an investment and getting the return out?

I never thought it could be long term. I was enamored with Jim Cramer. I mean, Jim Cramer really invented a lot of this stuff. Little did I know that he was backed by people who now are my mentors, like Michael Parekh and Fred Wilson, who was a CEO for an hour at TheStreet.com post-2001—such a small world. TheStreet.com invented a lot about what you see today. Cramer was blogging, TheStreet.com was taking on *The Wall Street Journal* and the establishment.

What would happen for the rest of us at Web 2.0 if Jim Cramer decided not to put on makeup and go back to Web 0.5, which is yelling stuff at the TV like a carnival? There's nothing innovative. We're just like all these other people who moved on, and that's finance in general. It just keeps getting further and further behind despite what the innovators are trying to do because of 1929 laws.

It's easier and easier to cheat, which leads to my philosophy, but it's becoming dumber and dumber to get closer to the pipe and smarter and smarter to stand farther away, now that it's clear it won't last forever. I see an end to this pretty soon and I am going to have to reinvent how I read the tape and do things, but if I can learn how to hold something for seven years, anybody can. I'm shocked at some of the stuff that I still hold that's doing well.

I still have a habit of selling things early whether it's Twitter or some other mistakes that are made in this bull market, but if I can learn to hold something like LifeLock, GolfNow, or TubeMogul, anybody can do it. You have to just learn about yourself and be realistic about what percentage of your net worth you're willing to trust to your long-term instincts around people and it's not easy. This is not something you learn overnight.

What do you think of the online angel platforms like AngelList, SeedInvest, or FundersClub?

I think Naval Ravikant and company have continued to just blow people's minds with software as an investing service. Half the investments I pass on because I dread the paperwork and I dread the bullshit that goes along with it. Software should remove all that. If I'm willing to invest and can get access to the paperwork quickly and everybody has access to the same paperwork, I'm all for it.

I look at AngelList and I say, "That's the new small-cap OTC stock market. Why do I want to invest in this stuff if I don't trust any of the paperwork? I don't know where the potential liabilities are and no social understanding of who the people running this company are. I don't know where every share is." I mean, that's ridiculous. If you're trading in OTC markets, you might as well put bullets in a gun and just shoot yourself. At least on AngelList, I can see who I am investing with, and everybody has the same paperwork.

I know how to reach everybody at one time. I know someone can theoretically steal the money and wire the money to himself. Then they aren't going to be doing business again in our town. There's still buyer beware and there are still rules of engagement and you could lose all your money, but it's a much better OTC market. The OTC market as it is now doesn't work. It's broken. The small-cap market is an unregulated complete mess. AngelList should be replacing all that.

We're talking ground up, AngelList is a better restructuring of the markets. It's not going to replace NASDAQ tomorrow, the CME, or the CBOE, but it sure as hell can replace the NASDAQ and small secondary departments. That's wonderful. If we can get some organization that helps to create more products, more opportunity, and more choices for people to invest their money into areas they're passionate about, that's a good thing.

Do you think the ease of investing through crowdfunding platforms lessens the ability for investors to have an edge?

This is what makes ESPN point/counterpoint stuff so fascinating to watch. If we have attacked this from both ways, you're going to give certain people who shouldn't be investing more ammunition to blow themselves up, but you can't protect that person. You just can't protect that person. That same person will get in a car and text while he's driving and drive right into you. There are no rules to protect them from that. You can't protect people from stupid people and you can't protect stupid people from themselves.

I don't know where you draw the line. If we're going to draw the line there, I am very anti-gun. If we're going to get into politics, I am anti-gun. As Chris Rock says, charge a lot of money for bullets. If we're going to go there with the stock market we're broken. Basically, we've been broken from the beginning because we use these 1929 rules in a 2014 stock market. It's the most dangerous set of rules I know of because they are packaged in such a way to make it feel like they are protecting you. You can't protect people from themselves.

You *can* educate them. You can give them case studies and examples of stupid people and tell them, "Don't be so stupid." You can drill that mantra into people's heads just like yoga. People like yoga because it's meditation, a mantra. It's continually doing stuff in a good pattern over and over again.

What are some of those lessons or mantras for a new investor?

I don't like Wal-Mart. I don't like retailing [for investing], but when I used to walk into an Apple store it always felt like everything should go into my cart. I can only imagine entrepreneurs just made some money and decide they didn't want a Porsche. I can live with Uber for the rest of my life, which makes sense. Now they have all this extra money because the math works.

I think this tech world is helping us live with less stuff. Live less connected and more connected at the same time. What you have to do is get some kind of control, so you can focus. If you can come onto AngelList and say I want to do clean tech, say. I want second-time entrepreneurs who have already been successful. I only want to invest when this VC also invests. You can curate it to the point where you could control it and get stuff sent to you.

You can step up or you can lean back and let the product work for you. When you get something delivered to your inbox, you're pretty much assured that it should be interesting enough for you to spend some time on. That's a harder thing for people. That's a different way to look at the world.

I have my interests, I know what I'm good at, so why shouldn't I just continue to focus on that? I also have my pet projects that I'm willing to gamble with or take some higher-risk money and place a few bets whether it's biotech or health care. That comes down to money management, but with these tools and mobile phones and push, we're entering a world where people are going to have so much more time but less stuff to spend it on. It's a hard product to be able to measure, but that's why this market keeps going up.

We're in this era in which we don't understand the productivity gains yet. They're not measurable and economists who are useless are trying to measure something that's in such a new territory. It's an impossible metric, the leverage from these networks, so why think about it? Just start participating and stop worrying about it.

How do you think about the investment vehicle, equity, convertible notes, and so on?

I think that's up to the entrepreneur. They have to be single-mindedly focused, which is why they are so successful. If you want to invest in product, you can go to Kickstarter. If you want to help people pay the medical bills, you can use GiveForward.com. If you want to invest in a startup, you go to AngelList. If you want to learn about the stock market and find people who love talking about stocks all day, go to StockTwits. You know what I mean?

If you want news, you go to Twitter, if you want to talk to your old girlfriend because your wife is fighting with you, you go to Facebook, those type of things. Boy, don't you and I wish we had Tinder? Can you imagine what we can do with Tinder? I just imagine not having Tinder. People are worried about the wrong things.

How many angel investments have you made?

I think we're closing in on a hundred since 1999.

* * *

Howard provides an interesting insight into the intersection of angel investing and public stock investing, with the understanding that there are many similarities in the principles of investing in public companies in OTC markets and investing in private companies. The main similarity is that the devil is in the details. The investment vehicles, legal documents, and agreements that are used to make the investments make all the difference in the world. In both situations, investing in high-quality people with good intentions is more important to focus on because there remains too much room for greed to overcome the great investment.

BUILD A COMMUNITY WITH VC DAVE MCCLURE

"You can't relate to a superhero, to a superman, but you can identify with a real man who in times of crisis draws forth some extraordinary quality from within himself and triumphs but only after a struggle."

—TIMOTHY DALTON

"Usually, people say that the team is most important. I say that's bullshit because most people don't know the team very well. "

—DAVE MCCLURE

I REACHED OUT to Dave through mutual friends. He is an incredibly busy guy, so actually scheduling a time for us to meet was difficult. He was incredibly gracious and found some time for me during a commute and I did everything I could to make sure it worked. Dave very much takes a momentum approach to his early-stage VC investments.

Dave is well known in the early-stage tech startup business. He has been focused on this space since 1994, after a few years consulting for a variety of larger companies. That includes PayPal, O'Reilly, fbFund, and most recently running 500 Startups, which is investing in early-stage tech companies all over the world. You can find him online. You can also see more on our website about Dave as well as a profile of Rui Ma, who runs the 500 Startup investments in Asia.

How do you view early-stage investing?

Certainly more accessible than in the past. Platforms like AngelList, FundersClub and others, as well as pretty widely available information, are making it easier for people to participate. That doesn't mean that they are dramatically more educated and knowledgeable. There does seem to be a lot of folks jumping into angel investing in tech. There should probably be a little bit of caution or concern there, given that some of those folks have starry-eyed expectations about returns and investing in the next Instagram, WhatsApp, or Facebook. The reality is probably a lot less exciting. I think most people don't take advantage of as much portfolio diversification as they should.

There is a tendency to think that five to 10 investments means that you're diversified. I would say that depending on stage, it is probably more like 20 to 50 investments are diversified. Certainly 20 or more would be my suggested target for a lot of new angels. Unless, of course, they are just prepared to lose all of their money or they are only doing one deal or investing in a particular thing they know a lot about. I wouldn't say that those are the typical cases.

What should you do to make sure the group of investments that you're diversified in are quality investments?

Generally, don't pay too high of a price is the one guiding principle. Obviously, if you're getting into very high-quality deals they are going to have some higher prices. The average angel investors' ability to get into great instead of good deals is pretty limited, so paying too high a price for perceived great deals is likely a fool's game.

In general, sub–$3 million investment valuations for most areas would be the price. In Silicon Valley those may be $5 million or even higher. In most parts of the country, it is closer to three, and in some parts of the world it is less than that.

Of course, there are a lot of different judgments about where they are at—is it just a PowerPoint presentation, is there product, is there revenue, and is there a team. There are probably five to 10 questions that could add half a million to a million in valuation, depending on whether they check off yes. Assuming you have some access to quality deal flow, you should be in at least 10 but more like 20 investments. That is likely to give you a better return.

For the average investor, does determining who the other investors are make a difference?

A little, unless they are particular. Unless the terms are differentiated, perhaps. It only really helps if there are celebrity investors who attract others. Sometimes they can pull the price up to a place where it isn't affordable. Assuming the terms and the investors are reasonable people, I would be more concerned with customer traction than who the investors or advisors are.

What about team versus product versus market?

Usually, people say that the team is most important. I say that's bullshit because most people don't know the team very well. Unless you're investing in a very experienced team, they may look great on paper, but they may not be so great in practice. There may be people who don't look so great on paper, but they have great behavior patterns.

We tend to look at product and customer traction most. Market we can assess a little bit, but it is harder to predict market. We look at unit economics and margins and guess at what those might be. Most of the time we try and understand if the product solves a problem and are there customers who would be interested in using and paying for it.

Most people haven't had two to three years with the team to really understand them enough to make a difference. Most people are looking at what's on their resumes or where they went to school, which isn't enough of a predictor by itself.

Do you try to model what the unit economics and exits could look like?

That is a little bit of crystal ball gazing as well. What we try to find is evidence that things are working—functional product and some kind of an active user base. Ideally, some revenue and retention metrics. Some understanding of customer acquisition cost and margins. Those are the things that we try to understand. We understand that those are going to be guesswork and we're going to be wrong a lot. In addition, we're looking for some scalable methods of marketing customer acquisition.

It's a pretty inexact science. We're mostly looking for evidence that things are working and try to make an informed guess as to whether that will continue, and hopefully, if we were right, we double down early because we invested first.

We're probably wrong three times out of four, if not more. Hopefully, between 20% to 40% of the time we find some success and probably double about a third of the time. Out of those, maybe half of those we continue investing in further. Ultimately, we probably end up with around a third of our investments having some form of exit and maybe 5% to 10% have a larger multiple. When the majority of your return is coming from 5% to 10% of your portfolio, you should be diversified into at least five to ten investments, if not more, to ensure you have a good shot at the winners.

How do you view doubling down, maintaining position, or just making a new bet?

People think about pro rata way too much. We don't care about ownership percentage, except in relation to our existing position. Most of the time we are making a $50,000 to $100,000 bet at a lower or earliest valuation as possible. When we buy more, we buy a minimum of 50% of ownership and ideally, 100% to 300% of ownership. Ideally, that's at not more than 3x to 5x or our original cost.

A good deal for us is when we can buy 200% incremental ownership at 1.5x to 2x our original cost. Unless we're doubling or tripling our ownership, higher multiples of cost isn't worth the risk on our capital deployed. Even though we are still high-risk investors.

I don't think doubling down on investments is a good idea for most angels. It usually isn't worth it for most investments, and it is putting a lot of capital at risk because it is so hard to determine which companies are going to generate wins. It's not usually easy for angels to do pay to plays. My experience as an angel when I wasn't doing funds is that I didn't tend to do follow-on investments.

BIRD DOG THE BEST DEALS WITH VC CHRIS DEVORE

"Remember that just because other people agree or disagree with you doesn't make you right or wrong - the only thing that matters is the correctness of your analysis and judgment."

—CHARLIE MUNGER

"It's having a sense of conviction about where the world is going in terms of innovation, and then talking to lots of people, not to steer them toward your convictions, but sifting the world to find people who believe what you believe and then backing them."

—CHRIS DEVORE

CHRIS DEVORE is the co-founder and general partner of Founders' Co-op, a seed stage fund based in Seattle. He is also the managing director for Techstars Seattle. Chris is an avid supporter of the startup economy in Seattle and backs it up as the chair of the Economic Development Commission for the city of Seattle and as a member of the board of directors at the Washington Technology Industry Association. The list goes on of boards and advisory roles that Chris has, but you probably get the picture that he's really focused on fostering an environment where large-scale companies can be built.

I was lucky to get some of Chris's time and walk through his views on early-stage investing.

How did you get started with early-stage investing?

I've been in the software business since the early 1990s, first inside big companies, then as a bootstrapper, then as cofounder of a venture-backed business, with some success and some failure along the way. One of the key things I learned was that early-stage investors were the ones who enabled innovators to get off the blocks.

I like innovation. I like ideas. I like people and I like being part of winning teams. I don't gamble, I don't watch sports, I don't do any of those things. What I like to do is bet on people in the innovation business, so as soon as I had the capacity, that's what I started doing as an individual—writing some small checks, and then some bigger checks.

My business partner and I started a fund in 2008, partly because we wanted to be able to make bigger bets than we could by ourselves as angels, and also because we saw an opportunity to help fill the early-stage investment gap here in Seattle. There was a lot of angel money, but there wasn't enough angel money focused on explosive outcomes, venture-scale outcomes.

I should be clear that my views on angel investing are very much about venture track companies, because there are lots of good companies that are a good fit for angel investment but aren't focused on creating venture-scale outcomes. I wouldn't want my comments to be overgeneralized to all angel investing. The kind of angel investing that I care about is in technology and innovation companies that aspire to making a significant cultural and economic impact in the world.

Looking at just those type of companies, how do you think about finding them?

Having been a professional investor for almost six years, there are a lot of things that are very different from an angel to being a VC. I run money for other people. As a fiduciary I have to go about it differently than if I'm just investing my own money. I'll try to tease apart the institutional side versus the angel side:

As an angel, when it's your personal balance sheet and there's no obligation or expectation, you want to make money, but you don't have to make money. It's easier to fall in love with a team or idea and write a check and be like, "Oh, if I lose all my money, I don't care. It was fun helping people."

As professional investor, I can't do that. My job is to turn money into money, and the more the better. It's the same discipline but it has a tighter screening and probability requirement. Having made more than fifty investments as a VC, I have a bigger pool of data to leverage than most single investors because I've just done more deals.

As investors, we believe that we're in the talent business, first and foremost. We're not in the ideas business and we aren't the money business, we are talent scouts. We are trying to find teams of people that have the rare combination of insight, skill, grit, persistence, vision, and drive to take a good idea in an interesting category, and do all of the things that are required to drive that idea to scale. The opportunity has to be interesting, but it really has to be a team on a mission, a band of pirates going out to conquer the world. That's the most important characteristic, and everything else falls out of that.

How do you really understand if they are in that band of pirates, or if they just talk like they are a band of pirates?

A lot of it is seeing prior success. There are a lot of people who aspire to be an entrepreneur but the only experience they've had has been inside big companies. It's hard to tell whether they have the emotional resilience and the ambition to really do it, because they have always lived within a framework that supports them in all kinds of ways that they don't even see.

People who've done it before or tried to do it before are easier to understand. People who achieved some success as a founder, meaning they know what success looks like, and people who've failed before and have learned some hard lessons from that. So you're biased toward people who've been in the game for a while, because then they know more. Do they really want to be an entrepreneur? Do they know what it looks like to build a real company? Do they know what it looks like to have everything blow up around them, and they are still coming back for more? That kind of experience and appetite puts you way ahead, into the 90th percentile of people who might be able to build their own company, versus just taking a flier on somebody who has never done any of those things before.

If you're working with somebody who's just smart and passionate, they need to be over-indexed in some area. Either they're really deep in their area of expertise, or they have an incredible track record of building really beautiful products, even if they've never had to sell them or fund them before.

Does running other people's money make it easier or harder to find those people?

The great part about running a fund and being a repeat investor is that people know what to expect from you. They know you write checks. They know you write them often. People are a lot more aware of your track record and stuff you've done, so it's much easier for entrepreneurs to triangulate on you. Is this someone who says they were going to write a check but never actually gets off their wallet? Is this someone who's going to be a good actor or bad actor in the long run for my business?

If you're a professional, with a track record of activity, they might not like the way you do business, but at least there's evidence. Angel investors are quirky and there's a big distribution and there are really good people who are good actors and helpful and knowledgeable, and there are people who are grasping, greedy, obstructionist, and disrespectful. It's hard to know those things if they are just an individual, because they haven't exposed themselves to the world in the same way.

From an entrepreneur's perspective, there are lots of people like me, on the West Coast at least, who I do what I do. It's a target-rich environment of known entities. If I were an entrepreneur, I'd aspire to work with those kind of people because this is what they do for a living. I know that they have incentives aligned with mine. Versus with an angel, because I don't always know why they are doing it. They might have the money, but they might be doing it for reasons that, ultimately, aren't congruent with my needs.

What do you do once you make the investment to help them become a successful business?

There is a value chain of entrepreneurship. On the supply side, you're going to help people become more capable professionals. Whether it's things like Startup Weekend or Techstars, what's all the machinery that you could put in place including individual mentorship, making introductions, creating opportunity for people to have experiences? All the ways that you can develop talent even before they've done anything to start a business. That's one end of it. At the other end is after they've built the company and raised a bit of money and they want to raise venture capital. How do they successfully go through the capital markets gate?

There are a whole bunch of things that need to be done at different stages, whether it's helping people build teams, helping people think about go-to-market strategy, helping people think about fundraising, or storytelling, or leadership, or management or governance, to how do I get the Series A done. Depending on where they are in their cycle or where we engage with them, we are able to help in many ways, not only through our efforts as a fund, but also by connecting them with our limited partner base and the extended mentor network of Techstars and Founders' Co-op.

Because this is what we do for a living, the breadth of connections that we can make on their behalf and the pattern recognition we can offer them allows them to accelerate their learning and reduce the degree of error in their decision making through many of the key decision points on the path to a venture raise.

By the time they've raised Series A venture, they've probably exhausted most of what we can do to help them, and our goal is to connect them with an investor who really understands what it takes to get from A to B, and we can be helpful in doing that. We continue to stay involved and offer support past that point, but really, seed to A or founding to A is the valley of death for a lot of companies, and that's where we focus our efforts. A to B has its own mechanics, but it's a different risk profile.

Where do you end up spending the most time helping?

A lot of our energy is spent in making sure we get our portfolio companies the best possible Series A raise. Best partner, best firm, best terms. Not to over-optimize, but making sure they get fair terms, and a firm and partner match that's congruent with the needs of the business.

A successful growth business is probably going to need to raise capital four or five times on the way to acquisition or IPO, and many of the preferences and governance mechanics get established at the seed stage. If you, as an investor, over-optimize for your own interests at the seed stage, you're going to eat your own over-optimization when somebody else does that to you later on. That can still happen to you even if you haven't over-optimized, but at least putting people on the right path to fair, transparent, equitable terms at the seed stage radically increases the odds you're going to get fair, equitable, transparent terms at the Series A and beyond.

Do you think the structure of the deal plays into that at all? Are some structures optimized more for investors?

There are all kinds of gearing and things that entrepreneurs need to focus on. Often, valuation is not the most important term. There are all kinds of levers that investors can and do use to create an advantage for themselves at the expense of entrepreneurs who don't know any better.

To help entrepreneurs understand how that game is played, Brad Feld's book, *Venture Deals,* is his attempt to help entrepreneurs with that. One thing I love about Brad is he's incredibly transparent, in the spirit of, "This is a partnership, this is a long business, it's a repeat business and you don't go in by trying to over-optimize. You go in by just being transparent about your incentives and machinery."

There's a lot of information asymmetry because people only raise venture capital a few times in their lives versus venture capitalists who do it for a living. Trying to break down some of that asymmetry as a good-faith gesture to get to the right deal is something that I think smart investors do. It's too easy to take advantage, and if they begin by taking advantage when they write the first check, you can expect they're going to keep taking advantage in other ways along the length of the relationship.

What are the top three mistakes you see angel investors making?

Number one is falling in love with a deal and not the founders, accepting founders who are probably not the right people to execute an idea, simply because they love the idea. In my experience, 99 times out of 100, the idea matters much less than the people.

Number two would be over-optimizing on their own math. Being a grinder on valuation or terms where they're so focused on managing their own downside and making sure they don't lose money that they wind up fucking the company for the duration, because they burned the company with terms or they've diluted the founders to the point where as time goes by, the founder's incentive and motivation to grow the business go away. It's the lack of perspective, it's acting in their own interests without having a view to the long-term life cycle of the company.

I think the third mistake would be not playing well with others. Usually, angels don't act by themselves. Even if they're a good actor, including people in the syndicate or participating in syndicates where other people are acting in unconstructive ways. Being selective about the co-investment pool and making sure the co-investors' values are aligned, in terms of how they want to help support the business.

How should angel investors think about managing their risk?

I think portfolio theory applies to angel investment like anything else. If you expect to write one angel check and have it be Google, you will fail. To manage risk you have to think about each investment as one in a portfolio of deals, not as a one-off.

The bad part about angel investing versus stock market investing is it's highly illiquid. Once you write a check you can't get it back. There's nothing you can do to back out of a trade for the most part. You live with these things a lot longer, so you have to be much more selective about what you actually do. You only have so much capacity, and once your capital is expended, you can't get it back.

Angels have to enter the journey with the intention of constructing a portfolio and not just doing one deal a year. It's sort of like buying one stock a year and trying to construct a portfolio.

Is it better to do more deals and be less engaged in each?

I would say set a pace for yourself. If you want to do two deals a year, five deals a year, or ten, whatever your capacity is, set a goal and try to stay on pace. Then once you've done a deal, do what you can to be helpful, but understand that it's part of a larger portfolio.

Stay engaged in supporting your portfolio. To some extent, investors are often counterproductive in their interventions. Don't attempt to micromanage your investments. Do provide help and support, do stay close and be informed about what they need, but approach it as a mentor and supporter, not as someone who having written the check has the right to tell the team running the business what to do. I think a lot of angels misinterpret their role as investors. They are backseat investors and somebody else is on the ground running the business.

What new things have you learned to do as an investor?

We are most focused as a firm on constructing investments that we have deep conviction in and have a very long time horizon. Meaning it's not about what's hot today, it's not like everyone's doing social mobile chat apps, we should do a mobile chat app. It's having a sense of conviction about where the world is going in terms of innovation, and then talking to lots of people, not to steer them toward your convictions, but sifting the world to find people who believe what you believe and then backing them.

It takes a long time to build real value in a company, probably five to seven years on average. Believing deeply in the people involved, believing deeply in the opportunity, and being prepared to stay engaged at moments of crisis and moments of opportunity, over the long term, is something I've had to learn how to do well. It's hard to appreciate it at the beginning as an angel investor. It's easy to fall in love with a team or an idea and not appreciate that you're going to be living with that decision for a long time. Be prepared to stay engaged for the duration of that journey. Make sure the reason you're doing it and the convictions behind it are going to have some durability as well.

Fashion comes and goes. If you're investing based on fashion, you'll get bored with the deal and it will probably fail because it was chasing the trend rather than creating it.

With conviction like that, are you anticipating building concentrations in some of them?

Yes, that's something we've gotten clearer about, that in general, investment success is based on concentrated positions. While you want a diversified portfolio, you want to own as much of those businesses as you can afford to.

You need to make sure that you put yourself in a position to do that over time. This is why pro-rata rights are one of the least-appreciated rights for angel investors. When a business is working, you want to be able to defend your position, or if possible increase your position, over time. You don't know what's going to work in the first instance. You have to be able to keep buying into your winners as you cut your losses on the ones that don't work.

Having both the capital reserves and the rights that allow you to defend or extend your position is one of those fundamental, structural things that angel investors should appreciate more. If you're going to write an angel check for a dollar, you better have at least a dollar, if not two or three, stacked up behind that. Make sure that when the time comes you have that money available and liquid.

How do you think companies like AngelList and SeedInvest are changing the landscape for angels?

I'm glad those things exist. We view ourselves as principal investors, which is sometimes acting as lead and sometimes helping to put together a syndicate on those platforms. I'm glad there's a way for our companies to get more liquidity into their deals. The more money, the better.

How do you think about interacting with those angel groups or angel investors?

Because we're a small fund, our limited partners—the people who give us money—are usually angels themselves. In their mental accounting, they take a fraction of their angel investment allocation and give it to us. In exchange for paying us, they get access to a diversified basket of stuff they might not have seen.

We are part of the angel ecosystem, even though we are a fund operator because of our money, and our community is made up of angel investors. The people we like to deal with are regular long-term systemic positive actors in the angel ecosystem. They think about it in terms of long-term viability, fairness, sustainability and don't over-optimize.

I think it's hard to work with angels who don't play by the same rules. I know I'm going to support my company's needs, whether it be a bridge round or taking pro rata in the next round, because I believe in business, and it's in my interest to do so. Not every angel thinks that way, or has the capacity to do that.

In a moment of crisis, what other lessons have you learned in dealing with either the companies themselves or the other investors?

There's hard stuff in those moments and I'm sure I haven't always behaved perfectly in those stressful situations. I like to see both founders and investors who behave gracefully in moments of crisis, whether it's accepting more dilution, taking money at a prior round price, trying to get a new price, or doing whatever it takes to just keep fighting. Even when you reach the point of no confidence, where you no longer believe in the team or their ability to execute, being transparent about that and explaining your reasons why and taking your lumps.

Would you do a future deal with someone who left at one of those moments?

Yes, depending on if they're clear and honest about their reasons for doing it, like "Sorry, I'm out of money," or whatever.

It is definitely a relationship game with all the other investors.

This is a very small community focused on early-stage software investing. There are probably a thousand people who do it seriously. And that's a small number. You all have been in business long enough to know each other. They'll know you by your prior behavior, by your reputation, by your actions. There is nowhere to hide in this community. And that's a good thing. Better for the entrepreneur, better for the investors, better for everyone. Transparency and liquidity are good. Investors like opacity and information asymmetry because it generates return, but it's not good for the health of the system.

Do you fight for larger exits? Do you end up trying to look for that?

We try to select founders for whom that's the default course of action, where that's their desire, too. When I think a founder is like "I had hoped to get a bunt on this one so I can make enough money to go fishing," then those aren't the kind of people we prefer to back. We wind up with them by accident because they didn't know at the onset or they didn't know themselves or they weren't transparent with us.

That's why the question at the beginning is "Do these people want to be on the same journey that we want to be on?" The journey that *we* want to be on is, "I want to go build a big fucking company, and I want to go build a big public company." Great. Me, too! Let's do that together.

THE VALUE INVESTORS

THE VOICE OF VALUE WITH CHRISTOPHER MIRABILE

"Investing without research is like playing stud poker and never looking at the cards."

—PETER LYNCH

"In my experience, momentum and social proof can be extremely poor indicators of round quality."

—CHRISTOPHER MIRABILE

CHRISTOPHER AND I SPOKE in April 2014. I connected with him about the same time I connected with David Verrill, Jim Connor, and Allan May, all of whom are on the board of directors at the Angel Capital Association. All four of these angels are leaders in the angel group community and have spent a fair amount of their lives thinking about how to improve the practice of angel investing. I was glad they all operated in their own space and had their own opinions and approach to angel investing. Christopher and I got into an interesting discussion about investing on momentum and investing on value that I'll include here as an introduction to the value investors section.

At the end of the interview, Christopher told me, "I think you should throw this book away and write a book about this investment dichotomy instead. I would get up and defend the value investor who's not chasing fads. I think Warren Buffett said, "You find out who's swimming naked when the tide goes out." Right now, the market is hot and there's all this happy bullshit—I don't know if you've looked at some of the extreme cases of people just indexing the market."

Obviously I didn't scrap this book, but you'll note that what Christopher is saying is exactly one of the insights I found through all my interviews and one that this book is structured around. To understand more about value investing, I wanted to explore how Christopher thought about his portfolio.

How do you think about angel investing in the context of portfolio management?

I will say that virtually everything that's been written on the subject, whether it be a blog article or a book, is deeply unsatisfying because the reality is that angel investing differs so much from country to country and region to region within a large country like the United States, and from industry to industry, that people tend to write about what they know, speak about, or pontificate about what they're familiar with, and invariably their perspective omits other key perspectives, so you end up with advice that's only good for someone coming at it in the same way as you, and irrelevant for everyone else.

You're probably wise to go with a multi-perspective approach the way you are because I think it gives you at least a fighting chance of writing something that's relevant.

By way of example, one of the biggest dichotomies right now is there's this rift between this somewhat consumer-led, consumer-mobile kind of deal flow that is prevalent in Silicon Valley and the rest of the world. In Silicon Valley, you have all these young investors who have money from big success stories like Google and Facebook. They are chasing trends similar to what they know. Some of the resulting deals are almost like popularity contests and it's all about moving fast, and there's really no emphasis on diligence or helping the company do anything other than "growth hack". There are lots of good investors and good companies amongst all that hype, but a lot of it just feels really bubbly and insubstantial. There's this perspective that you could almost analogize to day trading or momentum trading.

Then you have the angels who have been in the game a bit longer, maybe a bit more group-centric and process-centric, who are more similar in behavior to value investors or stock pickers, if you were going to use that same stock-picking analogy.

This second group of angels aren't day trading or momentum trading, they aren't trying to play the market. They're trying to find great teams and great opportunities at good companies—need-to-have products, rather than nice-to-have products, and do it in a thoughtful process–oriented way, and then – and this is crucially important - help the companies afterward. I've done a number of interviews, been on Frank Peter's show, blogged about this, and talked about it in various contexts.

For me, it kind of boils down to this idea that angel investing is a lot saner when done analytically and on a risk-adjusted basis, where you've got a reasonable expectation of return for the amount of risk you're taking. To me, angel investing is more analogous to adopting a puppy than buying a lottery ticket. It takes time and work with these companies to help them become successful over a number of years. There's a lot of people buying lottery tickets right now—they have this idea that they can sit at home in their pajamas and their bunny slippers and they can be an angel investor by clicking their mouse. I sometimes worry that "curation" is becoming the new due diligence. Might work for a while in a cresting market, but needless to say, I see that ending badly.

I think the lottery ticket mentality a very dangerous way to go at this, and it's going to lead to a lot of people getting badly burned when the cycle turns. Now, in a rising market, like in 1998, 1999, 2000, you could have bought a basket of any tech stocks and as long as you got out quickly, you could survive. It may be that some of those people who are angel investing today will make out okay just because they got diversified enough and something will succeed in a big way. But they're probably taking on an awful lot more risk than they need to for the overall returns they're generating.

The funny thing is the two schools of thought appear not to have a lot of respect for each other. The momentum guys are like "if you're not in the cool rounds with Ashton Kutcher, you are missing out – it is all about who you know. If you're not investing in mobile and consumer, Instagram and WhatsApp, you're doomed to failure." That crowd also invests in a lot of stuff that by its very nature is hard to do diligence on because you can't really call up a customer demographic and ask how they like the product, right?

To me, it feels a bit like chasing hit records or hit movies. Plenty of money gets made in the music and movie industries, but it's awfully hard to predict which ones are going to be successes, and those who do succeed tend to need a lot of capital, so they're taking on a lot of subsequent financing risk, and they're very much sort of feeders for VC. Whereas I think that those in the other school of thought are being a lot more deliberate around issues like: who is going to lead this, how do we stage capital, who is going to sit on the board, do we want to bake VC dependency into our deal?

For example, at Launchpad, we're pretty careful and analytical about doing a deal that's really going to need a lot of capital down the road. Sometimes we will decide not do them or, when we do, we try to identify strategics or non-dilutive grant financing that's going to come in, or where we understand who the VCs are going to be and if possible we get them to all invest with us at the same time on the same term sheet. The type of angel investing where the basic model is, "Let's just throw a little bit of money at this deal, they can mess around for a while and then we'll go get real money" - that's crazy investing. Unless you have a very good sense where the big Series A is coming from, you're likely just throwing your money away.

Keeping the options open is the key. You can always go big if the situation merits it, but once you slam a ton of capital into a deal, there's no reversing that. We had a classic case where we invested in a mobile analytics company. We found and seeded this company that provides analytics for mobile apps that are similar to the kinds of web analytics that are common—if you're a publisher of a web page you need analytics to figure out what you're doing, what's happening on your page, and if you're a big publisher of an app, you need analytics to figure out what's going on with your user base and your app—and so we invested in these guys, and at first the investors and the founders capitalized the company pretty lightly.

Everyone kept the option of selling early by not putting too much money into the company, and we decided we'd play it by ear. But what ended up happening is they really took off and they found an adjacency to what they were doing that was even bigger than the original market.

They began to get tremendous traction and landed some really major customers, and so it made sense at that point to say, never mind, we're all going to go big on this thing and so the founders and the investors agreed to bring in a VC round with a 12x greater valuation and then later the company brought in a bigger round at a 5x greater valuation than the previous big round. The lesson here is that you can always add money quickly later if it makes sense but you can't take it out – once a company is over-funded and its cap table is ruined, you cannot go back and fix that without pain all around. But you can always quickly and easily pour coal on the fire if called for. Epilogue to the story: at this point, the company's tools are on nearly three billion mobile devices and counting.

The interesting thing a lot of people don't really understand is that if you take a million bucks from somebody modeling a 10x return and you give away half your company to do that, you need a $20 million exit or they're not going to be happy. And $20 million, coincidentally, is what the average M&A deal in this country goes for, and that's just for $1 million in capital.

A lot of people blithely throw money into companies and put two or three million bucks into a company at four, five, six, eight, nine million–dollar valuation, which is what's going on in very hot markets like Silicon Valley, and they don't even understand that they have no reasonable prospect of a big multiple unless this thing gets sold for two, three, four, five, ten times the size of the average M&A deal. The farther above that average you go, the lower the frequency and likelihood goes.

Now they may say, I don't care. I want to make 100 bets because I only need one to deliver a thousand times and I'm made. That's fine. It's their money, they can do that if they want.

That is the common argument that, statistically, making enough small bets will pay off. Isn't that true?

They'd better get really diversified then, because those big exits—you'd think they come up all the time if you read TechCrunch; you'd think those exits are falling out of trees, but the reality is statistically, they're one in a million. These things are called unicorns for a reason, and you better be putting a lot of money into a lot of deals. And you'll need one 100x hit for every 99 mistakes just to break even. Not to mention the amount of money you're tying up and the amount of uncompensated risk you're taking.

We take a slightly more deliberative approach. You try to share the risk with the entrepreneur and capitalize the company lightly so you have some options, and allow them to take a little bit of money, de-risk the company, increment the valuation up a little—take a little bit more money at a slightly higher valuation—so they can keep control and don't really pour on the rocket fuel until we figure out what's going on. And as I said, we also tend to invest in stuff where it's a need-to-have for the company, for a particular identified customer, rather than nice-to-have for a demographic. We tend to look at and try to understand buying priorities of the targeted customer segment.

I think this mouse-click, lottery-ticket stuff is an accelerating trend. It's getting a lot of coverage - it's the "it" topic right now - and I think it's only going to accelerate with various forms of crowdfunding. Which is not to say that the proposed title three rules as they're written are workable—I think as currently drafted, they are dead on arrival. But that's a whole other topic. I just worry that this is going to lead to a significant angel crash and possibly even some fraud and the result will be regulatory reaction and backlash. It has some of the makings of a tulip-mania in some areas.

Are platforms like AngelList accelerating the potential for a mania?

I have nothing but positive things to say about Naval and the team at AngelList. They're good guys. I like them and I think they're smart and they're doing interesting stuff, but the design of their platform and the model of their syndicates certainly does put a lot of emphasis on social proof and momentum in rounds. It can be difficult to figure out what, if any, due diligence has been done, let alone read those reports. You also cannot really tell who is truly leading the round and who is really involved with and committed to helping the company. I think those are really important questions. In my experience, momentum and social proof can be extremely unreliable indicators of round quality. In rising markets it can work for a while. But the music stops. Just ask the last lemming to go over the cliff whether it was a good idea to follow all those other lemmings.

I also feel like a new investor needs to keep an eye on the fine print. Depending on the platform, all the carry, the fees, and intermediary expenses can really add up and take away value. I don't know if you're familiar with the Fortune Magazine article Buffett wrote in 2006 about the fictional Gotrocks Family. In it, he talked about how the financial services industry is this massive industry, completely feeding on America from all these fees on fees on fees, and there's something to be said for that perspective in the increasingly layered and curated angel world.

Human beings are drawn to perceived shortcuts and they always want to think that there's a shortcut available. In life there really aren't many true shortcuts. Angel investing is a lot of work, and most of the real work starts after you invest. Sure, there's a lot of work at the beginning if you properly and diligently do a deal. There's a fair amount of work, but a lot of the work starts afterward. Somebody really has to sit on the board. As the first round is being designed, someone has to think about staging capital into the company over the long haul. Somebody has to sort of give advice and coach and grow the CEO and help them try to figure out how to position the company for exit. Someone has to help find A-players to hire, and find introductions to customers. Those returns don't just materialize.

Now maybe in certain consumer- and mobile-oriented spaces it is different. Maybe you can come up with a good idea, and go through this farce of forming a company, getting backing, doing a little "growth hacking" as people love to call it, and really it's all just theater to force Facebook or Google or Apple to buy them. Maybe that's sort of a crazy weird way of productizing tech ideas, but in the real world, the things that drive real exit value are things like revenue, or eyeballs, or earnings, or huge customer lists, or undeniable strategic positioning - for example, if you want to get a good company's attention, you steal a couple of their customers.

Those things, all of those things in that list—eyeballs, revenue, earnings, customers, strategic position—none of those things happen overnight in the real world. I mean, they might happen overnight with a downloadable app that gets really hot like Flappybird or something, but in the real world all of those things on that list generally take some time to develop. And so this idea that you can just get in and out really quickly, that angel investing results in get-rich-quick returns like you read about in TechCrunch—it's not real life.

Are the entrepreneurs and investors who're written up in TechCrunch different from those who aren't?

I think that Silicon Valley has a disproportionate number of young, tech-centric, mobile-centric startup founders who've never had responsibility for a P&L or run a business or done anything professionally except sling code in their whole life. That type of founder occurs everywhere, but they probably occur a bit more frequently in Silicon Valley, and that really is a very web- and mobile-centric world. There are plenty of great mobile and web deals, and many fortunes to be made in that space, but it's not the whole world—it is just one subset.

Just by way of one point of contrast, in a city like Boston, we are the preeminent city in the world in terms of life sciences and med tech. That's a whole world of investing with a completely different set of rules, which brings us back to the beginning of the conversation, about how different players have different perspectives. Most angel investing writing and advice either is exactly on point or totally off point, depending on your perspective.

Getting a medical device through the FDA or getting a drug through human clinical trials or getting a diagnostic tool built—these things have a whole bunch of different challenges and take a lot of capital. It can be hard to do on the angel level and nearly impossible without true experience and expertise involved. The scale can be large - we're in a company right now that has raised $20 million in angel funding from 200 different angels. They are surrounded by a lot of expertise, and it is helping them make their way. We think to a good place: I'm not saying they're on a path to do it this second, but they have the potential to be the first company to ever go from angel funding to IPO with no institutional capital at all.

So what is this divide really about?

When you think about it, the gulf between the sort of momentum investors and the value-picker investors, this sort of schism between solo angels tapping their buddy networks to get into rounds versus angels who are collaborating in established angel groups, it comes down to leading versus following. This is something that Fred Wilson, Chris Dixon, and Hunter Walk have written great pieces on, talking about leading versus following, how it's easy to follow someone's deal but it is actually really hard to lead a deal.

When you jump into one of these hot deals as a momentum investor working remotely, do you really know much about the round? Who created that round? Who's in charge of it? Who's going to sit on the board? In contrast, when you think about the angel group model, the basic atomic molecule in an angel group is, "You sit on a board for me, and I'll sit on a board for you and we'll each get two properly supervised investments." I think a lot of people don't really get that. They kind of assume someone else will structure the round and they assume they've done a good job of it and someone else is going to sit on the board, someone else is going drive the exit, all they have to do is ride coattails. The old poker rule applies here: if you cannot spot the sucker at the table, it's you.

I come at it from a different angle. We prefer to lead rounds because we can be certain that a proper amount of diligence has been done and we understand what we're getting into on a risk-adjusted basis. We understand that there's a strategy in place for putting capital into this company and there's somebody sort of measuring what the milestones are and whether it makes sense. We know that quality people are going on the board because we put them there, and we know there's somebody in charge. We've all had the bad experience of getting into a party round where you had nobody in charge and the CEO starts to go off the rails and the company could be saved but there's nobody who has enough skin in the game to even bother trying to fix it.

In those situations, unfortunately nobody cares, and the thing just becomes something to laugh at over beers. But that's 25 grand or 50 grand that you lost that you didn't have to lose. I guess that both camps think the other camp is crazy, but to my way of thinking, these types of investors are a lot crazier than I am.

The group model has its challenges, but it has its benefits too. The reality is every time you hear about a company, you're like, "Wow, that's awesome. That's a good idea that could totally work." I don't know how many thousands of pitches I've heard over the years and I'm still a sucker for that first description like that. Every time I'm like, "Oh, that's a pretty good idea." Then you start going around the network and different people ask questions and make observations and you're like, "Oh, I didn't think of that. Oh, I didn't think of that," and your perspective becomes much more rich and balanced. You may still go ahead and do it, but you will have a much fuller perspective on what you're getting into.

This ability to take in the perspectives of others during a diligence process really changes how you invest. Launchpad is one of the top groups in the United States, year in and year out, in dollars invested and deals done. And the percentage of members investing over the course of any given year is consistently nearly universal. But what's interesting is that when you look at our deals, even a runaway train of a deal where there's lots and lots of enthusiasm, really, really broad-based enthusiasm in the group, that particular deal is still only going to be 25%, 30% of the group. In other words, 70% of the group thinks any given idea is not great. That happens every single time.

Every time you invest, you're making a counter-majority bet. But when you spend time with the group of people and you have a kind of a professional process where you get a ton of deal flow and you put different scouts on it and you bubble up the good stuff and then you spend your time looking at that.

We have 150 people and one of the things that's interesting is we have two sessions a month where the same companies present. I'll have a morning meeting and then an afternoon meeting. Different days, different times, different locations and yet the list of issues and questions raised is invariably the same across any given company's two presentations. Two different groups of investors, two separate days, and they consistently come up with the same basic themes of what the challenges are going to be and we do lots and lots of deals.

Some critics have said, "Oh, angel groups are a way of taking three yes's and turning it into 30 no's." And it is certainly true that entrepreneurs would probably prefer to pick investors off one at a time in coffee shops using convertible notes. But there is real value in the collaboration that occurs in the group. One of the main values is that it allows angels to be more diversified into a greater number of deals that still have the proper amount of diligence and human capital involved.

True, it can sometimes be hard to go after a totally crazy black swan within the angel group itself, but that's not necessarily a problem because we have lots of deals where we just don't have enough broad-based interest to really start a process, and we're not going to want to give them the term sheet, but a few people will go chase it anyway and they'll invest in it and that's fine. In situations like that, where if enough people go into a presenting company on a freelance basis, sometimes we'll later add them into our portfolio.

Many investors, particularly those who've been out doing it on their own on a "onesey-twosey" basis, realize they would benefit from a little bit more process and a more human capital–centric approach. That's what we're about. We screen our applicants for membership carefully to focus only on very active investors. Some other groups, such as syndicates and funds may be focused on passive investment and that's fine—nothing wrong with it to centralize the decision making. We're just focused on active investors who can get involved with the companies. We don't do a deal if we don't have expertise and can't add value because we can't take the risk.

Which makes sense if you think about it. Our returns are basically a function of picking really risky, really early-stage stuff, with a low valuation because of the risk, and then getting involved and de-risking it so that the foundation of our returns is the delta between what we paid and what it's worth with our help. And that delta? It's human capital. A lot of people don't get that. They think you just buy the lottery ticket and then somebody else will figure it out or else it's magically going to be worth something. It makes me shake my head and wonder.

Do you try to make sure that there's someone in the group who's really great at international expansion or something?

Yup, we do. We think about the topography of the skill set in our group all the time. Our group has been full and had a waiting list for years now. We bring people in selectively based on where we need additional skills. And in terms of the companies we select, we tend to only get involved in companies where we have value add and we know what we're talking about.

Now we don't substitute our judgment for the judgment of a great founder. It's not one of those "Oh, we're here to help, we're from the government" situations. Our investors are professional and they know what they're doing. I think angels tend to overestimate the value of their help at times. There's nothing worse than an angel getting underfoot when they're really just a pest, so our people are thoughtful about whether they have anything to add. If they do, they help, and if they don't, they stay the heck out of the way.

As a general matter, we're not investing in stuff we don't understand. We don't really do any consumer-packaged goods and we haven't recruited those skills. We don't have those skills, so we don't want anything to do with that space. We have a little tiny bit of consumer web in our portfolio but, as a general matter, we think that's a picking hit records thing and it's difficult to do it well on a risk-adjusted basis. We think it is really hard to get compensated for the risk that you're taking on in those deals. It's just not our area. If you're Jack Dorsey, or you're Mark Zuckerberg, or you're Marissa Mayer, maybe you can pick consumer web technologies better than average, but there are a lot of people who really can't, and when you look at the studies, it's actually extremely difficult to figure out what's going to resonate with kids and what isn't.

And that matters because kids are a big driver and people will say that for every WhatsApp or Snapchat, there are 50 clones that didn't go. Think about how many exact copies of Instagram there were—for a while it looked like Hipstamatic was going to win, and yet out of nowhere came Instagram. And it goes on to get bought for a ton of money per active user. So we tend to be careful about doing those deals. Similarly, we tend to be careful about doing drug development deals because they're so expensive—that is, capital-intensive.

To return to the analogy, we try to pick value stocks. We try to pick a really good team, solving really important problems for really significant customer bases, and you can't go too far wrong with that approach.

What areas do you tend to invest the most in?

We're in Boston, so traditional tech, Internet, telecommunications, networking, mobile, enterprise software, green tech and EdTech. That's our bread and butter.

Big data, data analytics, storage, that's the stuff that's really Boston's backbone. Life sciences is the second big vertical for us. Our group of members with life sciences expertise is as big as many entire specialty angel groups who are devoted to life science investing. We have somewhere in the neighborhood of 40 people with various kinds of really deep expertise in that space.

We can't always invest in them, but we look at a fair amount of green stuff. We do a lot in the life sciences. The way it breaks down is we do about one third life sciences, one third tech, and the final third is green, edTech and miscellaneous. It's the skills that are indigenous to the area. It really depends on what we find that we like.

Is there a typical profile of investor in the group or are they pretty varied?

They're pretty varied. I mean there are some common themes. The vast majority of them, if not all of them, have operating experience, so our typical investor has owned P&Ls and had to make payroll in their career, so these aren't super young coders for the most part. We have a lot of engineers in the group so they tend to be people with pretty meaningful business experience. Seventy percent-plus of them have had a CXO title of some kind—CEO, CLO, CFO, CMO, and 70% plus of them have prior board experience.

In terms of the kinds of jobs we've had, we have people who've been head of engineering, head of product, head of sales, head of the company. We have a lot of former entrepreneurs who made their money starting companies and selling them, sometimes serially. What we *don't* have is the sort of clichéd kinds of angels: accountants, doctors, lawyers, or dentists as members. We don't have any of those people. We don't have any consultants or gig-shoppers looking for jobs or consulting work. Our group is made up of serious, large-portfolio angels who write a lot of checks. In any given 12-month period, we'll have 90% to 95% of the members in the group write a check and that's across a 150-member base.

Do you go through an interview process with incoming potential members?

We do. Our process is that every new member has to be recommended by one or two existing members. They have to come as a guest to a meeting and then we sit down and we have an interview process where we go in depth into their background, in their skills, and their motivations for being an angel - why they want to be in the group and what they can bring to the group. If there is a good mutual fit, they go on the waitlist and we tend to check references and find out a little bit more about them and if we're still comfortable after all that, we let them in when space allows. We like to think it's a privilege to be in the group. People consistently say this is a powerful network of interesting people.

We work hard to make sure the members know each other so that, over time, they understand who to trust and who thinks the same way they think, so when it comes time to rally support for a deal, the members are inter-networked pretty well. They get to know each other in the meetings, on diligence teams, in various training sessions, and in a handful of social events in the course of a year.

We're different from some of the more low-key social club–type angel groups. People sometimes joke that it's more like having a drill sergeant. I mean we're extremely serious about maintaining a level of professionalism. Our meetings start on time, they end on time. Entrepreneurs show up prepared. They understand what they need to do, they know what to expect. Their pitches are of almost uniformly solid quality. They don't get extra time. They deliver a pitch in the allotted time. The Q&A goes according to schedule. It's extremely crisp and professional. But we are always certain to be respectful of the entrepreneur and tolerant and respectful of each other's opinions.

That is an important distinction. In some angel groups, entrepreneurs come in and they're belittled. The questions are asked in a way that attempts to make the angel look smart and makes the entrepreneur feel stupid. That is absolutely not tolerated in our culture. We have a really strong code of conduct that everybody signs and reaffirms annually, and at the core of our code of conduct is respect for the individual. We treat entrepreneurs with respect in our meetings and in all of our dealings. Our members are out in every area of the innovation economy in Boston, and every single one of them is a brand ambassador. They add value and they show respect in every interaction they have with an entrepreneur.

What advice would you give to other angel investors?

There's probably 10 really common early mistakes. I've blogged a lot about this on the Seraf compass blog, but let me make some observations. I think one mistake that you see a lot of times is people tend to write a little bit too big of a check in their first couple of deals. So I guess what I'm trying to say is, "Don't be impulsive. Being decisive is necessary but be thorough too—don't be impulsive."

The other thing I would say is, don't look for shortcuts. Don't invest in things that are too good to be true, because nothing, nothing is as good as it looks. Be a bit more penetrating and don't be lazy.

Double check the company with somebody who knows something about the company's area. You may choose to ignore it, right? That's okay, better to know than not know.

Probably the other main thing is really going to be about the CEO. Get a lot of blind reference checks on the CEO and figure out whether they're quality or not. We've all had a CEO flake out on us.

Picking the right team is critical. When the market goes crazy on you or it just doesn't materialize, there's not a lot you can do on that. You paid a low valuation because you were assuming a lot of market risk and it's just a timing thing. That's okay. The issue is that the old saying about an A team with a B plan will outperform a B team with an A plan is really true. An A team is reading the market all the time and they can tell that it's not coming together, and they pivot before they've gotten themselves into such a capitalization hole that there's no way the company can ever deliver a good return for early investors.

The only thing worse than being wrong is being expensively wrong, and a great team says, "You know what, this isn't working. We're not getting the data," and they'll start to move early and decisively before the company has raised and spent so much money that the cap table's just irretrievably screwed up.

Once the cap table gets really screwed up and you've got a whole bunch of investors who are crammed down or pissed off or unhappy or lost faith in the CEO, the whole thing's a disaster because it's just hard to get new or returning money back into those companies and the whole thing's a write-off and all of it could have been avoided if the CEO was reading the market and said, "I'm going to have to make some changes here in a timely way," and they can even go out and raise before the money's gone and go, "Look, we're doing a pivot fund raise here," where it's out in the open and everybody gets it.

CEOs get credit for admitting they're wrong. You'd think some of them learn in CEO school to never show doubt or fear or admit they're wrong. Which is odd because they get so much credit for admitting they're wrong.

* * *

You can see that Christopher has strong opinions. Even though I'm a 35-year-old angel (with operating experience, at least), I can appreciate the difference that he is raising here. There is a small gap between active value investors who are doing a lot to improve their chances of success and active momentum investors doing the same. When they're more passive, the gap widens.

Christopher's Launchpad Venture Group meets regularly in Newton and Boston, Massachusetts, and invests $350,000 to $1 million per round in companies around the Northeast. Their current portfolio includes a wide range of companies such as Localytics, Boston Heart Diagnostics, Crowdly, ezCater, Groupize, Mobius Imaging, Pixability, QStream, and PunchBowl.

BE METHODICAL WITH ANDY LIU

"Success is a lousy teacher. It seduces smart people into thinking they can't lose."

—BILL GATES

"If I look at all my investments, the ones that were successful, every single one of them had pretty darn close near-death experiences."

—ANDY LIU

I'VE KNOWN ANDY for quite a few years and was excited to reach out to him to interview him for this book. Andy is one of Seattle's local notables in the field. He is an entrepreneur, an investor, and a relentless supporter of the startup community here. Andy was excited to participate in the interview and shared a thoughtful approach that many others profiled can learn from.

Tell me how you got started in investing.

I started out as an entrepreneur back in 1999 and sold the company in 2004. I kind of started because I had some great angel investors in my first deal and liked hanging out with them. I wanted to dabble in it and really started in earnest around late 2007, early 2008.

I think what got me interested was hanging out with entrepreneurs, hanging out with angel investors, and I thought I could just dip my toes in. I did and then got pretty engaged and excited about the whole thing. Since 2008 I've continued to invest and now I'm in just over 50 deals. It's fun, and it's turned into a passion of mine. I can see myself doing it for a long while.

You make it sound like so much fun. How did you find these great entrepreneurs and investors to hang out with?

When I first started, I was just a part of syndicates. A buddy of mine, Geoff Entress, said, "Hey, you should take a look at this deal." I was brought into deals and didn't lead any, I just wrote checks, kind of participated, and I learned. In the beginning, it was mostly just what was brought to me.

Once you start doing deals and your name is out there, all of a sudden, you start getting bombarded with pitches and entrepreneurs. Now, I think I get almost all the deal flow that I can handle. Right now I'm averaging maybe 10 to 15 a week, but I try to meet with one entrepreneur a week.

When you're just being brought in, were you doing much due diligence, or were you just kind of saying, "Hey, I trust you, I want to go for it"?

In the beginning I did want to do some work because I didn't know what I was doing. I always met with the entrepreneur. I wanted to at least look at the materials. I wanted to look at deal structures. I wanted to be in an area that I was interested in as well, where I might be able to add value.

In the beginning, those were the kinds of things I was doing. I wanted to be intellectually stimulated. If I want to just blindly follow, I might as well invest in ETFs or the stock market, but the reason it's interesting is because I could really learn from and help the entrepreneurs I engage with. I think the biggest jump is from there to leading a deal. Once I started leading deals, then I got really engaged, sometimes sitting on the board and all that.

How did you make that jump? Did you meet a great entrepreneur and say to yourself, "Oh, that's it, I want to lead the round with these guys"?

Yeah, I would say the first deal I led was actually I Can Has Cheezburger. When I led that deal, I had met [Cheezburger founder] Ben Huh earlier on and thought highly of him. I thought that he'd do well in an entrepreneurial type of opportunity and early on we spotted the Cheezburger asset and I said, "I can pull this together and I want you to run it, let's see if we can make this happen." The rest was putting the team together. Our attorneys went all the way through on pulling the whole deal together.

What inspired you to work with Ben on the Cheezburger deal? Was it just Ben as an individual?

One of the things where I think there's an opportunity is to spot talent. You can tell someone's got a lot of the tools to be successful. That kind of opportunity makes an impact and I get inspired personally by it. Whether it's like someone who's currently in a position in Amazon or Microsoft and then one cocktail conversation can lead to another.

I think a lot of people have ideas about becoming an entrepreneur, but only some people can hack it. You can tell if someone can hack it. You really want to kind of push him out the door and see whether he can do it.

What do you pick up on for people who can hack it versus people who maybe want to try it, but they don't know if they could hack it?

The biggest thing is my gut feel. How likely they are willing to walk through walls. When it comes down to it, startups are really hard. You see all the glory in *Fortune* magazine and when you read online about a $19 billion acquisition and all that, it's very challenging. When you run startups you have near-death experiences. You have to think and rely on your own experiences and trust your gut when it says this person might want to run away from their near-death experience or if they can stare right at it and try to break through it. If they're able to break through to it, they're going to be much stronger. They're going to have the capabilities of becoming the only player out there.

There are a lot of good things that can happen if you can break through near-death experiences. I would say not many people can handle much fire, but some people can. If I look at all my investments, the ones that were successful, every single one of them had pretty darn close near-death experiences. So I'll look at why I invested in the company, what the great opportunity was, the great idea, and so forth. It always comes down to the entrepreneur walking through walls.

What do you use for your scale that you grade people on?

I start with the idea, how likely I think this idea is going to absolutely crush it. I would give it an A if it's a great idea. The team is based on experience, and I factor that in. There's a couple of other things, too—the "it" factor, being able to run through walls, dealing with adversity. And is the entrepreneur somebody who's a hustler—you know, somebody who is just out there pushing and willing to get in the face of others, realizing that you have to get above the noise, too. If you're not willing to get above the noise, it's hard to get attention.

I'll grade the leadership of the entrepreneur and his experience. I've invested in young teams I would say lacked experience, and after all is said and done is probably a B-. The idea would be like an A-. It's not as good as an A team with a C-, D+ idea. I've invested in companies where I didn't really understand their business model, but I figured they would figure it out, they're smarter than I am. And sure enough, they did.

How do you decide where on the scale each measurement lands?

You can kind of pick up on some. Have they failed in the past? How did they deal with that? Look at their propensity for risk. One of the things would be you're more likely to walk through fire if you put in a million dollars of your own money into it and your net worth is $1.2, or $1.1, right? The guy who's very wealthy, did very well at Microsoft and is writing a $25,000 check. I'm like, "Eh, he doesn't have too much to lose if things get tough. He's got the big job ready at Microsoft." There are some things you can measure. Then the other piece is really a gut feeling.

Do you spend a lot of time with them before you invest, or do you invest quickly?

I invest quicker on something when a friend of mine whom I like a lot is leading the deal. There's a few guys like that—Geoff Entress, for example, whom I like doing deals with and I know that they're doing a lot of diligence on it. If I'm going to lead the deal, I want to know an entrepreneur really well. I spend a lot of time with them over several months before leading that deal. If I lead the deal I want it to be very, very competitive and solid.

Is there a structure you prefer on your deals?

From an entrepreneur's point of view, yes. As an entrepreneur, I would prefer to do a convertible note with caps and so forth, primarily because the legal fees are smaller, so I can get it done very quickly. I like doing that as an entrepreneur, as a seed round. As an investor, I prefer doing a priced round to get the equity. I want to start the clock on capital gains, I want to get to know what my price is and so forth. My preference is a capped structure. If the deal is good, I will do convertible notes too.

Do you care about pro rata and future follow-ons?

I do. That's an area I've been learning more about. I would say overall I wish I did more of mine pro rata. There are a few deals where I had the chance to participate in pro rata. Honestly, I undervalued the pro-rata rights. I think in future I will value it more.

As an angel investor, you're taking in a lot of risk. To have the option to just be able to say, "Hey, I want to buy some more shares";

that's a valuable option. While I did have that in a lot of my deals, I just wish I exercised it more.

Some of my exits could have had higher cash on cash return. It would be a lower IRR because it's at a higher valuation, but there would have been much higher cash on cash returns, so it would have been much better.

How many positive exits have you had?

Six, so far.

How many negative exits have you had?

Right now, three fully closed. The rest of them are live. Some of them are more live than others. We'll see.

How long are you expecting to hold the companies that you invest in?

I'd like to see something in five years. That would be a nice average to hit. Some are shorter and some are longer. I had one with Dan Shapiro that was six months or something like that, and that was a great deal.

How engaged do you get in the startups after you've made your investment?

The ones I lead, very. The ones where I am a part of a syndicate, I am much more in the background. If I get an email from them, I generally find ways to help out, but otherwise, it's much more hands off.

The ones that you do lead, you're usually taking a board director or observer seat?

Exactly. Right now, I am meeting with one entrepreneur a week, and then sitting on a couple of boards is plenty.

Even that can add up. How much time are you spending?

Well, for sure one hour a week on meeting an entrepreneur a week. I enjoy it, so on my off time I might spend three or four hours. I think that's about right.

How do you think about angel investing in relation to your net worth?

Mine is a rolling thing, so if I have a rate of return more than I put in, I put that back into angel investing. Some think it is kind of being crazy, but I put that back to work. I would say my initial investment size is 10%, though.

Are you going to run into a point where you have too many companies in the portfolio?

I don't think so. I'm going to probably stop if there are no exits going on. If I'm not seeing any exits coming in, I'm going to slow down dramatically, and just let things marinate and help out what I have currently. What's nice is, it's not like a stock that I have no control over. I might be able to say, "Hey, you know what? I can designate some time to focus on this company. It seems like it's on its breakout or might be able to sell or where I can add value." I feel like I can impact the returns by getting involved.

When they struggle, do you invest more if they need it?

Yes. The ones that I have participated in haven't been successful yet, though. Two of them are completely closed, and I participated in two down rounds there. I've participated in other down rounds, but the epilogue hasn't been written yet, so we'll see.

Having seen the two not make it and the rest waiting to be seen, do you think you would still do down rounds in the future?

I can look and see where I've made mistakes, I can see where I should've bet more on the winning companies and less on the losing ones. That's very clear, based on a set of 50 companies. Would I still participate in down rounds? I probably would, but I'd be a lot more thoughtful about it, maybe put less in.

If they're doing well and I get the opportunity to put some more juice into it, I should. Before, I was just afraid because valuations got blown up so much. I think to myself, "My money isn't going to do anything there." On the downside, I'll think, "I'm owning a lot more of the company, but this company is worth a lot less than I thought."

At the end of the day, it is the data that matters. If the data from my past investments show to invest, I should.

Out of six, you put more into two of those, so that's interesting data that some angels don't do a great job of tracking. You mentioned mental stimulation and engagement with the entrepreneurs as well. Are you tracking both returns and stimulation?

It is definitely both. I want to make sure I get the returns. Otherwise, I can't keep investing and invest more. It becomes philanthropy. I can't do it anymore. It's like a one-time injection. That's not what I'm about. I want to be sustainable. I'm the kind of guy who will take returns and reinvest it. I want to keep doing that.

I also don't want it to be an S&P strategy. I have a portfolio set aside to do that. I don't want to do that with this side. This side is because I actually am more focused on consumer Internet, more focused on entrepreneurs I like to hang out with. Honestly, it's also great conversations with folks too, like talk about companies that are doing well. It's fun to be a part of that ride. Those stories being written are a whole lot of fun.

I don't usually talk about the companies I invest in on the public markets or the ETFs with as much passion as I do regarding companies I'm involved with.

Looking back, are there things you could identify now that you're more experienced?

Absolutely. One of them, I graded the entrepreneurs to be very green. I thought that they had what it took to make it happen, though. I think it was a combination of inexperience and not enough risk taking. At the end of the day, I would blame it on the leadership and not on the idea. I graded the idea much higher.

Another one that did turn out great is one where I did the first round, then the next couple of rounds, which were down rounds. I really thought I shouldn't do it, but the lead investor made several calls to me and said, "This is a really good deal." I went against my gut on it. I made note of that, just because I wanted to know when I put in the money, "What was I thinking?!" Then I can check back and see whether it was a good move. It turned out to be a terrible move. I lost all the money on that deal. I could have stopped my losses there. That one was pretty clear. Those are the ones that popped in my head as to what happened.

Do you keep a written log, or is it a mental log of your analysis of the investment and what you were thinking about the investment when you made it?

Yeah, I do take notes. I want to have a written log. It's fun to take a look, anytime I want to take a look and say, "Oh, I haven't thought about these guys in a while. How are they doing?" Or "Hey, we exited. I'm curious to what happened when I first made the investment." Sometimes it's like four years or five years, and you kind of forget. What were you thinking? Or if they close, you're like, "Okay, why did I do that deal? What can I learn from it?" I hope my hit rate improves over time. Maybe I'm just lucky. I don't know. Who knows?

You're the first to bring up a written log. If a new investor came to you said, "Hey, what should I know about early-stage investing?" What would you tell them?

There's a few things. I would say, "It is high risk. I wouldn't bet the farm on it, personally. I wouldn't want to go into financial ruin doing early-stage investing. I do think that having more deals is a better way to start. I may start getting more concentrated because I already have a large portfolio, so I may say instead of doing just a bunch of small deals, maybe now start picking them off and taking larger positions, getting more involved in it. I may be switching into that kind of phase. I've been thinking about what is more interesting for my investment style.

I would say you should definitely have a more portfolio theory, spread it out. You'll be able to see what's going to do well, and so forth.

Finally, I would say, find where you have a passion in a certain space. If it's stressful, it's not enjoyable. If it's not stimulating, if you're doing it purely for financial returns, there are better places to put your money.

Do you think having a particular expertise in this space is a requirement?

I think an expertise in the space that you're interested in investing is a requirement, or at least a passion for it. I think the angel investing side of it could be picked up pretty easily. You can get to understand the deal terms. All that stuff is a given that that can be learned. Passion for the space is harder to learn. It has to be interesting.

Do you end up sharing a lot of the connections that you have, or the experience that you have, with those entrepreneurs?

Absolutely, and vice versa too. I learn a lot. They're learning a lot. What's working, what's not working, and so forth. All of that's useful for both sides to learn.

What do you think about AngelList?

I get so much deal flow, I don't have as much interest to drive more deal flow at this point. Maybe when I find a way to do this full time, I'll want to look at more deals. Right now, I feel pretty comfortable not looking elsewhere. I've had some trusted friends bring some AngelList syndicates up, but I haven't done one yet.

What are the biggest mistakes a new angel should avoid?

I'd be very thoughtful about the down rounds. Think about how comfortable you feel. Do you feel like they've made optimal decisions, given the information they had? Do you feel you've been kept in the loop? I'd just spend more time figuring out if I would participate in a down round and be more selective there.

I think it's easy to say yes, harder to say no, depending on your personality. Maybe the mistake that I would say would be if you start right away is if you say yes too much. There's always another deal. Take your time kind of thing to get your skis on and all that.

You do a lot of investment with other angels. What makes working with them easier or harder?

As you work with more angels, and I've worked with a lot of them, you get to know which ones that you would do deals with and which ones cause undue stress on deals. I don't like working with them. This is a fun thing for me.

I think startups are already stressful for the entrepreneurs. I'm probably more on the entrepreneur's side. I want to see a success. Troublemaker angels, even if they're well-intentioned, make it less fun for me.

For example, if the deal is about to get done, either with a financing event or a transaction, and they start throwing up red flags, and most people are on board. Everybody is on board, ready to go, let's do this transaction. The entrepreneurs are on board. Then they bring up a bunch of red flags, I'd say no, just get in line. Let's trust the process. This thing is a good deal. Don't railroad it. You're just one investor in a group of investors. Let's get this thing done.

That's the thing. I'm doing it for fun. I don't want to lose money, either. At the same time, let's all try to make the company more valuable by not putting stumbling blocks in front of the company.

How many red flags are you avoiding up front? Do you do background checks or anything like that on entrepreneurs?

I should do background checks, but I definitely do look at all the LinkedIn profiles and I go deep into the search and then I try to find out who knows them. Generally speaking, I like to know who the entrepreneur hangs out with, then hopefully I know some of those folks. If there's some peer trust, then I'm okay with it.

What about insurance on your founder or the accounting team?

That's a good question. I don't think we have it for most of the companies I invest in. I don't know if I'm experienced enough to know. I don't even think that we have insurance on here. Yeah, I don't think I have a very strong and formed opinion on it.

* * *

Andy takes a methodical approach to angel investing that many other investors ignore. Having a slow approach to investing while keeping a solid investment log is a practice that's commonly used by investors such as Warren Buffett and Mohnish Pabrai. Yet Andy was the only investor to talk a lot about this process in his investing procedure.

FIND SOURCES OF HIDDEN TALENT WITH DAVID VERRILL

"Without continual growth and progress, such words as improvement, achievement, and success have no meaning. "

—BENJAMIN FRANKLIN

"We try to focus on companies using capital-efficient models. It's become cheaper to start a company but not necessarily cheaper to grow one. "

—DAVID VERRILL

THROUGHOUT MY INTERVIEWS, I kept running into these guys from the Northeast who used all these baseball analogies. I don't watch much baseball, so I had to look up all these terms to figure out what they were talking about. David was one of those guys. For those of you who aren't familiar with the sport, batting average (referred to as batting a .XXX) is just hits divided by at-bats. If we translate that into investing, we're only talking about positive exits divided by investments. You'll see that David talks about his batting average being .400, which is that 40% of his investments have had a positive exit of some kind. That is impressive, considering many of the investors in this book have had much lower percentages of successful exits (while some have had incredibly high returns with a lower percentage).

David is the chairman emeritus of the board at the Angel Capital Association. I reached out to him for exactly that reason. I figured, hey, a guy who's been the chairman of the association for angels must have some interesting insights into angel investing. He was incredibly gracious and responsive to my request, I don't know if it is because I'm a fellow ACA member or because he's just an incredibly nice guy. He set aside some time for me and we jumped on the phone to chat.

I learned a lot during the interview and was thrilled to gain insights from David that weren't echoed by other investors. It was also great to hear from an investor who hadn't started a company, had a huge exit, and then went into angel investing. Many of the angels that I meet don't follow that path so it was refreshing to hear from such a high caliber investor who didn't follow that path either. We started in the usual place, but as you'll see in the interview we explored a lot of different areas to some of the other interviews in the book.

How did you get started with early-stage investing?

Necessity is the mother of invention. When opportunity knocks, open the door. I had been working at a small division of a large company that was divested. Rather than retain the hundred employees on the East Coast, the private company acquirer on the West Coast decided to let everybody go the week before Christmas in 1997. I found myself without a job.

I had previously worked in corporate fundraising at MIT, tech transfer, and sponsored research. I sort of cut my teeth on how the industry was using universities to fund cutting-edge technologies. A colleague of mine at MIT who raised money from individuals was also leaving the institute, so the two of us started a third-party marketing company. We basically raised money largely from the MIT alumni network, on behalf of hedge funds, and venture capital funds. Many of the investors were family offics, or chief investment officers for large entities. We were working within a pretty interesting little ecosystem.

I found that many of the alumni, particularly those outside of the region, were complaining that they didn't have access to this dynamic innovation area around MIT. The only way they could have access to those startups was by being an investor in a venture capital fund and that wasn't appealing to many of them because there was really no transparency in the venture portfolio. They were just financial investors.

Around the same time, I had a couple of MIT faculty members who were starting a company. They said, "Hey, you raised money for us before. Would you help us raise some for our company?" So I had two people within the same ecosystem looking for each other. They just don't know how to find each other. So in April 2000, another fellow MIT Sloan alum and I did an experiment. We brought two companies in front of four angel investors, three of which were MIT alums—and Hub was born.

Within the first 18 months, we'd grown to 25 people and made five investments and put $5 million to work. We looked at each other and said, holy crap, we have something here. Let's organize and structure it. That's how Hub was born.

How many investments have you made since Hub was founded?

We've been investing since 2000 and made 35 investments.

Are there particular types of companies that you invest in?

Our first investment ever was ZipCar, which had a pretty spectacular IPO, albeit ten years after we made our investment. We decided that we should be looking mostly at tech deals, but because both of us had a life sciences background, we have a minor focus, if you will, on life sciences. Only particular parts of life sciences. A little bit of devices. A little bit of diagnostics. A little bit of health IT. No therapies because the capital required for pharma is so large.

That became a little bit of a philosophy for us. We generally look at companies that have pre-money valuations of far less than $10 million. We've used $10 million as our cap for making initial investments. Almost all of our investments are in Massachusetts. A couple others in the New England states and two in New York. While we creep a bit from that scope, we expect the majority of our investments to be local.

We try to focus on companies using capital-efficient models. It's become cheaper to start a company but not necessarily cheaper to grow one. We're hoping that we can connect with companies with relatively low capital requirements. If a company comes to us and tells us they need $20 million or $30 million or $40 million, we cannot take a look at them because we know we're going to get lost in the shuffle as they go through their rounds of financing.

Do you invest just once in companies with lower capital requirements or do you follow your investments in future rounds?

We purposefully structured our group as a fund for two reasons. One, we wanted to have money in good times and in bad. Many angels sit on their wallets when the economy is tough because they worry about their second home and their third kid in college or something like that. We always wanted to have capital.

Two, we wanted to be able to follow our money. Most angels tend not to do that. Most of them are one and done. We've found that in following our investments, we've been able to tune the returns a bit. So we don't necessarily worry about dilution with companies that are doing well, because we own our stock at a much lower price and are happy in that position. We are able to invest when there might be a cram down to protect our position—but only if there's still merit to the company.

One way that we mitigate that potential issue is that, on average, we fund each of our portfolio companies three times during their lives. It's usually a seed, an A, and a B. After that, we tend to lose our appetite, typically because the company is doing so well that a dollar invested in an earlier-stage company might give us more bang for the buck. That's a pretty progressive approach to angel investing to reserve at least a dollar for every initial dollar of investment; although there are angel investors who reserve a lot more.

Do you invest the same amount in each round or maintain your percentage ownership?

It depends upon the circumstance. Sometimes you cover yourself in a down round. Fortunately, we haven't seen many of those in the last five years in our portfolio, so I believe that tells us we're getting smarter about pricing. When you have a company that's doing well, you want to double down on it if you can. We use the follow-on financing in a variety of ways.

How many positive and negatives outcomes or exits have you had?

We're batting above .400, which is pretty good compared to most. We had one spectacular exit when ZipCar IPO'd, but honestly, IPOs are likely the outlier in terms of our exits. All the rest of the exits have been through acquisition, although we do have two pre-IPO companies in our portfolio right now. One in 10 in an IPO is probably an expectation, but we don't try to shoot for the grand slam every single investment. We might invest in a company that's a bit later on in its life and solidly in revenue and headed toward profitability in the near term toward the end of one of our funds. We try not to hit a moon shot with every single company, although we do try to convince ourselves that we can get at least a 5x out of each investment. So a slightly different take at the outcome.

How do you go about finding companies to invest in?

We're out in the marketplace. We're judges in business plan contests. We're mentors. We go to events. We speak at events. We host events. We are friendly with the service providers. We work with venture capital groups. We work with angel groups in the area. We use that network to screen companies. You can't apply on our website. There's no way you can submit your business plan. In fact, our personal emails aren't even on our website. You've got to network to find us. In doing so, there's this natural filter that for those people who know us, they know that if you're developing a drug therapy for Alzheimer's, they're not going to recommend your company to us because we don't do therapies.

If you're developing some fantastic robotic device that's going to require $30 million intake in capital, those people in our network know we're not going to look at it. It automatically culls a lot of the things that aren't central to our interests.

Our members bring in leads as well. People in the marketplace know that our members are wealthy and their nephew or their next-door neighbor or former colleagues are asking them to look at business plans all the time. We also offer the charity killing of a deal. If one of our members is looking at something that they know sucks, but they don't want to tell the person themselves, they'll use me as the grim reaper.

Do all of the Hub members invest the same dollar amount? Or does everyone invest different amounts into the fund?

We focus on being a group of equals. So everybody invests the same amount of capital into the fund. Now if somebody wanted to co-invest in a particular portfolio company along the way, they certainly would be welcome to do so. They would write that check directly to the company rather than through the group or through the fund. It has a lot of benefit to the investor. For a relatively small amount of investment in the fund, they get access to eight or 10 companies. Then they can cherry pick those for co-investment without any tax or carry or fee put against it.

We run the fund in a very traditional fee structure of 1.5% on the management fee and 20% on a carry. We pay ourselves a monthly stipend that's pretty modest and our expenses are very small. We're motivated by the carry, and that's a tradition that has been lost on many people in the venture capital community that built these big funds and sort of got fat, lazy, and happy on a 2% management fee off of a billion-dollar fund. You don't have to have exits to live comfortably. You can just sit on the management fee. In our case, the management fee is so puny, we have to fight, scratch, and dig for successful exits so we can participate in the carry.

Do each of the members participate in due diligence equally?

Not entirely. The 80–20 rule prevails. My Hub partner and I run every single due diligence team, so we have a very fixed process, a methodology, and we're going to run that through our due diligence process every time. We do invite volunteers from the group to participate. Usually we have at least three, sometimes six, seven, or eight people who join each due diligence team. Some do a lot of it. Some do none of it. Usually somebody participates in some shape, form, or manner at some point during the process.

Do the members worry about you taking a management fee and the carry even though they participate in due diligence and deal flow?

Not at all. They're happy to pay us. There's so much deal flow in this marketplace. There's so much work to be done in due diligence. It's difficult negotiating terms. Most don't want to do any of that. They want to participate as much or as little as they like. They're more than happy to pay us a relatively small fee to have access to what we hope are eight or 10 of the better companies in the Boston ecosystem.

How long is your due diligence process?

It's pretty lengthy. What we try to do is tell the CEO within 30 days if we're making really good progress or if we're finding deal killers along the way. I think 30 days is a reasonable period of time to give somebody a measure of interest or disinterest. If we're interested, we turn up the due diligence a notch and try to complete it in another 30 days and start to put together other like-minded individuals who might be interested in that deal and try to start pulling a syndicate together.

We share our due diligence with others freely. We tend to do more diligence than most of the other groups in the area, so they appreciate our sharing with them. They pledge to make their own decision and hold us harmless. We actually have a due diligence treaty in the New England states where all of the angel groups have agreed to share due diligence but hold each other harmless.

During the due diligence process, what are you looking for?

All the basics on any venture capitalist due diligence list. There's the standard background stuff. Check references. Interview the members of the team. Interview the investors. The board. Then there are the more interesting parts where you talk with competitors. You talk with customers. You talk with prospective customers.

Often, we like to introduce the company to a prospective customer to see the sales cycle. We spend a lot of time vetting the management team. Which means not just checking references they give us, but talking with other people in the ecosystem who know them. Over the course of 30, 60 days of due diligence, you meet with them four, five, six times, and you really get a good feel for how they respond to certain questions. How they react in certain situations. I think it's an important part of the decision-making process to develop that relationship. We look at the financial model. We try to find analyst reports about the size of the market growth rates and things like that.

It's just pretty thorough. In fact, I just finished a due diligence report today. It's 60 pages. It's got notes from 15 interviews. It's got a financial analysis, a strategic analysis. It's pretty darn thorough.

Do you always syndicate?

We tend not to have deep-enough pockets to take a full round in the rounds that we're doing. In the last four years, we haven't done a round of less than a million dollars. When we're putting in $250,000 to $500,000, we need somebody else at the table. More often than not, it's other angel groups or angels in the area. Sometimes there are some venture groups that are doing some seed investments. Polaris and Atlas have done a few deals with us. There are a few of the bigger VCs that are allocating some money at the seed stage and we're happy to have them at the table because they reduce the financial risk of the company going forward.

How would you compare that to some of the other groups you share information with?

We're at the anal retentive end of the spectrum of due diligence. There are a couple of other groups in town that do that level of due diligence, but the majority of them just don't. They'll put together a due diligence team and the members will make two or three calls. Then they'll write up a self-assessment of the company in two or three pages. That really doesn't work for us because we're a fund. It has a measure of required rigor in everything we do, not just the due diligence but the other processes we use.

It's a good day when we partner with LaunchPad, Common Angels, or Golden Seeds because they also do an extreme amount of due diligence, and we appreciate that. Nonetheless, whatever other groups have done, we'll certainly accept that as input for the process.

Do you have rigor around the structure of the investment terms?

We're almost always investing in preferred equity to start our relationship. We are in a couple convertible notes begrudgingly. We'll do them when there's a lead who prefers to do it that way. Atlas is doing only convertible notes for their seed investments and we're happy to ride those terms because they bring with them some other benefits to the table. Normally, we only do preferred. Otherwise we'll use a bridge note for an existing portfolio company to help them get to a better place and a better valuation. Our preference is to focus on preferred equity.

We use standard NVCA documents for our term sheets to keep the costs of closing low and to keep our closing documents very vanilla. We don't want to have any bells and whistles in there that will scare away any future investors. We want to keep it simple.

How do you handle the valuation conversation with the entrepreneurs?

It's part science and part art. Most of the companies that we invest in are on the edge of revenue. Either they've got a pilot with a company that's going to purchase or they've got their first $200,000 of revenue. You can pretty easily convince yourself of the next 12 or even 24 months of revenue.

At the end of the day, it's obviously a negotiation, but we try to be fair. If we screw somebody over, the word's going to get out, and we're not going to get the quality of deal flow that we want to get. It's obviously a point of fairness. If both parties walk away from the table feeling like they didn't quite get everything they wanted, then we probably found the right price.

How do you engage with your portfolio over the life of the investments?

We've got a two-pronged approach. If we do have a board seat, it's more likely that one of the members of the group will take it. Although I serve on a couple of boards, it is mostly our members who take board seats. Our focus is always to find the right person for a company's board rather than just taking a seat because it was in the term sheet. Having that board presence is important for information rights and also allows us to be in the right conversations at the right time when the company is making difficult decisions.

On a quarterly basis, whichever partner originated the deal and ran it through the due diligence process will create a quarterly report. It shows our holding. It shows any up or down rounds and the implication on our valuation. It shows the financials, the performance of the last quarter and year. It includes a narrative that's a couple of paragraphs. I call it the warts and wonders of the company's experiences in the previous quarter. All the good things that are happening and commentary on the things that they've stumbled on. Often, there's a call to arms—"Does anybody know the chief marketing officer at Fidelity? Does anybody know an iOS developer who could work on a project for six months?" So on and so forth.

We use that as a mechanism of communicating with our members every quarter. Then we meet six times a year. So every other month, every quarter, and at the end of the year, we have touch points with the members of our group.

How do you go through figuring out who should be engaged?

It's almost always somebody who has participated in the due diligence process, and they've participated in that process for good reason. They know the industry. Or they know the entrepreneur. Or they know a lot about the ecosystem that the company is playing in. We don't put people on the board just because we've made a financial investment. We want to put the right people on the board. If we're in a syndicate and either we don't have the best person or we're not planning to lead, then obviously we're happy to have a member of another group sit on that board for our class of shareholders. In that case, we take an observer role. When we do have an observer role, it is usually me or my co-managing partner.

Most companies treat their observers as they would any other member of the board until it comes down to the voting process. I think most entrepreneurs want to limit the number of people in the boardroom. They don't want five observers, but one or two doesn't hurt. When you have a good group of people who have a level of trust and respect, then all the help that an entrepreneur can get is worthwhile.

Tell me about a company that you invested in that didn't turn out so well.

We invested in a big data company in the grocery space. They partnered with the large grocery chains to download purchase data from loyalty cardholders. They then performed analysis on that data and provided valuable insight for the merchandisers at the large chains and the consumer product brands who want to know what's going on in every retail store but who don't have visibility into that data.

The company wasn't able to ramp all that quickly. Grocery chains are very, very boring when it comes to technology and technology adoption. The merchandisers aren't particularly sophisticated. The company slogged it out for a couple of years. Generated revenue but not at the growth rate we would have liked.

We got to the third round of financing and realized that we weren't likely to attract another venture source outside of the company. The internal investors were getting tired. We decided we should probably try to sell the company. We engaged an investment banker and they brought a half-dozen people to the party.

We ended up selling the company to Google. It was essentially an acqui-hire, which you hear a lot about these days. Very typical of Google. It had some very interesting economics for the key members of the team, particularly the technical people. The two co-founders who were younger, first-time entrepreneurs are still at Google.

All of the key people of the team got very interesting new jobs, basically exploiting the technology that they had developed in the startup. The investors came out with something shy of a 2x return on their money. So it was a win-win situation for a company that really didn't hit the cover off the ball but nonetheless had some very talented people and created a very nice engine that could be repurposed.

How many years did it take to sell?

Four years.

Was there a point that you saw signs that indicated this would be the path?

We saw that pretty early. The company wasn't able to ramp its revenues, although it was slow growth. Probably two years in, we recognized it was going to be difficult educating the purchaser. We just weren't able to educate the merchandisers and the management teams of the grocery chains. There's a generational change that needs to go on there in terms of management that embraces technology. They just don't know the power of the data that they have. They'll figure that out sooner or later. We were just too early in that marketplace.

We gave them one more round of financing to at least get them to a point where they became a little more attractive to an acquirer. We spent six months in the process of selling the company. It took us three months to close the deal once we'd started the purchase and sale.

Have you done very many acqui-hires like that?

We've got two in our portfolio right now that we're starting to have those conversations with them. They're interesting companies, but they're not the rapid growing opportunities that we'd hoped they would be. They're not going to attract additional venture financing. We're looking at reasonable outcomes that will give us some liquidity and hopefully give our money back, if not low multiples. Ideally, they will give the members of the management team an opportunity to either move on to their next gig or move on to a more interesting company.

Is that result being driven by the time frame for the investors or mostly by the progress of the company?

Mostly the progress of the company. I wouldn't drive a company to an exit just because I wanted them to have an exit. There are other mechanisms of generating liquidity if we need it. It's really the company's lack of growth. The lack of ability to raise more capital, fishing or cutting bait with a reasonable exit rather than putting more money in and eventually losing it all. Getting cents on the dollar rather than zeroes is a very important concept that I think angels need to put more focus on.

Tell me about a company that you invested in that turned out great.

I think it was the first year that Techstars was in Boston. There was a company called Localytics that was a graduate. One of the other local groups gave them some seed financing in the form of a convertible note. For the first preferred round, Hub, New York Angels, and Launchpad put together a priced round. There actually was a term sheet from a venture capital firm competing with us. The management decided to go with angels because they wanted to preserve the opportunity for an early exit. We very much appreciated the optionality that the CEO showed.

Localytics are providing mobile app analytics. Of the 30 apps that you have on your mobile phone, most of them are using Localytics to send data about your use and my use of a particular app to the app developer. Everything from what device I'm using, what carrier I'm using, how long I spend on each page. Whether I go from a particular page to an e-commerce site, and everything in between. It does so basically on a real-time basis, which is really, really interesting.

They're now adding another revenue stream in providing in-app advertising because they know precisely when I'm doing something in-app. They can send me a very precise ad that's appropriate for where I am in that app. Really interesting company. We've funded them a couple of times. Polaris actually came in during the seed round and has subsequently participated in a Series A and B. They've just closed a Series C round, which was just made public about a month ago. They raised $16 million from Foundation Capital on a valuation that was a very nice increase from the previous two rounds that Hub participated in. They're off to the races.

With West Coast and East Coast VCs, there will probably be an additional round of financing. We've put our last dollar in. We're happy with the exposure we have. We invested two times. I was on the board as an observer. We lost that right in the B round. Now we're happy to sit back and watch the venture capitalists take the company to what's hopefully a very big exit.

Did you guys know that might be a path they would take based on your earlier due diligence?

It was a pleasant surprise is how I would characterize it. The CEO was a first-time CEO, but an older young guy. He was thirty-something. Just a bright, bright person. I think he bought himself an option for an early exit without causing any harm to the company whatsoever. To his credit, and we fully agreed, because the company was doing really well and had the opportunity to add another important revenue stream, we felt it was appropriate to shoot for the fences and raise significant venture capital. Then it became important to choose the right VC. They had multiple term sheets from VCs in this last round. From absolute top-shelf VCs, and that's the situation you like to be in.

What made you excited to invest in that company?

Techstars was a great platform to launch them. They basically developed the product while they were in Techstars and honed their strategy. They came out and they were ready for funding. Because they were so early, the VCs were not paying attention to them. It was serendipitous that we participated in the demo-day presentation and liked the company. We met the CEO and he had two other co-founders with him. The technical co-founder was spectacular, and still is the heart and soul of the product. They had a marketing/sales co-founder who had been around the barn with two previous startups, one of which was successful.

They had all of the makeup that you like in a team. Even though the CEO was a first-timer, he was very thoughtful and had been in important operating roles and had worked with Apple. He had a very clear sense of the ecosystem for apps. We felt like that team of people had unique knowledge of the space, and that's what we look for in a team. Unique knowledge.

What advice would you give to other angel investors?

I think that a group offers a new angel the opportunity to see a rigorous process. To see screening. To see presentation. To see due diligence. To see term negotiation and governance. That's an educational process. I think groups do a very good job of educating people. Although my group is structured as a fund, I often get first-time angels attracted to it because it allows and encourages participation, and that's education.

It also offers other things such as diversified portfolio. An investor in any one of my funds is going to get exposure to at least eight companies. I believe that in any asset class, diversification is key. If you can get into eight, 10, 15 companies, then the portfolio effects of a diversified strategy are going to take shape. I think groups are very important.

I think the new disruptor in the marketplace are the accredited portals—AngelList, SeedInvest, FundersClub, and so on. I know that the Foundry Group has been experimenting with a piece of their fund on AngelList. I think it's a really important player in the ecosystem. It gives newer angels the opportunity to follow people that they perceive to be experts or super angels. If I want to follow Ron Conway or Brad Feld or somebody else on AngelList and put my money into deals that they're looking at, I'm getting some of the best deal flow in the country. I think that's an interesting approach.

Those are two ways that newer angels can introduce themselves to the marketplace. I think that, if you're a new angel, and you don't make a number of investments that gets to a portfolio effect, you're likely not going to be an angel for long, because losses happen before winners. If you're not reserving money to follow, it's a riskier strategy. If you're not finding a way to educate yourself on how to do this process, then you're doing yourself a disservice. Finally, you need to figure out where the best deal flow is and make sure that you're seeing the better deals in your ecosystem. Hopefully people are doing that.

I'm also the chairman emeritus of the Angel Capital Association. I think the ACA is a tremendous resource for new angels. In fact, we're inviting accredited angels as individuals to join the ACA. It's not just a place for groups. The accredited portals, all the major portals, are members of the ACA. Family offices as well. There are resources at the ACA that every angel can benefit from.

* * *

David has a unique perspective as the chairman of the trade association dedicated to angel investing. He also describes an interesting way to organize a group of angel investors that is unique amid the other types of angel investors and angel groups profiled here. His insights into deep due diligence and learning from great investors is a theme that you'll hear again, but not from all investors.

David also brings up the major portals as an important part of the possibilities. Investing alongside great investors is a way to learn to invest as well as a way to diversify a portfolio. There are many partnering with the ACA such as AngelList, DreamFunded, FundersClub, Healthios, and SeedInvest. The options for joining a group and learning from angel investors as well as not joining a group and learning from angel investors are expanding, and David clearly is trying to steer the ACA to be a connection and learning point.

DEVELOP A PORTFOLIO STRATEGY WITH JIM CONNOR

"Details create the big picture."

—SANFORD I. WEILL

"As you become involved in funding startup companies and tracking growth, you look at the bigger picture and say, "This really is having a dramatic effect on the economy."

—JIM CONNOR

JIM CONNOR IS A FASCINATING GUY. He's on the boards of both the Angel Capital Association and one of the top angel groups in the country, Sand Hill Angels. He has a decade of angel investing experience and much more experience operating companies in the financial software space. Most recently, Jim built SymPro and sold it to JPMorgan Chase.

I reached out to Jim due to his expertise and investment style. The early investments made by the Sand Hill Angels often have other recognized investors involved, such as 500 Startups, Health Tech Capital, Life Science Angels, Launch Pad and Tandem Capital. There is clearly something valuable about the domain expertise and talent network that investors in the group have developed. After talking to Jim, I understand more about what it is and why so many top angel investors who aren't angel group members are investing so often with Jim and the Sand Hill Angels.

Let's start with how Jim views angel investing before we get into how he started and explore some of the good and bad experiences he's had.

What do you think about the process of getting into angel investing?

Angel investing is a stimulating and rewarding experience. I tend to see three categories of angel investors: angels who've been investing for one to two years, three to four years, and then five-plus years. I think everybody knows what the one- to two-year investor feels like. You say to yourself, "Wow, this is interesting!" You're stimulated by the intensity of the group, the skills of the group, and the group's experience in speaking to new companies and understanding their unique innovations. It's a great experience! If the new potential investors find the company compelling from an emotional perspective, they are very likely to invest.

The members who have three to four years' experience tend to recognize the reality that generation of a positive return from angel investing is a little harder than it looks. Meaning, they have seen a couple of companies become insolvent. They've seen some of the disappointments. They've seen some promising starts, but they realize that exits only come from a smaller subset of startup teams. Essentially, if things don't happen in the first three years, most companies enter an extended, longer-term life cycle.

Then, at the six-plus years, most angel investors usually step back and recognize that they really need to think about how far they wish to go with this asset class. By this time, they have established a portfolio, and have formed a policy regarding their decision to commit new money to an existing portfolio company versus continuing only to invest in new opportunities. For most angel investors the time horizon for positive returns on the portfolio has not been reached and they probably haven't reached a point where the proceeds from liquidation events is greater than the total principal invested. However, most early-stage investors probably have some winners that continue to work towards an acquisition or an IPO. There is a period of self-analysis—how is my portfolio structured? Do I have too much concentration in one company due to follow-on investments? Am I too sector heavy? Are some of these companies firmly on the path to become lifestyle companies?

Most of your investments that are going to fail will do so in the first two to three years. As you reach the middle stage of being an investor, about three to five years, you start to have the perspective that generating a positive return takes a serious effort. You have to focus on which of those companies can get an exit, whether by natural growth or by personally putting some effort into how the company, the board and the investors are focusing on an exit.

There's a big debate about how much investors can do to help shape an exit in a portfolio company, especially if the company has not maintained the preliminary work and a "state of readiness" in the first one to three years. If you're not doing the work to ensure the company is prepared to engage with an acquirer, or the company does not have a definitive product strategy, revenue strategy, sales execution, and culture, then it's hard to affect any change at a later point.

What work needs to get done in those early years?

For the individual company, angels put forth efforts to establish strong corporate governance, good investor communications, and a culture that attracts talent and is inclusive of a broad range of perspectives.

For the investor who wishes to build a diversified portfolio of emerging technology companies, it is extremely challenging to know which companies will succeed and which will fail. Investors believe that they're applying intellectual or analytical skills to know which company will succeed, but everything I've seen is unpredictable. This process is similar to the inability to predict if the stock market's going to go up or down for any specific time horizon. There are internal and external events that you have no control over. Even with all the analysis, computational horsepower, and professionals focusing on the US stock market, it is difficult to predict the individual winners and losers with any significant accuracy.

You can apply that same randomness to private equity. The fact is, there will be external events over which you have no control, which will affect the outcomes for startup companies. You do your best, focus on the basics such as the size of addressable market, the potential evolutionary or disruptive potential of the products or services, the quality of the team, competition and defensibility. The most important factors are the people and the capacity of the company to be very good or to excel at some execution or product deployment. This is a very subjective assessment, and it's a crucial indication of the potential for success. I ultimately come back to the question, "Is this team really good at something, maybe one of the best at something?" Ultimately, you're making an evaluation of the team to build a company that delivers significant value to a large market and is a scalable operational model.

Do you have to have been great in the past to recognize something great now?

It's the team's personality and culture in the company that matters, which is established by the values of the founders and extended by the management team. You need to recognize teams where the culture of the company is able to first have the confidence to believe that they can be the best at something. When you've been very good at something, you understand what it feels like to compete, to persevere, to get the lead and maintain a lead in some discipline, to have the recognition and the confirmation of the results. This experience will help a young company persevere through the struggle to emerge with a great app or a superior technology. You know how it feels each step along the way from being a contender, to persevering to be recognized as one of the best, then the step to being the leader. One of my key subjective evaluations is assessing if the founding team culture has DNA to attract strong people who'll find the culture compelling, leading to a commitment and alignment to the company's success. This is one reason that I look at the level of adversity in the background of the founders, overcoming adversity in past experiences can be an important indicator of future success.

Startup companies are made up of individuals but, overall, it's the culture of the company that determines if a company is going to be successful. For investors, it's very important for the company to build a culture where they are the best at something.

How did you get started with early-stage investing?

One day I was part of a 25-member team that was eliminated in a reorganization. In the transition period, I decided to pursue an emerging need in the early local area network integration. The company encountered challenges and migrated or pivoted to become a pure software company and build a great product for the capital markets. Eventually the company was stable, profitable, and I felt that the window was open for a sale. It was the right place at the right time; the company received three exit opportunities and the right one worked out.

After you get an exit, there's a honeymoon period, when special powers and special skills are attributed to you. People ask you to help them out, evaluate their business plan, be an advisor, and even give your opinion on pending decisions. Sooner or later, they're going to ask you to help on the finances. Then you have to decide if you want to be an investor.

If you find the idea of investing in a startup exciting, then the second thing is, how do you want to invest? You can invest as an individual or you can invest through a group. Group investment for new angel investors is, in my opinion, the best strategy, unless you have so much money you can lose a lot of it in the learning process. Investing through a group, learning the best practices, and participating in the investor education process is an essential component. Understanding how early-stage private equity investment is structured, learning about term sheets, stock purchase agreements, convertible notes, employee stock option allocation, cap tables, board roles, and taxes is all part of the process.

After a few years, some angel investors will start their own micro VC fund, or break off to dedicate themselves to one or more new startups in an operations role. The education provided through an angel investment organization as well as the practical experience is unique. In my opinion, the education delivers skills that can be applied to a wide range of management, advisory, and leadership roles.

I felt that remaining a part of the Sand Hill Angels was the best strategy for me, because I enjoy having the benefits of a diversified portfolio and I didn't have the skills or time to evaluate the various other sectors necessary to build a diversified portfolio. Investing as part of a group also has some unseen advantages; for example you build investor friends, share perspectives, insights, and you learn from others. If your group is the lead investor, you can participate in creating the term sheet and working on the due diligence. Periodically, you may have an opportunity to serve on a company's board or serve as a board observer.

As you become involved in funding startup companies and tracking growth, you look at the bigger picture and say, "This really is having a dramatic effect on the economy." As young people are coming out of universities, they're getting good jobs leveraging their creative outlook and skill sets and most important, they are getting fantastic experience in the most challenging time of creating a new business. Maybe we have to take some chances on the companies, but the macroeconomic effect of all these companies receiving funding to grow and using the products and services of other startups is enormous. This is one of the key multipliers of innovation and value creation being spread throughout our society.

A smaller subset of the startup community will be tremendously successful along the lines of Google and Facebook and Yahoo. These new tech companies are a product of the American enterprise and capital markets system. If you're a person who has the means to participate financially, you get the perspective that being involved in the funding of startup companies creates enormous contributions to our economy and is a very worthwhile way to spend your time.

Tell me about a company that you invested in that turned out great.

Think about the business model of skiing. You decide to go skiing a week to a month in advance, but it's not until you get to the ski resort that you buy a lift ticket. You waste significant time, 30 to 45 minutes or more, just buying the tickets. The physical ticket office sales model is a challenge for the resort operators. They don't know how many people are going to show up any given day and they're running a fixed-cost business.

Evan Reece and Ron Schneidermann founded Liftopia back in 2005. They previously worked for Hotwire, both were active skiers or snowboarders, and the idea of selling discount tickets for ski resorts was a pretty standard idea that depended on excellent execution. They're really smart entrepreneurial guys. They evolved that model into providing a platform for the advance purchase of lift tickets just like you do for an airline ticket. By offering advance purchase discounts and time savings to customers as well as revenue predictability and marketing presence to ski resort operators they created a market for their product.

Over five or six years, the company changed the whole model in the ski industry from people thinking "I will go to the resort and buy a ticket" to "Of course I get online to buy ski tickets before I go to the resort." Overall, the company has done very well. They've grown, had several of financing rounds, and established direct one-on-one relationships with all the ski resort operators. Today, they're the dominant provider of advance ticket sales within U.S. ski resorts.

While this service appeals to the consumer, it has even more appeal to the ski resort operators, because now they've engaged the concept of yield management of revenues. Now the ski resort can manage and fine-tune the demand parameters such as price, day of the week, multiple day sales, and the revenue results of that demand. They sell tickets early because advanced purchase tickets are discounted for two, three weeks out in the future. As you get closer to the day of skiing, the prices of a ski ticket tends to rise or the available inventory of tickets at a certain price is sold out. The ski resort operator know they will have a certain number of people on the hill for a specific date and can count on the average revenue that comes from the sales of food, equipment rentals and concessions from skiers on any given day.

Liftopia provides a dynamic revenue model and product strategy platform for the ski resorts to offer compelling deals to skiers based on the day of the week and the number of ski tickets sold. Ski resorts started to view Liftopia as a must-have revenue management and marketing program, and that's when the company experienced consistent growth. They went from a nice-to-have to a must-have product for the ski resort sector.

What did that team have to make that work for them?

The Liftopia management had a number of key skills, both founders had worked at Hotwire, they were avid skiers, they had the ability to be very diligent about who they brought into the team. Once you have money in the bank, you need to get people. You often start to compromise. It's so easy to do. It is quite common to have job applicants figure out what you want to hear and then tell you. You get caught up in the timing and pressure to get somebody in a critical position, so it becomes easy for you to make unfortunate decisions.

If you don't address the performance issue quickly, then pretty soon you notice this mediocre team, and ask, "How the hell did we build this low-performing group?" Evan and Ron were able to keep that intensity of demanding very high quality and performance from all members of the team. They hired stronger people who could bring skills and superior results to the company.

Did you recognize their ability to bring on the right team members?

I felt that Evan and Ron were unique and had natural, entrepreneurial talents, but I didn't immediately know if they could build a dynamic, strong team. There's so much unconscious messaging that goes on in an assessment. We all intuitively know if we like somebody within the first one or two minutes of meeting them.

The next thing is, can you recognize and filter out that bias in your analysis when you're thinking about adding a new person to the team? In my experience, this is a very challenging process, one that I personally found difficult to do when I was making an assessment of a founding team's strengths.

What led you to decide to work with this company?

I had met Evan and Ron at several startup events. I liked them for their personalities, their spirit and commitment, and because I liked them, I spent time with them continually refining their business plan. Eventually their business plan, research and traction was recognized and they got a seed equity round that lasted for 18 months. That was really what happened. You've got to be likable enough that someone will spend time with you.

The next question is, can you execute on the business plan? Their ability to execute on the business plan was totally unknown at that point. It was up to them to show proof, persevere, whatever it took, to execute on the business plan to make progress. I don't think anybody can know the answer. You make the investment. Then you watch and see if they can execute the business plan or they require moderate to extensive supervision. Do they communicate with investors? Are they transparent? You look at past behavior patterns, business skills, competitiveness, and you make the best decision you can.

It worked out. Liftopia as a company and the management team have evolved to be a leader in their space. The team is accomplished, confident, has a strong culture, and can hit bumps in the road but they keep moving forward. You can take a look at liftopia.com. They dominate the space for pre-purchase of ski tickets and ski resort services.

Did you have existing expertise in the space that helped you decide to invest?

No. I had the minimum requirements of knowing the space in that I'd been a recreational skier for many years. I understood the inconvenience of standing in line at a ski resort and buying a ticket and the advantages of buying a pass or ticket online and then walking up, turning in my receipt, getting my ticket and going to the ski lift without any waiting line, down time, or fumbling around for my credit card.

Tell me about a company that you invested in that didn't turn out so well.

Let me give you some perspectives on the companies that did not work out. In general, the business concept or idea did not have market validation, there was no significant feedback from a customer who adopted the idea or was in a beta process. The quickest failures are when investments are made prior to having customer validation of a product, the pricing or the solution. The second most common failure point is an inability of the company to generate revenues in a sustainable way. Earning revenue by delivering value is crucial to any company. Unfortunately we often find that a startup can hit their expense targets but fail to come close to the revenue targets.

What advice would you give to other angel investors?

The most important thing to decide is if you're going to be a one-time investor in the company or a multiple-round investor. I think it's important to decide at the beginning, "I'm going to put in $25,000 and that's it. That's my strategy" Or "I'm going to put in money now and I'm going to continue investing as long as the company continues to grow and hit its milestones up to some point."

At a certain point, as a company grows, you might decide it's time to stop investing because you're starting to dilute your share prices by purchasing shares at higher valuations, giving up the opportunity to maintain your ownership percentage. On the other hand, if the company's doing great and things are going well, continuing to participate in subsequent rounds is a good sign to the new investors. If you haven't thought through your investment policy and strategy, you will have to engage in an analytical and emotional decision later on when the company comes back for its second, third, fourth round. Sometimes the rounds are relatively flat from the price of the prior round or have a modest step up on price and sometimes there are big upgrades in terms of valuation.

I think it's important to develop a strategy in your first two years because you're going to be encountering this decision when your first investments come back for another round. Just because a company has a term sheet from an investor doesn't mean it's a good investment for you. You should define what aspects of a company appeal to your investor sentiment, values and your sense of commitment and then limit your consideration to the companies where you can find a compelling reason to invest.

The other point is that early-stage investors should realize that it's okay to pass on an investment opportunity. There is always tremendous excitement around new companies with new products or services. My experience has been that in the next three months, there will be another company solving the same problem and maybe with a better team or better technology. Sometimes they're only weeks apart. Watch the older investors in the group. They pass all the time because they recognize that really sweet, hot deals come and go all the time and you know what? It's okay to pass if the terms aren't right for you, if the valuation is too high, or there are too many high expectations out there for this company.

As an angel investor, you have to define how much time and energy you want to put into this effort because it can become a full-time activity for you. Many people are still working and you have to decide if you really want to become a focused investor or become a full-time investor. There are discussions along the lines of how early do you want to be? When you're at the early bleeding edge, often you don't get rewarded for taking the early-stage risk. As much as you might think it's exciting, you don't get rewarded financially for investing at that early stage because of the dilution in subsequent rounds and the continuous risk of a failed execution, or because of the high failure rate of the first innovators in a new technology, only to have subsequent entrepreneurs find the right combination of resources to execute.

How much of your portfolio do you allocate to early stage?

Five percent is the accepted number and, considering the risk, most investors should not exceed 10%. If you exceed 10% in this sector, you either have a continuous high income or a significant trust fund. Most angel investors started out with a five-year plan—1% per year over five years—but couldn't hold their allocation to 5% for a variety of reasons; some assume they will have positive realized returns over five years to reinvest proceeds from earlier investments.

Does the allocation change over time, especially as average valuations change?

My personal opinion is most people who're doing this don't think about an allocation model, unless they have experience in the structuring of a portfolio, a portfolio advisor or a financial advisor of some type who's laid down a strategy and an allocation model to follow.

I think venture debt is also a viable way to go. I invested some funds that lend money to mid-tier startups that are cash flow positive but need funding to grow and do not wish to be diluted by a standard VC investment. I like the consistent interest rate of return of venture debt. It's a stabilizer. It generates a quarterly check and there's a sweetener because debt funds will purchase warrants or options in the company, which allow for participating in a liquidity event, and this will raise the overall return.

Is that part of your fixed allocation or is that an addition?

It is part of the fixed allocation. The venture debt funds have risks, but I'm comfortable that the management of that fund is sufficiently knowledgeable to manage the risks. They're going to have a few losses but given the nature of debt, the fund has security claims on the company's assets for some level of recovery.

How do you like to structure the investments you make directly?

Most angel groups don't find convertible debt to be attractive. There are many reasons why. In the first year or two as you begin investing, you don't see the downside to convertible debt. If a startup company is too small or too limited and doesn't accept a valuation on the company by investors but instead wants convertible debt, the founders are not recognizing how many downsides there are to investors in convertible debt. Many startups have been incorrectly advised that the easy way to get angel group traction is to offer investors convertible debt.

Most angel groups realize that convertible debt is simply not a great structure for them. The startup companies will say, "We want to fund with convertible debt, with a valuation cap on the future equity round when the note will convert to preferred stock." I've heard companies say that all the protections are available to make convertible debt very much like a seed equity round, but the reality is that with a reasonable effort, the company can design the investment as a seed equity round and they will tend to receive better traction from angel groups.

How do you handle the valuation conversation with the entrepreneurs?

Angel investors have a sense of risk–return in early-stage companies. If you have been in a group for 1 to 2 years, you can research the competitive offerings, one can observe the group's approach on the valuation or the cap on the [convertible debt] conversion price. Angel investors are generally aware of the competitive alternatives among similar companies in a specific sector with a valid technology, product and actual prospective customers. As a group, angel investors can find a valuation that provides a rationale for making an investment. There is research available, known as the Halo Report, available through the Angel Capital Association that collects actual data on completed deals among the angel groups since 2011. The Halo Report has good participation among the angel groups and provides a reliable indication of valuations in these early-stage transactions. The average valuation for an early equity round with individual investors and angel groups across the US is $2.5 to $2.7 million, and it's been that way for a number of years.

Silicon Valley, Boston, and New York angel-funded companies are at the higher end; they have early-stage valuations upward of $3 million to $3.5 million, and $4 million occasionally. Places like

Indianapolis have lower valuations such as $1.1, $1.5, and $1.8 million. Overall, it averages about to $2.5 million.

Companies who want to be funded through angel groups need to be comfortable with that valuation range. Companies should understand that angel investors make efforts to find companies that are providing a viable, scalable solution to an identifiable market with a mature, coachable management team at a reasonable valuation.

Do you see company success tied to valuation?

I don't see a correlation between valuation and success. Raising an early-stage round depends on organizing a credible, compelling story and competitive conditions can push valuations beyond a reasonable risk-reward trade-off. There is plenty of hype and a group of influential investors can get carried away and push the valuation. Much can happen competitively in a year; both investors and the company learn that the sales cycle or adoption rate is taking longer than expected and revenues are not being received at the projected rate.

The high valuations might make the founders feel good for the first round but high valuations put tremendous pressure on the company management to swing for the fences, creating many strikeouts. We often see markets evolve, and a company might be in the space where they need to develop longer-term engagement with the customer, such as we see in the enterprise application marketplace.

The higher valuation also increases investor and company risk. If the company doesn't hit their milestones, their next round is going to be difficult sell for any new investors. The only game left is with the existing investors, and the company's pitch goes something like this: "We're really desperate. We can't raise any money from new investors. Can you keep us alive?"

You take out your checkbook and you think, "I should have seen this before I invested?" You write the check to keep the company alive, to keep the game going, hoping that the company will get enough traction and validation to be able to attract new investors into the next round and that the next round will be at a higher valuation. That's why I'm saying that investors need to realize they are likely to write two checks. Every time you write one check, be prepared to write a second one of equal or greater size to that same company before they get to a round with new investors.

Do you always follow on, even on the down rounds?

I look at each follow-on independently and determine if the company's prospects and the valuation makes sense. On a down round, it depends on how down it is. There's the concept of trying to catch a falling knife, which should be avoided. Very few people will say they failed to execute because of structural problems in their team, wrong product, or wrong market. However, a structural problem, wrong team, or incomplete product is often the source of the disappointing progress and these types of problems are very challenging to correct. In my opinion, each investor has to determine if they can continue to financially support a stalled effort.

What advice would you give to angel investors?

Today, many angel investors have an operations background. Many currently run companies as CEOs. Many of them probably will realize that they are better company operators or they're better C-level executives than they are passive investors. This is probably one of the key issues today. As an angel investor, you have to decide if you want to be an active or passive investor. Maybe you give advice, you help out upon request in an areas where you can contribute, you do some mentoring, but that's all you can do because you're in a lot of companies and you have limits on your time.

My sense is that an individual coming into angel investing should decide on one of two roles. You're either going to be a truly broad, widely diversified angel investor who's not active in the various companies; or you're going to focus on a specific area of experience and knowledge, limit the range of investments to areas that you can have an effect on, and focus on those handful of companies or opportunities, where you can make a meaningful contribution.

How broad and diversified do you want to be? Do you want to be passive or involved in just a handful of companies during any given year? I think it comes down to the personality of the investor. Are they really a person who loves to be in business, solving problems, doing things, or are they a broad, diversified investor? I have evolved from being a broad, diversified investor to being a focused, active investor. I enjoy the focus. I don't need to be in every investment, I just need to pick the two or three companies that I want to work with this year. Then allocate enough time to engage to make that positive contribution, maybe only as a board member, maybe only in an advisor role, but a role that is stimulating and you're excited about the opportunity and the company's mission.

* * *

One thing Jim brings up that's incredibly important for investors looking for exposure to early, growth-oriented companies is the possibility of investing in the space via tools like venture debt. There are a lot of other mechanisms beyond investing with equity or a convertible note that can be used to reduce risk in an early-stage portfolio. This is important because as Jim points out, early-stage investing can be hard.

The company Jim discussed, Liftopia, is still running strong with relationships at most major mountains in the country. They raised a $5 million Series D in late 2013 from a variety of VCs and a few private individuals such as Spencer Rascoff (the CEO of Zillow) and Marc Benoiff (the CEO of salesforce.com).

STRUCTURE MATTERS WITH PETER WEISS

[The market is] "the only place where when things go on sale, people get unhappy."

—WARREN BUFFETT

"After 35 years of doing finance, I know that things go up, things go down, times are good, times get bad. I never expected what happened in 2008."

—PETER WEISS

I REACHED OUT TO PETER with a cold call as I had so many investors. Some were cold calls to a person to introduce me and some were direct cold calls to the investors themselves. Peter fell into the latter category and we set up a time to meet near his house. When we met, I was pleasantly surprised to find a New Yorker to talk my ear off and tell me the insides to angel investing. He went deep into his viewpoints on the technical parts of angel finance and it was a real treat to have such an opinionated viewpoint that often contradicted so many of the viewpoints I'd come across in my research.

We talked about capital markets, market cycles, options, warrants, bridge financing, impact investing, LLCs vs. C-Corps, debt versus equity, and of course…baseball. The conversation was incredibly interesting, regardless of how much you agree or disagree with Peter's views.

Let's talk about due diligence. What are you looking for in the process? What's the purpose of due diligence?

The purpose of due diligence is to find the reason to say "No." That's the only reason for doing due diligence. If you're not looking for a reason to say that, why are you wasting your time? Why are you wasting the company's time? If you have already pretty much decided you're investing, whatever you may find, unless it jumps up and bites you on the nose and you don't beat it off with a stick, you're going to invest in the company because you fell in love and you've got a head of steam and you're sure that you have seen something that's unmitigated pure truth. In which case you would be silly not to write a check.

The purpose of due diligence is to figure out why you want to say no. Not to find a sugar-coated excuse, you can say anything you want. Gee, it's not the time. Gee, I just made another commitment. The key is you do due diligence long enough to say, "Nope, I don't want to be involved with this anymore," and you cut your losses. Why does Rob Wiltbank's chart relating due diligence time and returns peak and then decline as you do more due diligence? Why does it decline as you put in more and more due diligence? [Author's note: see the resources or glossary for more information on Rob Wiltbank's research]

You start discounting the reasons to say no?

You're trying to convince yourself. You know you should say no. Now you're burying yourself in data so that you no longer see the forest because of the trees. That explains Rob's correlation between returns and due diligence to hours. Obviously you want to do something, you want to make sure that the company exists. You would like to know they can at least spell the name of the product that they propose to sell. There are a few kinds of basic things.

That's the first hour or two and then maybe you do want to do the other things you asked about. In my mind that first set of time, it's the first one to 20 or 30 hours that's spent answering the question, "Can I find any reasons to say no?" How much you put in—I forget his chart exactly, but it's 25 to 30 hours. After 30 hours you're doing your darnedest to talk yourself into something that you know better than to do.

I have been involved with organizations that wanted to say as matter of policy that everyone on a due diligence team intended to invest unless they found some reason not to, and I always said that's ridiculous. Why walk in having prejudiced the outcome? By putting it that way you immediately removed most of the skepticism that you need to make an intelligent rational analysis—not that most of these things are that subject to rational and intelligent analysis, anyway—but once you have removed the skepticism, you have removed one of the major brakes, and then what's the purpose of due diligence?

By the way, this leads to a corollary. A lot of people say, "How do you make decisions?" I trust my gut. Do not trust your gut if it says to invest. Trust your gut absolutely if it says *don't* invest. Even if you can't put your finger on it. If something is saying to you stay away, pay attention because you know what, highly likely six months or one year, two years, or four years later, you will find out what it was that you were aware of but you weren't aware that you were aware of.

I have never, ever regretted passing on a deal where I listened to my stomach about passing. I have regretted many deals where I have continued on a deal where my stomach said to stay away. I have regretted passing on some deals, but they were things I had other reasons for passing, including I had other things I felt were better deals, or I didn't have cash or whatever, didn't have time.

I guess that leads us to another corollary. As an angel investor the default position should always be "No." There is always another deal. There is always another opportunity. You don't have to be in this one. If I had $10,000 for every deal that was going to go to a billion-dollar IPO that went absolutely to zero that I have seen pitched, it would have covered the value of my rather nice house on Mercer Island free and clear with plenty left over.

The default position is "No." The purpose of due diligence is to find a reason to say "No." If you're spending too much time on it you're trying to talk yourself into something that deep down inside you know you should skip.

All of this leads us to ask what's the best way to make money? Begin by trying to not lose money. You cannot say in angel investing I will never do a deal where I have risk of losing money, because that's not the nature of the universe.

What's the difference between a .250 hitter and a .300 hitter? A .250 hitter is a very average major leaguer. A .300 hitter is an All-Star. What's the difference? It's one hit out of 20 at-bats. How do you get that one hit? Pitch selection or, alternatively, defending the plate from the pitches that aren't great but are going to be called strikes. In other words, far from being aggressive as an angel investor, if you want to make money, be defensive. Doesn't mean hide your head. It means take a deep breath, slow down. If someone calls you up and says, "We opened this round a week ago and we're going to close it in two weeks, and if you don't get your subscription in the next week, you're out." Pass. Right then and there. Pass.

By the way, let's talk about front-loaded deals. If they are offering a bigger discount for the first X dollars, walk away. Walk away for a bunch of reasons. Number one, they're not fair. Number two, the odds are very good that they will fill the first part of the round, and then hit a brick wall on the second half because most guys will go, "Let's see, you filled the first half last night. This morning you want to charge me 20% more for the same securities, you must have had a hell of a good night. Would you please tell me what happened last night that suddenly your company is worth 20% more?" The answer is, "Well, we filled the first part of our round." My answer is, "You reached $500,000 last night, and suddenly this morning the next $1,000 is worth 20% less than the one you got last night. I'm not interested. Thank you very much."

By the way, most smart investors will take that position. I don't like deals that are front-ended like that. It shows the issuers are not smart. They will end up spending more on lawyers, and anyone who's doing that kind of financial engineering in an early-stage company is thinking about the wrong issues. They are thinking about how to outsmart and out-position investors rather than how they're going to use the money to build a great business and make a lot of money for everybody, including their investors, once they raise their capital.

What are some of the other tricks people play in early-stage finance?

Let's talk about warrants. Leave aside desperation deals where they must offer warrants to raise money. Let's assume it's a company that's in a position to do a normal raise. Warrants as they are generally done are one of the worst ways to induce investors to put money into the company. They are bad from the company's perspective, they are bad from the investor's perspective. Why? Because the typical warrant in an early-stage raise has a life of somewhere between five and 10 years. This means that the warrant won't generate capital for the company in any time frame that's meaningful for an early-stage company. However, it is a permanent or at least a medium- to long-term call on the value of the equity of the company. Put another way, a five or 10-year warrant is in fact a substantial discount on today's equity value. It also permanently, or in the long term, screws up your cap table. It is cleaner to say "I will value my company at $2 million with no warrants instead of two and a half million dollars with a whole bunch of warrants that won't bring me any capital in the future." Why? Because if I give warrants in this round, I probably will give them in my next round. Period, end of story. Each time I will be rolling forward. I will have the equity appreciation. If I get an exit in four years I won't have had any access to that capital, but I will give away part of my value on my exit. This makes no sense from the company's perspective.

Let's look at it from the investor's perspective. This is a terrible idea. Why? Because, number one, I own less of the company today. To the extent that it ever matters that my votes get counted, which it almost never will, I have fewer votes. Number two, if I want to maintain my sort of implicit ownership I have to write another check, whether or not it's convenient, whether or not I have cash, whether or not it makes sense at the time. The worst is if there's an exit, and I haven't exercised my warrant at least a year in advance, now on my equity appreciation I pay short-term cap gains rate instead of long-term cap gains rate. Gee, I would have been better off buying in at a lower valuation and getting long-term rates and just owning a little more outright from the beginning than holding a warrant.

Warrants are bad for the company, bad for the investor, everybody loses; oh and by the way, the attorneys get to charge more and the accountants will tell you that you need to do your 409(a) valuations, although for most early-stage companies that's not true. There is no obligation to have an outside person value your 409(a) until you have been in business for 10 years, or you have certain levels of assets and revenues. It doesn't matter. Your accountants and your attorneys win while the business and the investors lose, and so do your employees with their stock options and everybody else. It doesn't make any sense.

There is an appropriate use for warrants. The key is expiration dates. Warrants can make sense if the warrant has a relatively short expiration period, somewhere between 12 and 36 months. I would typically go somewhere between 18 and 24 months. Then warrants become a fast, efficient, and an economical way of bringing in more capital. If you do a good job as a management team of staying in touch with your investors, you communicate regularly, and you can communicate openly, good and bad, if you're making good progress, the CEO and the CFO can contact the warrant holders and say, "By the way, your warrants are expiring in 60 days. Here are all the cool things that we did with your money last time, and with our next valuation or our next raise, the value will be substantially higher than your strike price. Wouldn't you like to write a check now?" You can get extra capital and runway from the original capital raise. No need to spend a lot of money with your lawyers. No need to spend a lot of time going out and convincing new people. It's the cheapest, easiest way to raise incremental capital. Warrants with a short expiration, in the right circumstance, if you understand what your company's needs are and what your timing is, can be excellent. Warrants with medium- to long-term expirations are really not useful and they hurt pretty much everybody.

What typically happens where there's a bridge financing in between financing rounds?

Bridge financing. True honest to God bridge financings. Bridge financings that are truly bridges. In other words, you're building something that is going to get to the other shore. As opposed to what most so-called early-stage bridge financings are. They aren't bridges. They're piers. You're going to end up swimming. Those should never be debt. Those should be equity. Suck it up. Management team, you made some mistakes and you're out of money and you can't do a fully-priced equity round. Gee. Too bad. You shouldn't have screwed up.

Investors who're already in have two choices. Either way, you're paying a penalty. But maybe you can recover some. You pay the penalty for having backed a management team that for whatever reason, good, bad, or indifferent, didn't execute the plan and didn't bring in enough capital to make it to the other side. You have a choice.

You can either participate or you can take the consequences. Either way, that's the price of playing with the big boys or the little boys. But that's the nature of angel investing. Frankly, that's one of the reasons very few people should do angel investing, because you have to be able to deal with that economically and emotionally. If you're not prepared for that, you just shouldn't be doing angel investing, period. End of story. By the way, most people who do angel investing should not be doing angel investing.

What are your thoughts on pay-to-play provisions?

Pay-to-play says, "if the company does another financing and you don't put up your pro-rata share relative to your current ownership, either of the company or the round that you're in or whatever the definition may be, into the new round, your current position gets converted into common stock". In other words, if you have preferred, let's say with cumulative dividends, it all goes away and you get common stock. If you have convertible debt and they're doing another convertible-debt round or something that doesn't trigger the next equity financing, but it's got a pay-to-play division you get converted into common. Which can be very unfavorable.

You have no protection. This is a provision that should exist only in VC deals. It should never be in an angel deal. It exists and one of the problems with angel deals is the term sheets, the documents, the structures are venture capital structures, which have been inappropriately adapted for angels. Pay-to-play provisions are one of those things that are completely inappropriate in angel rounds. VCs do this because typically there are somewhere between two and six or eight VC firms in a round and they want to make sure that if more money is needed, all of their partners stay with them. So they have chained themselves together and anyone who says, "I'm not going to jump in the lake" gets severely penalized.

The VC firms are structured. They're holding reserve funds. They have capital to do this. They have expertise. They are represented on the board. They are receiving much more information than any angel is receiving. No small angel should ever be in a deal with a pay-to-play provision because they will get hurt if there's a big investor, because the big investor will often find a way to trigger that and push you down. If they don't, shame on them because they should. That's the way the rules are written. They're not breaking the rules, they're just playing tough by throwing an elbow. That's pay-to-play.

What about convertible debt?

Convertible debt. I hear all over the place, "Oh, everyone does it, it's a great way to raise money. Makes a lot of sense. Good for investors. Good for companies." Wrong on every count.

Let's talk about it from the investor's point of view. Convertible debt is a transaction where I give you money and you give me a blank sheet of paper. At some point in the future you're going to say to me, "Give me back my blank sheet of paper and I'm going to write something on it. Whatever I write on it, maybe with some very vague limitations, that's what you're going to have."

Now, there have been a few restaurants I've gone to that I've trusted the chef enough and trusted the waiter enough that I would occasionally walk in and say, "Bring me whatever you think is good tonight." I might even have the equivalent of a conversion cap by saying, "I don't want to spend more than *x* dollars."

I know the chef. I know the waiter. I trust that they're going to take good care of me. They know me well enough to know that if they don't take good care of me, I'll never come back again. There are only a few restaurants that I've ever gone to in my entire life where I would do that. Why would I do that with my money? Why would I do that with tens of thousands or hundreds of thousands of dollars? Why would I give anyone money in exchange for a blank piece of paper that they're going to write on later? That's convertible debt.

In a convertible-debt deal, if the next equity financing happens to have a pay-to-play provision, you're out of luck. You got it. Because you don't get to negotiate anymore. So from an investor's point of view, my simple summary, my epigram describing convertible debt is: "All the risk and a fraction of the upside."

Some companies say to me, "Well, we don't want to do a priced round." I look at them and I say, "You just don't want my money." Acknowledge that your company is worth whatever it is worth today. And if you're feeling that you can use my money to double the value of your company, why should I let you sell me half the stock at some point in the future? That makes no sense from my perspective. By the way, having explained it to you, as the issuing company, how can you look me in the eye and tell me that's a fair deal? And if you can, why would I want to invest with you because, frankly, your sense of fair and mine don't line up really well. You're not the kind of guy that I want to invest with. Thank you very much. I'm moving on.

Now let's talk about convertible debt from the company's perspective. Aside from the fact I think that in the case of someone who has been made aware of the inequity of convertible debt, it does raise questions about their sense of fairness, but I realize on this I'm an outlier.

Let's talk about it from the company's perspective. Convertible debt should have a maturity date. A well-designed convertible-debt offer, of which there are very few, should have an automatic conversion feature if they haven't reached a conversion event at maturity. To be well designed, it also needs to include a conversion price, which should be set at no more than today's honest-to-God value and discounted because they haven't raised the next equity round that they implicitly promised you that they would. They have failed and they should be penalized, or more to the point, you should be compensated for their failure. Yet, I don't think one in 50 convertible debt deals has a reasonably priced mandatory conversion feature on maturity.

Most convertible debt deals are aimed at angels but don't even have a mandatory conversion feature. So what do we have? We have a company that hasn't converted its debt. The debt has now matured. And what do we have? We have a company that's in default, a company that is now un-bankable at every level.

We have a company that really should not have been borrowing. We have a company that's subject to a smarter, more aggressive investor coming in and saying "By the way, I'm owed money. Pay me my money. I put $100,000 in your company; with the accrued interest, I'm entitled to $140,000. Oh, you only have $30,000 in the bank. Guess what? Pay me. Judge, may I have a judgment? I want all of the company's assets." This is a bad situation for everybody. No investor wants to be in a hostile situation, but no investor wants to be sitting there dangling trying to figure out how do I get my money back and what am I going to get for it?

So I don't like convertible debt because it's bad for everybody.

I have been professionally advising early-stage companies for 15 years now, since 1999, and we had a very nice couple of years, then we had March 2001, the tech crash. There were no exits to speak of and virtually no capital available until sometime somewhere toward the end of 2004. Some people found some money along the way. Things slowly got better but didn't get great until about 2006, and then we had the summer of 2008. After 35 years of doing finance, I know that things go up, things go down, times are good, times get bad. I never expected what happened in 2008.

We did not start seeing money flowing in any reasonable manner until late 2011. We didn't see IPOs again until late 2012, we didn't see exits until mid-2012. In other words, for half the time that I have been a professional finance guide for early-stage companies, there were no exits, very little capital, no IPOs. In other words, convertible debt is total Russian roulette for everybody. It's a terrible financing structure unless there's an extremely high probability the company has an investor who is strong, who'll do the takeout in a fairly limited amount of time and there's a specific reason they aren't funding today. It can be a specific event, they have a new fund closing or they have a sale that's signed and the conversion event will occur in a few months. If they are committed that they will fund in X months, that's the only time convertible or bridge debt makes good sense for all of the parties involved. Otherwise, it is playing with fire. At the least, the investors don't do nearly as well as they should for taking a risk and, at worst, it can blow up and everybody can get wiped out because you end up in a bad capital structure with people at each other's throats.

Let us not forget the words of some of the greatest financial theorists of the 20th century, Monty Python: "Nobody expects the Spanish Inquisition." There is enormous truth in that joke. You cannot build a business assuming that you have control of the external capital markets. That's foolhardy. By the way, the same truism applies to exits.

If you have a capital structure that has a fuse on it and you're compelled to an exit because of someone else's timing, regardless of whether it makes sense for your business, you're going to lose. So if your investor is a venture capital fund that has the typical fund structure of eight years plus two one-year extensions, figure when that fund is seven and a half years in, which may only be five years after you got their money if you were one of their last investments, there's going to be a conversation about, "Gee, don't you think it's time to sell this company?" and if you say, "Well, no, I think another four or five years would really make a huge difference in how much money we make," don't be surprised when they say, "No, we think it's time for you to start working on the exit." Your VC may have a problem. If they don't wind up the fund on time there may be penalties to the venture firm that are owed to their fund investors, which they really don't want to do. Their upside might be substantially reduced.

If you have maturing debt and if the capital markets are locked up, making it so you can't refinance, you could be forced to liquidate. Not a good situation. Capital structure needs to be stable in the same way that the foundation of a house needs to be stable. And if you're built on marshy ground, you better have pilings that go way down to bedrock.

It's never about the short or even the medium term. The medium term, maybe that's five to seven years. But if five to seven years happens to be January 2009, guess what, you better be able to hang on for another five years or you may be annihilated. And you may have a very good, successful business. But you and your investors will get clobbered because you have no other choice. You cannot have a collapsing or exploding capital structure. That's not a way to build a business.

What are your thoughts on the process of making an investment?

The typical angel pitch is five minutes, 10 minutes, or 15 minutes. All of which is a ridiculously, insanely short time to decide whether you want to put more time into doing due diligence. The odds are equally likely that you'll get excited, not having had enough time to figure out why this is a waste of your time or you won't get excited because they haven't had enough time to lay out something that would make it interesting to you.

The typical angel pitch spends a whole bunch of time talking about markets in some global sense and opportunities. Guess what, in the first few years you're not dealing in global opportunities, you're dealing whatever you're starting with. They spend all their time talking about the big idea. Most of that time is spent talking about how they came to the big idea and what they thought of the big idea. They spend relatively little time talking about what they're going to do with the big idea in detail. They spend relatively little time talking about execution. They spend almost no time talking about how much capital is really going to be needed. By the way, on any kind of tangible product business, they never spend enough time talking about working capital, inventory, and receivables versus when you have to pay your bills.

The thing that strikes me over and over again is you never get any meaningful time on capital structure. To me this is insane. An investor is not buying the company. You aren't buying the idea. You aren't buying the opportunity. You're buying the security. The process is called selling securities, it is not called selling the company. It is not called selling the idea. If you watch *Shark Tank,* every once in a while Mark Cuban will step in and say, "I will give you a very large amount of money compared to what you asked for to buy your entire company." That's fine, Mark Cuban can do that.

But as an angel investor you're not doing that. You're buying a security. And your only rights and your only upside are those items delineated in that piece of paper. Which, by the way, could be changed subsequently with or without your consent, depending on the details of what's in that piece of paper.

So the security is everything and capital structure determines a lot, including how stable the company is. If someone is selling you three-year debt and doesn't have the ability to repay debt in three years, you have an unstable company. If you buy Series A or Series B preferred stock, and you don't have a put provision—angels almost never get put provisions but VCs often do—you're locked in until everybody else decides that they want to sell. Could be 15 years, could be 20 years, could be never. And there's not a darn thing you can do about it, because you won't have the votes and you won't have the power, and I guarantee you won't have the contractual rights to do anything about it. You're along for the ride, enjoy it, I hope it's going to be fun.

I have this story that I tell CEOs on this topic. I say to them, "Let's say you have a company and I invest and this company ultimately ends world hunger, cures the common cold, and brings peace to the nations while also making it possible to have foot massages just for wishing it. You will become famous, respected, admired. You will be asked your opinion on all kinds of things about which you know nothing, and people will take you seriously. You will be invited to amazing parties and you will sleep with as many super models of any size, sex, shape or other persuasion as you want every single night. You will have a fabulous life, and you will be honored and revered and respected. The day will come when you will be invited to Stockholm. On one day you will give the Nobel Prize acceptance speeches in medicine, economics, and peace. You will be deemed a great person. But if you don't find a way to bring this company back to cash so that my family gets something for having put our money with you early on and helped you end world hunger, cure the common cold, and bring peace to the nations, the only thing that we will have for the investment is getting foot massages just for wishing it" (which I admit is far better than the return I've had on many investments). But that's not enough. Make no mistake about it. I invest for my family's financial advancement.

I don't invest because I am an innately good person. I don't invest to end world hunger, cure the common cold, or bring peace to the nations. I invest to make money. If I happen to make money by doing any one or all three of those things, I am a very happy guy and I feel very good. But if I do those three things and I don't make money for my family, this is a failed investment and I am a very unhappy guy, again except for my foot massage.

Unless you can show me that in doing these three things you will also have a way to bring my family back to cash, I won't invest in your company. If this makes me a bad person I'm willing to be a bad person, because I believe that my first obligation is to my family, my friends, and my community, and part of the way that I take care of those obligations is by using my money to invest in businesses to create wealth so I can do charity, but charity is a different story.

People who get confused about the difference between the economics of investment and its possible social impact are confused. Do not pretend that an investment made to do good is anything other than an attempt to do good. It is by definition handicapping your economic outcomes. Doesn't mean you cannot make very good money doing good. You can do well by doing good. Let's move on to social impact investing.

I will tell two stories. One, I remember the day, I think it was in 1973, when McDonald's made a major change in the way it did business and was hailed as an incredibly advanced, environmentally oriented company. What was the innovation? The innovation was packaging the Big Mac in the Styrofoam clamshell. Why was this environmentally good? Because you were no longer cutting down trees to wrap hamburgers, and they were hailed for this.

Obviously when they stopped using Styrofoam packaging for their products in the early 2000s the view had changed. What is socially desirable at one time is not necessarily desirable at another time.

To take a somewhat different perspective, when Marie and Pierre Curie discovered the radioactive properties of radium they created a social fad. People would get X-rayed to see their hand glowing in the dark. They discovered a few years later that it was killing them. What seems like a good idea at one point may not be a good idea at another.

Let's take the flipside. Costco. Costco has always been very, very clear. They are in business to do business and to make money for their owners. They've also been very clear that as part of the way that they do business they will conduct themselves in certain ways. They will pay their employees well. They will give very, very good benefits plans. They will try to keep as much of the inbound packaging material out of the recycling and trash stream. They run very, very energy-efficient buildings.

They do all of these things because they believe it is the right way to run a business, to make a more profitable business that will ultimately make their owners wealthier. They have made a decision to do these things, most of which we generally would agree are social benefits. They've embraced them. They have been embedded in the way that they did business, pretty much from day one. Certainly the way they pay their people and the way they do benefits.

Avoiding recycling was actually a way to eliminate a very big cost because you had to pay to have cardboard taken away. So let's have a better idea. We don't need to buy bags. We'll just let our customers take these boxes home so that they can carry their stuff. Great. But Costco also has said, we want to be in full compliance with laws. We want to be in full compliance with our tax obligations. That doesn't mean they're not aggressive on their taxes. They want to be good citizens and good members of the community. They will help and support community organizations, but this isn't private charity where senior executives' wives get to go on the boards of organizations to go to good parties. When they support a Children's Hospital you see it all over their building. It is a way of building community goodwill. It is a marketing expense. This is doing good as you're doing well. It is not getting confused about the purpose of your business.

What about the businesses who are trying to change the food or energy in the world and organizing their business as a business with return for investors?

Let's talk about another local company, I think it's pretty much focused on the Pacific Northwest. Value Village. Value Village is a chain of thrift shops. What is their business model? When a charitable organization has a collection box, and it gets filled with clothes, they call Value Village. Value Village does a sort. Some of the stuff they keep and they put in their stores and they sell. Some of their stuff goes off to the Third World, some of it gets shipped off as rags, and they pay the charities a price per pound for the stuff that they get. They've built a very, very successful, hugely profitable business.

I know the family who owns the company. They are immensely community minded. They are very, very charitable and generous. They run their business as a business. Their business happens to create all kinds of ancillary good. So does IKEA. IKEA is a very, very generous company, but they do their charity really as an extension of their marketing. So these companies all have a sense of themselves as citizens in a community. Some of them, Value Village, very explicitly part of how they do business, seems to create inherent social goods. They're funding regional and local charities. They are moving stuff into a chain where some of it's being reused, some of it's being recycled. They're keeping stuff out of dumps. This is all good. But they run it as a business. They don't flinch from "We are here to make money."

Let's take Amazon. For years, people would go to Amazon and say, "You're a huge company. Donate." Jeff Bezos set a policy very early on, if this company is not cash flow positive, and we are still funding this company by selling equity, I cannot justify making charitable donations at the expense of the people who're backing my company.

I believe that has evolved now to him saying, "This is not my money, this is not the company's money, this is the shareholders' money. To the extent that we're going to do any charitable or social giving, it has to advance the business."

There is a knock on Amazon that they aren't a generous company. I think this is an interesting point. They've created an enormous amount of wealth and a lot of the people for whom they've created wealth do all kinds of giving, not least of whom is Jeff Bezos, who's consistently on the list of the most generous donors in the country, giving away tens, and sometimes hundreds, of millions of dollars a year, personally, not through the company. He doesn't make himself look good by giving away the shareholders' money. He gives away the money that he has earned by owning

Amazon stock and working for Amazon. That's a very, very different thing than giving away shareholder money. He's very, very clear on the difference between Amazon and Jeff Bezos. That isn't to say they aren't a contributing part of the community or they don't want to run energy-efficient installations. There's a social good there, but it's driven by a business objective.

If you say your business is supporting things that do social good, if I'm running a business that processes Little League registrations for the Boys and Girls Club, well, that's my business. Now maybe I feel good that I'm doing good things for kids. That's great. I still need to make a profit, I still need to pay my people and there's no excuse for not doing those things just because I'm doing good for boys and girls who play Little League.

So, to me, I find social impact as an investment motivator makes no sense. I will say, personally, I've seen a number of businesses that I've looked at and said, I think there's money to be made there, but what they are doing makes me uncomfortable, therefore, even though I think someone's going to make investing in this, I am passing. Because I just choose not to be part of it. That to me, it is a legitimate decision.

I've seen a lot of impact investment structures be in the form of an LLC with distributions to shareholders or in the form of buying back shares out of a portion of revenue. What do you think about those kind of structures?

Those are two separate issues. Let's just jump away from the social impact to structure. The standard model for an angel-funded startup is a C corporation. In fact, in almost every case, nobody even thinks about whether there should be an alternative. In most cases, they really should have thought about whether there should have been an alternative and in many of those cases they should have gone with an alternative.

The principal reason that everyone goes with a C corp almost automatically is that venture capital funds overwhelmingly, 98% of them or more, really have enormous problems with investments in anything other than a C corp because of tax issues relating to their funding partners, many of whom are nonprofits and have a terrible tax problem if they're being allocated earnings from profit-making businesses that are flowing up through a tax pass-through structure. If we had a different set of tax laws in this country, we quite likely would use different business structures. For example, private equity firms have very little trouble with LLC investments. Why? In part because they're in the cash flow businesses whose investors like current profits and distributions, as opposed to the bigger capital gains sought by ventures firms. They're structured differently and they have a different set of tax issues.

Most businesses will never be worth $10 million or $20 million. Most angel-funded businesses won't be worth $10 million or $20 million. They don't realize it, nor do their investors, but they won't for lots of reasons. Some of the reasons are screamingly obvious to someone with a sufficiently skeptical or knowledgeable perspective. Others don't get there just because the life of a young company is akin to the salmon cycle: you lay five thousand eggs and three fish come back to the hatchery. So many things, known and unknown, can kill a young business.

When you start a business, to me the first question before you do anything else is, "Where are you trying to get to and why are we doing this?" If you say the goal is that I want to be rich by selling this thing in three to five years, the odds are extremely good that you're going to be disappointed and you're going to lose your money and your investors' money. You're going to have a lot of upset people, because that's just not realistic. We already talked about economic cycles, availability of capital, and lots of things can happen. That's not a real plan. That's like me saying, "I'm going to drop out of high school barely able to read and I'm going to spend my days shooting hoops because I know that I can get one of those multiyear, eight-figure-a-year NBA contracts." As a guy who's five-foot-seven and a half, slow, and utterly unable to jump more than six inches off the ground, that wouldn't be a realistic plan for me to do. It doesn't matter how much time I spend practicing shooting hoops. If I were six-five with a decent jump and athletic ability, it would still be a lousy bet.

The number of companies that make it to an exit are minuscule. The number of companies that make it to an exit that are worth it for anyone other than the last round or two of investors is smaller. It's a tough way to do things.

I would have been the fourth generation in a family business. The only reason I wasn't was when I came out of college, my father was still very young, it wasn't time for him to move aside, and it was clear the business was not ready for two of us in there, so I went off. I did other things. I stayed involved, but I never took over that business.

We didn't open the door every day going, "What's our exit strategy?" We opened the door every day saying, "How we going to make customers happy? What products are we going to sell? Who's going to be working for us? What do we want the place to look like?" You do that year after year, day after day, and over time, you build something that becomes successful. It creates wealth. You take care of yourself. You take care of your friends, your neighbors. You take care of your community.

I'll never forget a conversation with my father. It was one of these things where years later you realize how important something was. I was a teenager. My father had the tax returns and showed them to me. Of course, every kid thinks his family and his father and what they do are important and the center of the world, and when I looked at the top line revenue number, I was surprised.

I said, "Dad, is that all there is?" Very quietly, very gently, he looked at me and he said, "Well, it's fed us for four generations. How much more do you need?" Now, that's a lesson that startup entrepreneurs should keep in mind. That's a lesson that angels should keep in mind, because you know what? That business fed us for four generations. That business allowed my family to make some investments, allowed my family to educate my sister and me, and allowed me to take the base created by the business and combine the assets we accumulated with my education and grow them substantially. As a result, my son probably won't have to worry ever about going hungry.

Now, maybe as it turns out, we may not be overwhelmingly wealthy, but my family is better off than all but a tiny, tiny fraction of the people in the history of this world. We're not rich. Maybe we're not even wealthy, but we're okay, and for four generations, we worked and we're better off than pretty much almost everybody in the entire history of the world. Is that such a bad outcome?

You know what? You don't need to hit home runs to get there, so ask yourself, "What are you doing, as an entrepreneur, as an angel investor?" Home run hitters strike out a lot. They tend to strike out a lot more than they hit home runs. Singles hitters, on a decent team, tend to score more runs than home run hitters, because you can't score if you don't get on base. Your team can't win if someone doesn't get on base and comes home. Would I love hitting home runs in my investments? Would I love hitting home runs with men on? Hell yeah, of course I would, but you know what? I'm okay with hitting lots of singles and doubles and making sure we end up with a winning team.

Coming back to structure, LLCs. LLCs are very tax efficient. LLCs allow companies to distribute free cash efficiently to their investors. An LLC structure in a business that is ultimately able to distribute cash is never going to be under the kind of pressure to find an exit that a C corp will be. A C corp can't efficiently distribute cash so it may have to sell, maybe at the wrong time. In fact, an LLC, in the right kind of business, and it certainly doesn't work in all businesses, but for the right kind of business, is like owning an apartment building.

You collect your rents periodically. You pay your bills. Maybe you pay off your mortgage, you split up what's left; in good times, there's a lot more, and in bad times, maybe there's a lot less or maybe there's nothing to get handed out. You sell it when someone offers you more to take it off your hands than it's worth for you to continue owning it.

Unlike a C corp where after six, eight, 10 years, your investors call you up, or if you're an investor, you're calling the CEO going, "I want my cash back." You've got the flexibility. In other words, you can use it to build a sustainable business. Now, you cannot use an LLC structure in anything that's going to be VC funded. That's most big-growth businesses, which are going to need large sequential investments of cash, so biotech, biomed, doesn't work. You cannot use it in companies that are going to need large amounts of ever-increasing piles of working capital, because it's just hard to get working capital into an LLC with a lot of passive investors.

Let's say you have a company that intends to develop intellectual property, and you intend to monetize it by going into a licensing model. An LLC is a fabulous capital structure. In fact, why would you want to be in a C corp for something like that? If you do a deal with a huge upfront licensing payment and a couple million bucks come in, wouldn't your investors rather get a piece of that rather than leave it all with you hoping you're not going to mess it up?

Isn't that a better way to raise capital? Hey, when money comes in, we're going to pay our bills, we're going to leave some reserves, and then we'll pay you without double taxation. By the way, when we sell the company, if we're not a huge company, if we're a moderate company, if we exit with a $15 to $40 million exit, which is the sweet spot for angel company deals, those deals tend to be asset sales, not stock sales.

Typical corporate asset sale deals, you have to do a lot of structuring to avoid getting taxed inside the corp on the gain on the sale of the assets, and then again on the distribution out to the owners. You can very easily get double taxation. It can sometimes be very, very hard to avoid. Oh, and by the way, you may even remit sales tax on the sale of some of those assets. Okay? You can easily take a 20% or 30% or 40% tax hit selling the C corp. In an LLC, you at least don't pay on the sale of the assets. You may have sales tax issues, maybe not, depends how you structure it, but you don't have the double taxation, so for some kinds of companies, with certain economic characteristics, LLCs can make a lot of sense.

There are other companies, other kinds of deals. I'm not a big fan of the revenue loans that I'm seeing right now. I think they're often being done with companies that are too early. It's not stable enough that they should be making those commitments. I also think that there are potentially some very, very significant tax issues that aren't being looked at.

When I did a number of revenue participation–type deals, and we really dug into it, we concluded that most of those, in fact, were a sale of a capital asset, subject to capital gains tax at the time of the transaction, which is something that no one is addressing, and I have asked a number of people. I did analyze it very, very carefully. By the way, if you have a C corp with accumulated net operating losses, revenue participation deals can make a lot of sense, because you can use your net operating losses to shelter the taxable gain, but I think many of these sales against future revenue are a sale of a capital asset subject to capital gains tax on the day that you do the sale, not in the future as you generate income to make your payments. It's the only way that you don't have potential for a nasty tax situation, something that most people haven't looked at. Is there a place for revenue-type financing? Absolutely. Royalties, could be. Profit participation, sure. Participating debt, sure.

There are all kinds of structures that can be done. They require creativity, and they have to match the business but it's not one size fits all—"Okay, here's your C corp. Here's your stock option plan." You know, here's this, here's that. Here's your form for your convertible debt. Here's your Series A. Here's your Series B.

I'll wrap this up talking about stock option plans in closely held companies. I believe stock option plans in closely held companies are usually indistinguishable from fraud. That's a very extreme provocative statement. What is the definition of fraud? The definition is inducing someone to give you something of value in exchange for something that you knew or should have known is of little or no value. In a young company, I use stock options to get somebody to come to work for me. Their alternative might be to go to Google or Apple or IBM or Weyerhaeuser or Staples. Places that are economically stable, pay a full market wage, have a set of benefits that are market competitive and are likely to continue in business. Yes, the world is uncertain, but your risks are substantially reduced.

In an early-stage company, I will often get you to take a lower than market salary, with huge amounts of employment risk, because who knows if we're going to be successful or if we're going to keep getting funded. You're taking, certainly, a much less attractive benefits package than at, let's say, a big tech company, and all in all, this gets a lot crazier. What am I giving you? I'm giving you stock options.

Now, in a public company, stock options are a lot cleaner, because there's a market for the stock. You know that it's going to vest. You can choose to sell them. You can convert them back to cash, if it's above water. If not, you don't exercise them until they are, but that's a reasonable risk.

There's a liquid trading market. You know if you ever do exercise, you can sell. You can turn it into cash. You can use it for a down payment on a house, but in a closely held company, the true value to most people of a stock option only happens when they can turn it into cash, which means upon sale or upon an IPO, assuming that they're not locked up and assuming that they can afford to exercise it, because of the tax consequences that happen on the exercise of stock options, which can be pretty ugly if they're not structured really, really well. Usually, they aren't, and stock options usually expire a maximum of 10 years after date of issue, and stock options have a vesting schedule, and normally expire a maximum of one year after you leave the company.

The one-year expiration exists because of IRS regulations and under most plans, the expiration is in 90 days. I've seen them expire in as little as 30. Think of it this way: you're married. Your husband gets a job in Florida and so you leave your hot startup in Santa Clara; but you've only vested 30% of your options. This company is nowhere near being sold, nowhere near going public to your knowledge, and now, you've got a choice. You can write a check for $26,000 within 90 days of leaving this company to own your shares, or you can say, "I don't have $26,000," or "I don't want to put it at risk, because I don't know how long it's going to be locked up." Your stock options go away, but you worked for 20% less for the last two and a half years, and what do you have for it? Absolutely nothing.

Every smart finance person, every VC, any financially sophisticated CEO, which unfortunately is not that many among early-stage CEOs, knows that the stock option pool is never going to be exercised to any significant degree. It just isn't going to happen.

Stock options—they're lousy. If the company doesn't get sold or go public, they have no value. You could be sitting on options to buy 200,000 shares at $0.05, and the company may be valued at $50 a share, but if you don't have enough money for a down payment on a house, your paper profits on your options won't help you get a down payment on the house. In fact, if you exercise your options, you will still be restricted. You won't be allowed to sell your shares anyway, and the tax consequences of doing that, both the exercise and then the sale, are nasty.

Stock option plans have their place, but largely in public companies, and they were originally created and intended only for the senior executives of public companies. It was really meant to be almost a C suite and SVP perk. It was never meant to be lower mid-level coders and developers. Never ever supposed to be that way. Yes, there had been people who've gotten immensely wealthy because they've been in the right place at the right time.

I have some friends who ran companies who made sure that the guys on the loading dock got options and I'm thinking of one guy in particular whom I just respect immensely. Every month he made sure he had lunch at least once with every single person in the company. He would talk to them about the company's finances, talk to them about options, and talk to them about long-term this and that, not trying to get them to do anything. Just explaining to them how things could work and he eventually made their company an enormous success, took it public.

It is a household name today and some of the guys who were on the loading dock making $6 an hour became millionaires, but you know what? Those stock options never were a replacement for them making their current income, supporting their families right then and there. That's the guy who did stock options right.

* * *

Peter is nothing short of opinionated on a lot of topics and he has done well for himself investing this way. You'll see many opposing views to Peter online and in this book. It is important to understand that Peter is a successful investor as are the people who have opposing viewpoints. You can be a successful investor with his approach, though, so don't confuse different opinions with lack of profits. As newer angel investors, we all need to find what aspects of the different investing styles we can truly use in a successful way.

MAKE DATA-DRIVEN DECISIONS WITH ALLAN MAY

"There is nothing so good that it can't become overvalued."

—HOWARD MARKS

"We put money in and the company went public. Even though they had millions of customers and a successful IPO, we invested at a terrible valuation and so didn't make a dime—a rookie mistake."

—ALLAN MAY

I REACHED OUT TO ALLAN because of his experience and background. I've looked at a lot of angel investments over the years and been pitched deals in the life sciences space. I've always shied away from them because I didn't understand how to perform due diligence. Angel investors in this space have a unique perspective and including it here is important. Allan is the Angel Resource Institute vice-chairman and treasurer. He is also the founder of the largest angel organization focused on life sciences in the US, Life Science Angels.

Allan helped to start the Halo Report, which is currently maintained by the Angel Resource Institute. The Halo Report tracks angel investing trends across the country from which angel groups are the most active, to which sectors are receiving the most investment, to what regions in the country are the most active. This data is incredibly useful for understanding things like the median pre-Series A investment valuation in 2013 is $2.5 million or that the median round size where angels groups invested has held steady at around $600,000 for the last three years.

The need to capture and understand data like this is an obvious sign of the investment style that Allan uses in his investing. As we talk about Allan's investment style more, you get a real sense that he integrates this data-driven approach into his investment style and offers plenty of insights into how any investor can do the same.

Let's start with how you got started angel investing.

Probably the typical way. I was running startup companies and hanging around a lot of venture capitalists and getting introduced to a bunch of entrepreneurs. In the startup world, if you have some successes all your friends know and they start coming around and saying, "Hey, I'm doing this, what do you think?" or they refer people to you. You start to invest, even if you don't know what you're doing but you like the people or the company looks pretty good; you start to invest and next thing you know you're an angel investor without setting out to be one. That's been since 1992 and I'm in more than 50 companies now, but I've never really counted them.

How many exits have you had with good or bad outcomes?

Interestingly, I've never run that ROI either. For the generation that started when I started, we were less focused on ROI and the hard-knuckle financial metrics than I think investors who are in the game today. There's been a huge, huge swing in that.

Having said that, I do have a rough idea. Out of something like 50 investments, I've lost around 20 to negative exits. Of the remaining 30, 18 are still alive and have some kind of shot and 12 were positive exits.

Were all 50 of those in the same space or similar area?

My first investment was in nanotechnology in the semiconductor field. I don't know shit about nanotechnology or the semiconductor field, and so as one would expect, I lost that one. The lesson there is sector expertise counts and it's a rookie mistake. As early-stage investors, you see some fantastic ideas and are tempted to write too many checks. Like with most angel investors, my first investment didn't work. In fact, I would say my first several didn't work. It's the usual learning curve. Most of the first investments of most investors don't work. I would guess out of the first 10, I probably had seven or eight losses.

Did you start to move to the things that you knew because you saw that as an obvious problem?

I didn't do it consciously, but that was the only non-life science investment I ever made. I moved pretty quickly to the things that I knew. Keep in mind, this was 20 years ago and we were not as sophisticated in due diligence as today. We were not as careful about things we looked at and went too much on gut instinct. There are just a lot of rookie mistakes when you're first starting out if you don't know better, which most people don't. You do things that later on you realize you didn't need to do.

What sort of lessons did you learn through that experience?

The usual ones, such as paying attention to valuation. A spectacular deal at a bad valuation is a bad deal. For example, I invested in Invisalign. It was a really "Big Idea" at its time. There were a lot of investors from Wall Street, a bunch of big impressive names. They had huge momentum, sales, a novel business model, and were attacking a sclerotic market ripe for change. We put money in and the company went public. Even though they had millions of customers and a successful IPO, we invested at a terrible valuation and so didn't make a dime—a rookie mistake.

What I'm saying is that just because you don't make a return doesn't always mean the company was a bad company or didn't do well. It can just mean you didn't do well. I was an in another company called Zogenix. We put the first million bucks in and the company went public. How does that sound?

Well, we got about 12 cents on the dollar. By the time it went public, they had raised $200 million on flat rounds, so early investors were $200 million diluted! So while it is a win for the company and for some investors, it can still be a disaster for early investors. I count those as negative.

Were these the most important lessons you learned?

The analogy I use when I'm teaching is that it's like hiring people. You can get pretty good at not hiring bad people, but you will never only hire perfect people. Perfection won't happen, but you can get pretty good at avoiding duds. I think that's the same paradigm in angel investing. I think you can eliminate the stupid ones, or at least the ones with likely fatal flaws.

One of the things I am proudest of is driving the creation of the Halo Report, which is aimed at collecting and analyzing real data on early-stage investments so that investors can understand correlations between behavior and returns. The data and the database are still relatively small, but it's getting better and it will someday be profoundly important. While it is still early to extrapolate significant and meaningful conclusions, it does show a correlation between diligence and returns. For example, it shows that a large number of people make their investment decisions in less than one hour and have subpar returns. Twenty to 40 hours is about the breakpoint where you can do pretty well, particularly if you're sector focused and experienced in the field.

Forty hours of diligence will improve your odds to the top of the return curve. You wouldn't be at the top of the curve, but you'd be at the high end. One could extrapolate and say "Well, okay, then you should do 400 hours or 1,000 hours, right? If I do infinite diligence, then I'll have infinite returns!" No, the impact of diligence is a typical U curve. There's an amount of diligence you can do to understand the known unknowns, to identify the risks inherent in the investment and to form a view as to the extent to which each risk can be addressed or mitigated. Then you have to decide whether those risks are acceptable risks to you.

Out of 10 investments, if you have weeded out the losers, you'll still only have five positive exits, three of which are return of capital, leaving two to make the returns in your portfolio. But with the right amount of diligence, sector expertise, and experience, you'll be on a curve where those last two can make the returns in your portfolio with 2.5x or better kind of returns.

The question is, how to decide which companies to put into your portfolio. Once you identify and understand the risks, you need to decide your personal risk profile to understand which ones to invest in. After that, you need to accept that the majority of companies in your portfolio will fail to make money for you, and it is virtually impossible to predict which ones fall in which category. You just carry on. If you have built your portfolio as just described, you can still return 2.5x on your overall portfolio.

In those 20 to 40 hours, what are the most important things to look for?

There's nothing magic there. Some people use a 100-page checklist. We start with people. Who are they? What is their track record? What is their commitment to the investment? How do they handle adversity? What is their experience? Are these the right people to make this company successful? Why these people? What is it about this team that separates them from the competition? If you're going to err on the side of any bias, err on the side of going with seasoned people with real track records and sector experience.

A good jockey can make a poor horse win, a poor jockey can't make a great horse win. In our world, we look for three fundamentals. A compelling clinical need, which implies a large market. A technological clear solution, which implies that you can build it at a cost that the market will bear at high margins, and that you can achieve strong, possibly blocking, intellectual property coverage.

Those are the linchpins for us. Beyond that, the focus is all on business model; specifically, how you make a company out of it, but those are the truly have-to-haves. You need an A or A+ in those three boxes.

Do you go as far as background checks on the entrepreneur and the founding team?

We don't do background checks, but I recommend you do. The reason we don't do background checks is the network we invest within. The Life Science Angels are in Silicon Valley. It has a hundred people in it. All hundred of those people have been in life sciences for 20 or 30 years and more. If we don't know you or we don't know someone who knows you, we're not investing. It's a kind of two degrees of separation thing. Either we need to know you or we need to know somebody who knows you. We don't invest in people not known to someone within our network.

Does it really matter if it's a trade secret over something patentable?

Night and day. The ability to successfully exit from a life science company is 100% directly correlated to the strength of your intellectual property. There are lots of businesses out there where you can make a million bucks a year and employ the kids and do great things. These businesses will never get angel funding and they shouldn't.

If you're going to be on the angel/VC funding trajectory, you need solid intellectual property enabling you to practice your invention. You need freedom to operate without having to license other intellectual property. Ideally, you should have a blocking patent as well, which means you can operate without licensing from anybody else and you can block anyone else from doing what you do. But no IP, no investment.

Are you analyzing their ability to patent or the patents themselves or are you hiring others to do that?

Generally, all entrepreneurs will have is a patent application or a provisional patent. We have to extrapolate whether we believe they are likely to get a patent and what kinds of claims would come along with it. We're pretty good at that ourselves having been in the field for decades, and we have some talented patent people in our group to call on as well.

If you go to the Angel Research Institute website, you'll see a study called the Super Angel Study that we did four or five years ago. We interviewed 30 or 40 people who had invested a minimum of $15 million to $150 million and were looking for a reason the so-called Super Angels were different from us ordinary angels. Of course there aren't any major differences, although all of them were incredibly sector specific and so plugged into the ecosystem that their ability to perform diligence was almost unparalleled in their field. The idea that your network provides a competitive advantage in terms of diligence and insight, that's the idea that our group Life Science Angels is based on. It significantly correlates to returns.

What matters most in the valuation?

The valuation is based on the exit premise—that is, the reasonably expected value at exit. Then we focus on understanding how much capital it will take to get to an exit. That allows us to guess at how many rounds there will be and at what valuations, and so tells us the financing risk we're taking. We generally educate entrepreneurs to the valuation methodology. We want it to be fair. We believe very strongly that the interests of founders, entrepreneurs, and early-stage investors have never been more aligned. If we make money, founders will make money, and when we don't make money, founders cannot make money. We are very transparent about how we go about that discussion and that calculation, and if founders can't agree with it, then we walk.

Do you get to that stage and walk away a lot?

There's always someone who just doesn't quite listen or believe. Their buddy is selling a company for $100 million so they think they're going to sell their company for $100 million. And they don't understand that a $100 million exit doesn't mean that the founders got $100 million; on the contrary, in life sciences it is common that the last investors take the lion's share of the exit capital and the founders and early investors get a small fraction. Generally, though, people have a really good reaction to it. We walk the team through the process interactively and build the valuation cooperatively. People are usually pretty positive through the educational process.

Do you have a preferred structure for your investments?

We prefer priced rounds, typically first institutional money invested. We prefer standard preferred shares but will agree to capped convertible notes in the right circumstances. We prefer standard terms without any financial engineering. Common stock is out of the question, of course. We won't invest in common and we won't invest in LLCs.

Are there particular terms that you focus on, such as registration or pro-rata rights?

The terms we're most particular about are pro-rata rights, information rights, board membership or observation rights, follow-on investment rights, and anti-dilution protection.

Do you normally follow-on in the future rounds?

We normally do. I think the data on this suggests that investors should follow on, depending on the sector. In life sciences there's an occasional one round and out, but they are fairly rare. That means there will be a next round, and that next round is often a venture round. If you want to run with the big dogs, you have to earn their respect. How do you earn their respect? You need to behave like a professional investor investing in high-risk, large-capital deals. You need to be there for the follow-on rounds. You can't just disappear and expect people will treat you fairly.

What are you helping these companies with after your first investment?

The answer to your question, in two words, is operating experience. We think the focus has shifted from picking good companies to making good companies. We will only invest in things where our members have commercialized in those areas. When the CEO gets in trouble on her commercial path, regulatory path, reimbursement path, we can put somebody in there or connect them with people who can help them solve those problems. We literally can help them be successful. It's not just the money. It's virtually never just the money. It's the ability to help them be successful. That is our differentiator.

Does how you differentiate yourself change who you invest with?

You hit it right on the button. Investor alignment is profoundly important to us. We will walk on a deal that has an investor we don't trust, hasn't behaved well historically, or we don't know. That makes us averse to crowdfunding deals. We don't want anybody on the cap chart that will be troublesome when difficulties arise. When a portfolio company misses key milestones, or when they come back and say, "Hey, that didn't work, but we think we know what will", we need to know all the investors will do what it takes to move forward and not freak out.

Does that mean most investments are with similar people?

Yes, in terms of sector expertise. We're in Silicon Valley and half of all the deals in the United States originate here. There is a core group of a dozen or less groups we invest with and the deal flow works both ways. The last time I looked, 25% of our investments were outside of California.

How do you connect with the investments that aren't local?

We attract national deal flow because we are so sector specific and have become pretty well known. For example, CB Insights just rated Life Science Angels the number one angel group in the US in all sectors. I'm on the boards of both the Angel Capital Association and the Angel Research Institute, and that gives us access to the top groups and most sophisticated best practices. It also facilitates familiarity and trust, which form the core of successful syndication. The ability to syndicate with such a high caliber of investment groups is a huge plus in the life sciences area, where deals tend to require larger amounts of capital to build successful exit valuations.

How do you engage with those companies that aren't local?

We require out-of-area companies to have the support and investment of your local group, wherever you are. We have to know the group and have worked with them. We need to understand their sector expertise and why they'll be able to help when the company gets in trouble. This is why we believe that angel investing is not endangered any time soon. Every time I get a deal across the web that lacks local angel group involvement, it might as well be in Nigeria. Trust is the key. It's two degrees of separation. This is really a business where we don't want to invest with people we don't trust. We'll inevitably pass in situations where trust is an issue that can be challenged.

I get deals every day. Somebody says, "Hey, I'm raising a million bucks. I've got 800 circled and only 200 left. Do you want in?" My answer is always, "No, good luck, that's not how we invest." I want to know who these people are and how they invest. If you can just understand that, you'll understand angel investing.

Tell me about a company that you invested in that turned out great.

A guy came to me with a device in the orthopedic area. He was referred by a good colleague of mine and I took the referral because of the colleague. We talked about it. The guy had incredible experience in this particular area of orthopedics. It was a relatively low-tech thing. We weren't taking much invention risk.

It was a relatively sure regulatory pathway without much regulatory risk. He had intellectual property around his idea that was established. It was a really straightforward investment. It wasn't a platform, going to change the world, kind of investment. It was a blue hammer and there was a particular way you could get intellectual property on a blue hammer. It was a discreet thing and the guy was just a bulldog, just absolutely one of those people whom you knew would walk through a wall if that's what it took to be successful.

We put the deal together. We thought we would exit in two years on $2 million. We didn't quite get there, but we almost did. We had a corporate acquisition set up on $2 million and the corporation ended up buying some other thing and didn't do the deal. They felt so guilty, though, that they gave us $2 million additional capital as an investment. We took that and exited on $4 million in about four years for $70 million instead.

How did the company you invested in get introduced to that buyer?

Through our network. We've got a lot of connections in our space. We have connections to people at the top acquirers in the world. A number of our members have gone on to key positions in major strategics in the life science space, and most of our members have sold one or more companies to those strategics, so we have personal contacts at most places that portfolio companies need to access. We also have corporate sponsors working with us to help them access early-stage technology. We now specifically look to target investment in fields where we have the contacts because we know we have a good ability to get the attention of the buyers.

Tell me about a company that you invested in that didn't turn out so well.

One of these deals we did in a biotech company was classic. A biotech team at Stanford, a breakthrough discovery complete with a cover article at a major science magazine. They had key patents and a bunch of patents pending. It was a new discovery on a channel for angiogenesis, and looked like they could form the basis for dozens of novel therapeutics. We put the first half million bucks in. It went on and within three years it raised $80 million in venture capital.

It got a $500 million buyout offer from one of the big strategics. The board turned it down as inadequate. They got an $800 million offer from another strategic with $80 million upfront and the rest of it on a milestone-based earnout. They took that deal. Then their lead compound failed in clinical testing and the company collapsed. That should sober up a biotech investor.

I have to say the only good news in that was the $80 million that they got upfront. They hadn't spent it by the time their clinical trial failed so they actually gave it back to the investors. We got back close to half our money.

Do you prefer teams that have experience getting successfully through trials?

Usually, it's better for everybody to have both successes and failures. This is a tough game and most of our folks have had both. It's just a tough business; that company had an incredible team. The science just didn't work.

How do you evaluate products when they won't be tested for so long?

Even on things that work, you still have a very, very expensive risk from a regulatory standpoint. Even when the products are successful, work, and do everything you predict, you still have to get them through the FDA and sometimes the FDA will say no. If you get lucky and obtain that approval, you also have to get reimbursement approval, which takes another two or three years, which is even riskier than the regulatory pathway.

Two out of three that apply for reimbursement get turned down and if you're not reimbursed in our medical system you die as a product. Maybe unless you're for erectile dysfunction or for plastic surgery or one of the rare things that people will pay money for. They won't pay money for 99% of the products out there. I think these things are quite unique to life science investing.

What are the top three things new angel investors should do to be successful?

Number one, study the data and reports that are at the Angel Research Institute site.

Number two, take one of the angel educational courses. The Angel Resource Institute offers some, other people offer some, but study angel investing. Let go of the pride that just because you're rich and successful or can operate a company that you know how to angel invest. There is a learning curve in investment just like there is in every other thing in life and so you need to understand that learning curve and things you can do to mitigate it.

Number three, focus on diligence.

Somebody who just sold a company for $100 million feels funny saying, "Hey, I don't know how to do diligence? Could someone teach me how to do this?"

I think it is the time of angel investors. I think historically, there has never been so much attention and focus given to entrepreneurship and early-stage investing. I think this is a pivotal time where guys who are now professionals in angel investing are moving it from being a club to an asset class. People are looking at best practices for syndication. I think it will be recognized as the driver of innovation in job creation in the US.

* * *

After the interview, I kept thinking I was sure glad I didn't do anything with the flyers I was given concerning life sciences businesses. There may be some similarities in the importance of who you invest with, how you analyze teams, and how you structure portfolios. It takes a lot of focus, though, to understand the risks, the ecosystem, and how to navigate those land mines.

For the companies that Allan invested in, I think Invisalign is not too far off from a household name, simply due to their commercials and advertisements. Align Technology, the company behind Invisalign, went public in 2001 at $13 per share and is now [2014] trading on NASDAQ under the stock symbol ALGN for $54.84 per share with a market cap of $4.44 billion. Compare that to the $130 million Align raised at their IPO.

Zogenix, formed in 2006, went public in November 2010 and now trades on NASDAQ under the stock symbol ZGNX (currently [2014] giving the company a market cap of $171.1 million). Compare that $171.1 million with the $200 million raised at the IPO. Remember, both of these companies had great exits from the perspective of the media and neither were huge windfalls for the early-stage investors.

BE PROMISCUOUS WITH MICHAEL DORNBROOK

"Money is like gasoline on a road trip. You don't want to run out, but you're not doing a tour of gas stations."

—TIM O'REILLY

"One of the companies I invested in at Techstars only took around $600,000 and they've never taken another dime since and they don't intend to. If you didn't get in at seed, you were never going to get in."

—MICHAEL DORNBROOK

I MET MICHAEL through one of the other angel investors I interviewed, Warren Katz, whom we'll get to next. Michael digs through his approach to finding companies in more depth than most of the others I interviewed. He talks a lot about the number of rocks he's turning over to generate deal flow. When you're on the outside looking in at what he's doing, you'd likely see a passionate guy with experience out there talking to startups, speaking at events, and generally participating in the community.

You likely see other investors using this same behavior in your own community; they're always doing what they can to give to the community because they know that the best companies will come to them first if they are both giving to the community and known for making investments.

Michael has been on the board and investment committee at Common Angels, who've been around since 1998, and in that time invested over $16 million into 40-plus companies (nine of which have been acquired and one IPO'd). You may remember from my introduction that 1998 was also the year I graduated high school and when my introduction to the tech explosion really took hold. Michael personally has invested in many more companies than that and continues to use both angel group and mentoring as his tools to meet great companies.

How do you go about finding companies to invest in?

I usually find companies through Techstars as well as a bunch of other startup competitions, accelerators, and incubators. Betaspring is an example down in Providence, RI; they are 65 miles away and are sort of an incubator for startups down there. They have a nice challenge and I'm a judge there so I see dozens of companies every year that come through that. About 1,300 apply to Techstars Boston and 12 enter. They encourage folks to come in and talk to those companies. I do a bit of that. There are a lot of different ways that I run into interesting companies.

There is the Cambridge Innovation Center in Kendall Square. I think there are 650 startups there. Common Angels actually has office space there so I actually have a card to get in. You know, just hanging around there, I meet a lot of great companies. They have the Venture Café on Thursday afternoons. There are also the few that are referred to me as well.

How do you start to filter so many companies from so many disparate sources?

There are certainly things that tend to attract me more than others. I try to be somewhat diversified and not put all my eggs in one basket. Common Angels, for instance, typically invests in software; they tend to avoid hardware. Every now and then they'll make an exception. Typically, they're more comfortable with B2B business models than with consumer, although they do some consumer also. There is a sweet spot of backend business software that they tend to love. The SAAS web-based monthly recurring revenue models, they love.

If I find somebody who's got traction with a monthly revenue model, I look for a reason to believe that it's a good team that will execute well. That for me is the most important thing. My sense is that the folks who are most flexible, the ones who are able to go with the flow and change their plans if that's appropriate, are the ones most likely to succeed.

How many changes to their idea do you see on average?

Typically, it's one. The folks who go to two or three often are the ones who don't succeed. There's an extreme in the other direction, clearly. Harmonix went through a few different ideas before it really started to click. I've seen it work with more than one.

Brad Feld has a great quote in his book, *Do More Faster*, about the various folks he brought into Harmonix, himself included, had all given up on ever getting any money back. Then, to their surprise, dumploads of cash appeared on their lawn. They had to wait 10 years before they really were the overnight success that people perceived them to have been.

I still feel like I'm very, very early. I haven't had a positive exit since then. I've had some folks go under already. That's to be expected. Probably my biggest investing years were 2011 through 2013; 2010, I was sort of getting going. You can't really expect exits in just a couple of years. Still, in that time I've invested in 77 companies, so I have a large portfolio.

Do you invest roughly the same number of dollars in each company?

I typically start with a $25,000 investment. I try to leave money for later rounds, partly because sometimes you need it just to protect yourself. Sometimes it's signaling if you don't invest, it looks bad. You're not able to raise money from others if the previous investors aren't willing to write checks also. I kind of count on the fact that future funds will be needed. Sometimes you need room to say, "Wow, these guys are really taking off and this round looks like a big deal to me, so I'm going to double down!"

Have you doubled down on most of your investments?

Some aren't there yet and others I've quadrupled or even more. I think the max is probably eight to 10 times initial. On an average it's a little over two, but probably half of them I've never done a follow-on investment.

When you follow on, how do you analyze that? Do you analyze it the same as your initial investment, or differently?

I'd say the follow-on is more about how are they executing. Initially, I might seed the company, so you can't necessarily expect any execution yet. Then it's what do the numbers look like? What's the caliber of the new investment coming in? How much more money is it going to need? I tend to shy away from folks who look like they're going to need to raise a huge amount of money, because I'm going to be such a tiny player that I won't really have any say. The really small guys, when you're raising round after round after round, often get screwed in the longer run. There is some cram down or something is done to push the early investors aside. I try to avoid those sorts of companies. If somebody is talking about "We're figuring we're going to need to raise $20 to $50 million out in the future," I shy away from those guys.

Are low capital requirements a must-have checkbox for you?

Yes, that makes it less likely that some major investor is going to be coming in with a huge amount of capital and cramming down or screwing all the early investors. It still happens occasionally, and I'm early enough in these companies that I'm sure it will happen again. One of the companies I invested in at Techstars only took around $600,000 and they've never taken another dime since and they don't intend to. If you didn't get in at seed, you were never going to get in.

They've got a very lean operation and they just continually grow quarter to quarter in a monthly recurring revenue business. They're profitable now and are plowing the monthly profits back into growing the business. They could take more money and probably grow faster, but that's just not their plan.

How do you weigh a company like that against one that will do everything to grow faster?

It depends on the business. Some would argue that you're opening the door to some much better-financed company just grabbing your market share. You see that happen sometimes. I mean these guys are in a market that's already kind of crowded, there are already a couple of players in it that are very well capitalized. They're just doing a better job of executing and keeping their customers happy, so they're slowly chipping away at the market leaders' business. That's a situation where a lot more cash doesn't look like it would necessarily benefit them.

I like the kinds of businesses that can create some sort of a barrier to entry without a huge amount of cash, whether it's patenting or some sort of network effect. One example of that might be CoachUp, for instance. I was the first investor in CoachUp. A lot of that was based on the founder, who struck me as a guy who could make this work. He is a very charismatic guy who has been able to put a good team together. They're creating a marketplace for private coaches. If you want your kid to get coached in tennis or basketball or hockey or whatever, he's got the marketplace for those coaches to connect with customers. No one else is doing anything like it.

There was clearly a need on both sides. The coaches, they could list on Craigslist, but there was no good marketplace for them. On the parents' side, they could sure use some checks on coaches to avoid things like child molesters. He's doing background checks, providing guarantees, taking credit cards, and handling all the paperwork. All this stuff that doesn't normally get handled properly is handled well in the CoachUp online marketplace. Once you get established in that, the coaches are signed up with you and they're building their reputation on your site, so it's really hard for somebody else to displace you.

How did you go about assessing the team and idea?

It was really when I met him, it was this one guy. He hadn't raised a dime yet. I met him at Venture Café, at CIC. I was there representing Common Angels that day so I was being mobbed with people with crazy idea after crazy idea. This guy just calmly stood next to me and didn't say anything for the longest time. Finally, things calmed down a bit and I turned to him and said, "So what's your story?" He responded, "Well, I'm a professional basketball player."

As it turns out, he was officially a professional but he played for Jerusalem, so not exactly NBA. He grew up in Cambridge. When he was in high school he'd gotten a private coach for basketball and that really changed him from being okay to being really good. He got a basketball scholarship to college. Afterward, he got the gig in Jerusalem. He concluded that he was never going to be an NBA star, but he got an MBA completely paid for by playing basketball.

He came back and he decided he wanted to be a coach. When he started looking around online for where to sign up to make his availability known, he was surprised that there was nothing available. He started talking to coaches and asking what their interest was in using a marketplace. He started talking to parents. He'd already done so much really good background work to determine if there was a market need. There were pain points on both sides. He was so articulate in describing the need and the pain points. I thought, "This guy's a winner!"

I thought I'd be perfectly happy to take a risk on him, at a reasonable valuation. I wrote the first check on a very good valuation. Then I actually recommended him to Techstars and he got in, which was another boost for him in terms of awareness, mentors, investors, and everything else that comes with it. He was a star at Techstars and he raised a couple of times, he raised a round midway through the Techstars stint and then at the very end. I invested day one, three months later, a couple months after that, and then a final investment within that first year. I actually wrote him four checks over the course of a year. Since then, he's raised two VC rounds. I invested first at a million-dollar valuation and his last valuation was for $25 million. On paper I've done really well.

Until someone actually exits, I'm not going to count it, though. He's got a pretty good-size team now—I think he's up over 20 people. He's got a lot of traction in a lot of sports, a lot of metro areas, and he's going after the top 30 US metro areas, trying to get at least 20 to 30 coaches in each sport in each area so he's got enough coverage in an area that pretty much anyone who signs up will be able to find someone who's not too far away. He's thought it through pretty well and he seems to be executing well. Day one I sensed that this guy was a winner.

Would you have invested if the valuation was higher?

If he'd said on day one, "I expect a $4 million valuation," I would have said, "Well, let's wait and see what kind of team you can pull together and see some traction." A lot of folks try to get too high of a valuation before they have made progress. They haven't put the whole team together or even some key member of a team is missing, like they have an idea but they have nobody to actually program it. That's a pretty big hole. Are you going to find a good person and can you work with them?

On the other hand, if there's a team that you believe can work well together, either because they've worked well together before or they've been executing well for the last 12 months, that will cause you to go with the higher valuation. Typically, these startups are looking for a $3 million valuation on a convertible note. The notes usually say 20% to 25% off of whatever they eventually raise a full round at, but with a cap of $3 million. If they raise money at less than $4 million, you're going to get a valuation of less than three, but that might be 18 months after you take the risk. In that time, hopefully, they've made a lot of progress, and riskiness for the company had decreased dramatically in the meantime. I don't really like notes, but you kind of have to deal with them. In the case of CoachUp, the initial note had a maximum conversion price of $1 million, the second note was at $2 million, the third note was at $3 million, and the fourth was at $4 million. At each stage along the way, there was enough progress that I felt comfortable. I still believed in these guys, they needed to raise more money, and the price seemed reasonable for the risk.

Do you prefer equity over notes?

Absolutely, for a number of reasons. Notes rarely have any sort of protection in terms of the corporate governance and I've been screwed on that already. One of those very early investments I made in a friend's business was just a note, no board seat, nobody overseeing what he was up to. To my dismay, and I've known this guy for a long time, he ended up screwing investors and if investors had better representation in the governance process, they wouldn't have let it happen. He ended up way overdue in paying the notes back and wound up getting a legal settlement that brought hundreds of thousands of dollars into the company. No one expected to get all the money invested paid back in notes at that point, but he took it all for himself and he was done. He took it all as back pay for an incredible salary and we had absolutely no say. We could've sued him, I suppose, but it's not worth it and that's not a path I want to go down. Having some sort of corporate governance in place is pretty important. If you're raising enough money through notes or you're working with a sophisticated-enough team, they'll often agree, "Yeah, we'll allow for one or two board members to represent the note holders while the notes are outstanding." It's pretty rare; very often these companies don't even have any sort of a board in place.

Another part is I really don't feel most notes compensate for the risk being taken at day one. If you're getting 20% discount off the first equity round in a couple of years, it's not a very good return on the risk you took in those first couple of years. Often those new investors come in and write rules that leave those early investors in pretty poor condition.

I invested $100,000 in a note two years ago in a company. A little over a year later, they raised a Series A round from two reasonably prominent venture capital firms. Even though a third of Series A ended up being owned by the note holders, the note holders had zero say. They wrote it such that only major investors had any board representations and they were the two major investors. They had veto over any significant decision, enough control to create a Series B that allowed them to leave out the seed investors.

You can end up taking a major risk, putting a serious amount of money at risk, and end up in a poor position, so I don't like notes. I understand why virtually all entrepreneurs are advised by their lawyers that notes are what they should do. Partly it's because there's more flexibility with notes. You can just keep issuing more of them.

You can change some of the terms like increase the minimum at which it converts along the way, or something like that. We'll change the discount, whereas if you raise money, if you're selling stock, you really have to have a closing date and you can't just keep issuing more shares.

If you want to do another round, you have to create another round of shares. They like the flexibility and it's understandable; especially if people are willing to give them money on those terms. If I want to get into these companies and that's the only way to get in, I kind of have to hold my nose and do it. I really don't like notes.

Is it essentially because debt is not participating in the growth of the business?

If the company's at all successful, those notes won't stay debt.

If it fails, it kind of doesn't matter either way. Only if there's some in-between, kind of barely hanging on to life sort of state where I think that it really has much impact. Even if they don't pay, I've never seen anyone turn around and sue the company for payment. Usually they don't have the resources to pay so you're just hoping things will work out. Maybe they've got an asset like a patent or something like that and you might be able to sell it or something, but it's just not worth the legal expense and the hassle.

Do you look at different things as a result of the experience with this founder?

Not really. Honestly, any sort of check on the guy wouldn't have turned anything up. I don't know that you can predict how someone is going to behave in a situation like that. I think I go by my intuition about the person. I had a good intuition about this guy. I've had good dealings with him in the past. I was honestly surprised he behaved the way he did. I think he was just so strapped for cash personally that he kind of bent his ethics.

How do you work with other angel investors?

I'm almost always investing with other angels. Often it is because some other angel I respect says, "Hey, I've been working with these guys for the last year and I have a really high regard for them." That alone can be enough to get me to write a check. I don't necessarily feel like I have to do due diligence in that case if I respect that other angel investor and they're saying, "Look, I have reason to believe these guys are good guys." For me, guys like Semyon Dukach or Brad Feld would give me confidence in a deal.

Do you prefer to be deeply involved in the companies you invest in?

I don't demand it. That's all some people want to invest in. I'm perfectly happy to help anybody who wants my help. I'm probably engaged with at least 20 companies. There is probably another 10 or 15 that at some point I was engaged with. Maybe they got to a point where they filled whatever hole I was helping them fill and they kind of moved on. I'm perfectly happy if you don't want my advice and I'm perfectly happy if you do.

I won't say that I go out of my way, but if somebody gives me a call and says, "Hey, I need your advice on X, Y, Z," I will pretty much drop everything and try to help them.

How much time do you think you spend with companies that you've invested in?

I don't really tally it up. I would say, even before I started my new company, I felt like I had a full-time job. Before I invested in very many companies, I had a reasonable amount of free time. I was doing some traveling. I don't feel like I have time to travel anymore. There's just so much going on at any given point in time. At times, I can pick up a book and read it. At other times, I am emailing at 1:00 in the morning, through the weekend, or having conference call after conference call.

I was in California for 11 days, in theory, out there first for the game developers' conference and then I would spend some time with some friends and then business meetings in LA. I found I was on conference calls pretty much all day the days I was supposed to be at the game developers' conference. I did go to some of the evening events and parties and dinners and things. One day, I was on the phone for eight hours. None of that paid.

I think I'm on about eight boards—four official boards and four advisory boards. The advisory boards don't tend to take as much time. A couple of the official boards are taking a lot of time. You get into certain places where you're trying to sell the company or you're trying to raise a major round or something like that, and there's just a lot of board discussion and extra meetings, emails, and looking at contracts. Just a fair amount of work.

Does that change how you think about investing?

There's just no way that I can both run my new company and put the same amount of time and effort into looking at new companies. I'm not going to turn off or turn down what I was doing for the existing folks. I think I'm going to be more careful about how much time I'm investing looking at new opportunities right now. Hopefully, within the year, I'm able to wind back my activities on the new company. The new company is not something I started to have a day job.

I saw an opportunity really based on another company I invested in. They've got some great technology. They're a bunch of professors. They're not very business oriented. They don't want to raise money or build a team. That's been holding them back. They just want to license their technology to others.

At some point, I turned to one of the other board members who's another business guy and said, "Are we just letting an opportunity of a lifetime dribble through our fingers here? Should we just license this and run with it and do the right thing and actually invest in a team and create software?" So we started this company and we're licensing their tech and trying to run with it. The plan is to put a team in place, find the appropriate management team, and then just step back and be board members and major investors. It isn't an area that either of us have past experience in. We're learning quickly. The company will become known in the not too distant future, I hope. We've been kind of in stealth mode so far.

What lessons do you think you've learned from your earlier investing that has changed the way that you do angel investing now?

I think the largest one I determined is that it's best to avoid friends. I invested in three early on and I don't avoid them just because they may go bad, if they don't go as expected it can hurt the friendship. There was another case where I invested in a guy who had an idea and for very good reasons it failed. I have no problem with that. I don't in the least blame him. He had a major medical crisis that just wiped him out for like two years. I felt sorry for the guy, but I don't in any way blame him. He has never been comfortable with the fact that he lost my money.

I can't make him understand that I don't care. I fully expect that half the companies I invest in are going to go under. It was a risk I was willing to take and it doesn't bother me, but it bothers him. I don't want to spoil a friendship over an investment.

I kind of knew this all along, but I certainly don't put too many eggs in one basket. I come from a games background, so everybody who's got a games business idea finds me. I don't want too many eggs in that basket, partly because I know how risky it is. I probably have too much of my portfolio in games already.

I think I would also underline people, people, people; it's much more about the people than it is the initial idea. It's nice to have a great initial idea, don't get me wrong, but it's more about can they execute on it and can they learn from the marketplace and roll with the punches.

What are the top things new angel investors should avoid?

I think it's been underlined for me that if somebody is going to need a lot of future investments, if I don't feel that I can continue to protect my share, I'll probably get screwed at some point in the future. I've learned to stay clear of those companies that are going to need a ton of cash.

I tend to like the lean and mean folks. The folks who aspire to quickly paying themselves hundreds of thousands of dollars a year if they're even slightly successful, I shy away from those folks too. What have I learned to stay away from? I said earlier that I try to avoid cross-country or faraway deals, but I do have to admit that the few that I've done that are further away are probably all doing well, so maybe I should open that up more. It is just harder to manage. Two out of the three I did through another angel who said, "Hey, I've got this opportunity, they're in North Carolina," or "They're in San Francisco and I really think highly of them." Based on his due diligence and involvement with them, I was willing to take the risk, and those both have done really well. Then another one was a company that I actually invested in while they were still here, but shortly afterward they moved to San Francisco. It does make it a lot harder to stay in touch with them. I still have a lot of lessons to learn.

* * *

You can certainly see why Michael turns over so many rocks—he's constantly looking for those companies that can truly be capital efficient and growth oriented at the same time. This is usually harder to find because so many founders have been trained by venture capitalists that they need a war chest in order to go out and be successful. Michael invested in CoachUp along with another of the angels interviewed, Semyon Dukach, in 2012. Since that $2.7 million seed round, CoachUp raised another $6.7 million Series A in November of 2013 and continues to grow.

ADD VALUE WITH WARREN KATZ

"Recognize reality even when you don't like it - especially when you don't like it."

—CHARLIE MUNGER

"...companies that don't listen to their customers and don't listen to the market, don't abandon their bad ideas quickly."

—WARREN KATZ

I WAS INCREDIBLY LUCKY to be introduced to Warren Katz through Brad Feld. Like many angel investors, Warren started his angel investing as an entrepreneur, having started a company and, shortly after, getting into angel investing with Brad Feld and investing in Harmonix. Harmonix the company became wildly successful nearly a decade later with the games Rock Band and Guitar Hero. Despite the many years of investing experience Warren has, this was still his biggest successful angel investment in the 20 years of angel investing between when Warren started investing and when we had this interview. That is a long time horizon to be thinking about, and it certainly lends itself to thoughtful investing and not just speculating.

How did you get started angel investing?

I was an entrepreneur myself, I started my company in 1990, and I guess my first angel investment was probably 1994/1995. Brad Feld introduced me to a couple of MIT media lab guys who started a company called Harmonix that made the Rock Band and Guitar Hero games. I am guessing you have heard of those. That was my first angel investment and really at the time I hadn't done anything like that, but it really was a friend who came to me with an idea, a guy I trusted, and said, "Hey, I am investing in this, will you invest alongside me?" It was mostly about trusting a guy who invited me in. I was an entrepreneur so I realized that it might be worthwhile to spread my risk around a little, invest some money in other startups, and try to capitalize in somebody else. It was kind of a lottery ticket. You have to do a lot of them to guarantee that you can have at least one hit. I had that one hit, Harmonix—other than my own company, Harmonix was my biggest hit, which has certainly paid back for all the losers. That is how I got into it, trusting a guy who came to me with a deal that he was confident in, and my desire to both give back to the startup entrepreneur community as well as hedge my bets, and spread the risk.

How did you go from just a deal from a trusted friend to spreading your risk around a bunch of deals?

I had been invited and introduced to all these angel groups. I am not a group kind of guy, because I have strong opinions about what deals I like, what sectors I like, my own opinions about what's going to be big, and what's not going to be big in the future. I haven't been right all the time, but I am a little turned off by group think. I'm not a big fan of giving my trust and money to some large committee or large group of other angels that have to all agree on an investment before they make it. I think that's a pretty high bar. I do have a lot of friends who're in angel groups; I listen to what deals they are doing, and at times I will co-invest with angel groups, or other people I have confidence in, but I tend to like to just do the individual deals myself.

There are two exceptions to that. I did become a limited partner in one incubator here in Boston, called Bolt. I think Bolt is the only hardware incubator in Boston. It is sort of a combination of incubator/accelerator that focuses on physical products; products that combine physical with electronics, and software. I did become a limited partner in that fund. But that's really not like an angel group.

There are classes, there are a dozen or so investments, and this very small committee of three or four guys who make decisions. Again, these are people I have confidence in. Although even their first class I looked at who they selected, and I would have only selected half of the ones they did. But I am willing to admit I am not always the smartest guy in the room, so in this small isolated case I am willing to trust somebody else's judgment over my own with my money.

We will see if it pans out or not, but it is kind of a small experiment. Even there I have invested in two of the companies directly, aside from the Bolt investment, so I am kind of using my position in the incubator just to get a better lead on the individual companies in order to further invest in individual companies.

Do most deals come from friends?

I have also been a mentor for Techstars for the last six years, and almost all of my deals came through that. I have volunteered as a mentor for all of the classes for the last six years. I would say most of my investments came from just having a personal mentoring interface with the 60 or 70 companies that have come through Techstars.

Is due diligence easier when you're a mentor?

Absolutely. I am very reluctant to invest in a company that I haven't spent a couple of months with. It doesn't have to be every day for a couple of months, it could be once every two to four weeks, just for a couple of months, so I can gauge their progress and focus. I can start to see results of marketplace acceptance, how fast they're progressing the product. It is different than growing my own company. I grew my own company for about 20 years. When you're in charge of your own company you can't see the forest for the trees. When you come back to somebody even once a week, you get asked, "What did you do in the last month?" You can see whether their progress is mild or whether they are making great strides, or they're repeating the same mistakes, or they're failing to abandon bad ideas quickly. When you get these little glimpses once every two weeks, or once every month, you get an interesting 40,000-foot view of whether this company is going anywhere. I very much like that and I really do like to spend three months interacting with the company after meeting them before pulling the trigger.

What things are you looking for over that time period that key you into making an investment?

There are several things. One is simple progress on the product itself. I like to see companies listening to the customer base and their potential market, rather than just listening to themselves in a quiet back room, which is a very common mistake in startup companies. The founders think they are super geniuses, they know what the customers want, and they refuse to talk to customers. When they talk to customers, they deny that what the customer is saying is true. If the customers say anything negative about their product or their offering they deny it, and they just blindly blunder ahead in their own stubborn direction. That is a classic mistake made in my own company in the very beginning.

Here's another thing: companies that don't listen to their customers and don't listen to the market, don't abandon their bad ideas quickly. I keep a pretty sharp eye on that one. Just basic progress. I have seen a lot of companies where they have conflicts within their own engineering team. If I see lots that they like to hide, don't want to release, or if the product is never done, that's a sure sign of death. When a company is afraid of their customer base, they don't want to hear the answers they can't stand to hear. Instead, they hide. So I keep a sharp eye out for that.

Another thing: bad hiring decisions, or bad staffing decisions that people don't want to deal with, because they don't want to deal with the interpersonal issues of moving somebody, or firing somebody. I keep an eye out for that. In a small startup company you don't have the latitude or leeway to keep somebody around who's not defined in a critical role. I keep my eye on that.

And finally, cash flow management, how they are treating whatever financial resources they have. I keep my eye on that. In general, I highly value frugality.

Do you focus much on the economics of the business itself, or the product unit economics?

I definitely look at that. I tend to like products that are going into an existing market, simply obsoleting an existing product that's already doing very well in the market. Those are the best ones. I don't see very many of those, unfortunately, so try to get as close to that as you possibly can. Somebody who's in a marketplace where people are spending a lot of money on a closely related product—that's also a very good sign.

I am leery of investing in companies where the marketplace doesn't exist. You hear all the same bullshit about "Oh, well, if Steve Jobs did that, we wouldn't have Apple" and "Well, if this company didn't do that, we wouldn't have the greatest breakthroughs." And Henry Ford said, "If I asked my customers what they wanted, they would have told me a faster horse."

In general, I like to see that there's a definite need, a lot of money being spent in a marketplace, and either you're replacing product that already exists, or you're investing in something, and putting out a product—if it is peripherally related to something that people are spending a lot of money on.

Somebody might walk in and say, "You know what, that's a feature in my product, I need to be competitive, and my competitor will come out with the same thing. I am just going to acquire it even though it is not financially viable on its own." That is another possibility in the grand eco-system, having something that's not independently viable, but still of value to somebody who's in the business, still connects with what I do.

When you find the right ones to invest in, are you leading the round?

At the dollar figures I play at, I would never lead a round. I just don't have the capital. I can't be drawing a million dollars or half a million bucks each deal. I play at a much lower level, so I never lead as far as the dollars go. I am not afraid to be one of the first people into a round, especially a small seed round with a very attractive valuation for a company that I like. I don't like to follow, because that means I might be a little too late. I tend to make my own decisions. I am definitely not a lemming. I don't wait to see who else is in. I will sometimes scramble if I see a lot of other people going in, but I don't usually like to be in that position. I tend to like to make my own decisions in the absence of knowing what other people are doing.

I have a couple of close friends who I send little notices to say, "Hey, I am doing this, just letting you know." Often they follow me in. Sometimes those same friends get in earlier than me, and I follow them. I have a small set of trusted people whom I share notes with, and sometimes we do the same things, sometimes we do different things.

Do you care about structure of the investment?

I will do a convertible note on the first round. Techstars does that with all the companies that are going through their program. The Techstars note has actually been the predominant way I have invested and that converts to equity on the first financing round with a discount around 20%. I've had a couple of issues where a venture capitalist coming into the first rounds tries to unwind some of the terms in the note and there's a bit of fighting that goes on there. For the most part, it has been very successful.

After conversion, how do you evaluate follow-on rounds?

I've done follow-on investments in four or five companies. Of the other dozen or so, it has been mostly just principal investments. I invested in a company called GrabCad, a Techstars company that I am investing in. I'm in two rounds of GrabCad—their original Techstars round, then I participated in the follow-on round. They're doing great and they're going to have a great exit. That is going to be my next big hit I am predicting. I couldn't afford to play in the follow-on round because of the valuation. They had a great valuation on their last round, and I am delighted that they are doing so well, but I can't play in this next round, it doesn't make any sense.

How do you stay engaged with the companies from your seed investment until it gets too big for you to be engaged?

I am on the board of a couple of companies that I've invested in and despite the fact they have acquired institutional investment, they still value me on the board. The VCs will throw me off as an angel, which is fine. All these other investments, I treat them the same as I treat my Techstars mentorship companies. I keep in contact with them. They send investor updates all the time. I keep in contact, and I tell them, "Look, if you ever want to meet with me, I am happy to meet any time sporadically, or on a schedule, or whatever." For the most part, most of the companies I have invested in have asked me to continue meeting with them. They don't have to and I don't pressure them to. These are informal meetings so they can bounce some stuff off of me; especially in places where the CEO doesn't want to always engage the board with every little issue that comes across their desk. They like to engage with a former executive who they can bounce ideas off of without exposing it to a larger group. I find the CEOs like to confide in a trusted mentor and I play that role for several companies.

How about on the operational side, recruiting, sales leads, and so on?

I had my own software company in Boston, so people often ask me, would I recommend an employee for this or an employee for that, references for recruiting. I do it all the time. If somebody is about to hire somebody, and they say, "Hey, do you know somebody at this company I can get a background check, a reference check?" I will often have a conduit into connecting people up.

I do sales calls and introductions. I was extensively involved in the military industry, which is not that common a thing in the Boston area. People say, "Hey, do you know somebody at Boeing? Do you know somebody in Lockheed Martin?" I am like, "Oh yes, sure."

I probably spend on a lighter side four hours a week and on the heavier side it might be 15 hours a week. I might average 10 to 12 hours a week. I have no complaints.

Are you more interested in an earlier acquisition type of an exit or more of an IPO type of exit?

Clean and quick is always better than long and drawn out. I would rather hit 10 singles than wait for one home run. Ideally you want to mix. If you do 100 investments I like to have one knocking out of the park home runs that's 100 to one payoff. Then you want five to 10 5x payoffs and then another 20 to 30 2x payoffs.

If you can get something like that, a nice hybrid like that, that's great. I do expect more than 50% of my investments to be worth zero, but I would like to get something back on the other 50%. I would never advise an entrepreneur to hold out if somebody is dangling a 10x return in front of an entrepreneur's face. I would never advise them to hold out for a chance at 100x. It is amazing that any deals happen at all. If you can get a good deal, take it, that's my mantra. It has to be a good deal, it can't be 1.2x your investment. It has to be something that's appreciable; at the same time I would never advise anybody to leave a good deal on the table to hope for a knock out of the park home run. On the rare occasions the company is going to the moon, and it is obvious they are going to the moon, then it may pay to wait a little bit. Still, if there's an inarguably good deal on the table, my advice is always to take it.

How much of your overall net worth portfolio do you allocate to angel investing?

I would say less than 10%. I can't give you an exact number, but I would say of my entire net worth, less than 10% is in angel investments. It is very high alpha kind of returns. If you're betting more than 25% of your net worth on angel investing, that means your net worth money must be very, very high, because you just don't care about losing 100% of that 25%. I am not at the point where I am that wealthy, that kissing 25% of my net worth good-bye wouldn't change a thing. That would change a thing for me.

Looking back at your portfolio, were there some clear mistakes you made along the way that you've learned from?

The ones that all blew up. What trends were obvious? That I should have known ahead of time? Well, there's one lesson that I always told myself and others that I violated, which is "Stick to what you know." I will give you one example. I invested in a company that made a golf app for smart phones. I am not a golfer. I don't play golf, I don't know much about the sport, and I don't know much about the tools, the techniques, the training. How much people spend in which parts of golf. All I knew was that people spend a lot of money on golf. I took that on faith that a golf-related app would do well if it was a good app. That company went out of business, and looking back on it, it wasn't sticking with what I knew. Although always sticking to what you know certainly doesn't guarantee that you will succeed.

If you see 1,000 deals, you should be rejecting 990 of them. You should be rejecting 99% of what you see. If you filter on things like big markets, a lot of money being spent, and an existing product there already. Team is good, they already have traction in the marketplace. If I know the market, and am comfortable with it, you can filter out 99% of the deals, and just get the ones that meet all of these criteria, ring all of these bells. If I am investing alongside somebody else, whom I really trust, who says, "I know this market, and I believe this thing is going to do really, really well," then you can get comfortable there. Wandering into places where you don't know the subject matter and don't know what you're doing is probably a lesson I have learned a few too many times. There are enough deals out there that you can stick to things that you know and still have plenty of deals as well.

There is no shortage. I am well wired into the Boston Angel community at this point. I am mentor at both Techstars and Bolt. Techstars and Bolt each get 1,000 business plans a year, and they only select 10 people. There's already 99% right there. Then I do another 10 [down] to 1. I usually invest in one, maybe two Techstars and Bolt companies a year. I already have 1,000 down to 1 selected that includes their first filtration, plus my second filtration. I still have no shortage of deals. No shortage. Even with that. Like I say, if you get down to that point, and you can have only 50% failures, you're doing superbly.

Looking back at your portfolio, were there some clear things you did along the way that you've found were keys to success?

My biggest successes unfortunately are the riskiest, and the investments that I should not have made. The ones that if I applied all of these rules, there's no way in the world I would have ever made that investment, yet it was the number one investment. So don't ever discount dumb luck. Unfortunately, my number one outlier, my number one success, was something that didn't have a lot of logic and/or follow the rules and I just quote you something I shouldn't have either. There should be something there, and maybe it is a trusted investor whom you can rely on.

What about GrabCad? They pretty much followed the rules that you set up for yourself.

That is a pretty textbook case and they did follow all of the rules. I did understand the subject matter. They are an online community of CAD/CAM designers and I am from the 3D modeling simulation space; this is one of the reasons they wanted me as an angel investor. They didn't accept all the angel money; they actually turned down a bunch of angels, and they let me in because I was of material assistance to them. They were growing like a weed. They didn't have revenue, but they had plenty of customer buy-in, and they have a million-plus users now in the CAD/CAM world, which is unheard of. There is no bigger community of CAD/CAM engineers anywhere. They started to sell, started to make revenue, but based on their growth rate and the kind of membership base they have, somebody is going to acquire them pretty quickly.

That is just too juicy a community to let sit out there not owned by somebody. Yes, I would say that for the most part, the CAD/CAM software industry is a space I was familiar and comfortable with. I liked the team; they seemed to be moving quickly. They listened to their customers, and I was comfortable after working with them for three to four months that they were going somewhere. So yes, I pretty much follow all the rules.

What do you think about crowdfunding sites such as AngelList, CircleUp, and others?

I am leery of group think and there's no way I am ever going to make a decision about a company that I just get email from. Somebody has got to bring the deal up to me whom I know and trust, and say, "I just invested in this. I think this is awesome, I would like you in as well." Then 50% of the battle is over or more than 60% of the battle is over. Then I will look at the deck and maybe make a decision without really knowing the company. Otherwise, I have to spend the two or three months with them, mentoring them, talking with them, and associating with them. It is pretty much only going to be companies that are in Boston. There are plenty of startups here in Boston; I don't really need to go outside of the city limits of Boston to go and find deals. If you take those five people across my own network and contacts, exposure at Techstars and Bolt, that's enough.

That is enough for me to have a 10 to 1 filter in quality selections. I don't need to join some big angel group. That is me; other people might not have the time to ever mentor a company. So that's a whole different dynamic, and other people might have so much money, or they don't have the attention or budget to meet with a lot of companies. People may just get lucky and have some money, but not the confidence; they don't trust themselves. That's a whole different dynamic. There are all kinds of angels. I am the successful entrepreneur type of angel who doesn't like to listen to anybody else, likes to make all his own decisions himself, and I have a few trusted colleagues I listen to.

Techstars has a hundred mentors and there's no way every company in Techstars can meet with a hundred mentors. What they are starting to do is match make a little more. Like this round with Techstars. I met with eight of the companies and after the first half-hour meeting, I would tell them, "Okay, you have had half an hour to learn about me and extract from me a bit. I have had half an hour to meet with you. The way I work as a mentor is I will meet with you any time after this if you want. I am not going to chase you." Sometimes they never call and I have no ego involved, so that's a good thing. There are a hundred mentors and only a few companies, so use your bullets wisely.

I leave it in the hands of the company whether or not and how often they want to meet with me. I would say out of the eight companies, six of them kind of fell off the map, and two of them kept calling me and that's pretty consistent. I would say in the last six years at Techstars and the one session of Bolt I have done, that's pretty consistent. So it winded up being this matchmaking dating process, and I think the entrepreneurs can quickly see—maybe it takes two, or at most three meetings. But they can see when somebody is adding value, or when somebody is just a blowhard, or pretending they know something they don't. When a company has a hundred mentors to choose from, they meet their core 30, then they can choose from those who're adding the most value. Those people you mentioned, those people who think they add value who actually don't, or are trying but really don't have anything—they get weeded out in the process, because the company has plenty of mentors to choose from.

Those people who have the money but don't have the value added are going to have to be just those kinds of angel investors who show up at the end when everybody else is in the round, and you just add their money, if they are allowed in at all. Sometimes the startup companies just want the capital. An angel investor who can plunk down $250,000—despite the fact that they have no other value—are just so much easier to deal with than 10 angel investors, who're each putting down $25,000 in the first round. A lot of startup companies think, "You know what, I have a couple of mentors, I have a couple of people I can ask. I would just rather go and get the heavyweight and make this first round even easier to just close." If somebody has got a lot of money, a lot of money is a very desirable quality. Advice, mentorship, and expertise is a different quality — you have to balance them.

Do you see some of the engagement with these companies as part of your interim reward for your investment?

I do get some pleasure. I do enjoy what I am doing, especially when a company is doing very well. There is a great deal of pleasure, sort of being on the team, at least from an arm's-length perspective. That is maybe 33% of the enjoyment, 33% of the reason I do it; the other 66% is I simply want to maximize the profitability and chance they will have a successful return on my money. Anything I can to do to maximize the profitability and the chance an investment will do well, I will do. I also do unpleasant things. I help other companies that aren't doing well, for the same reason. I want to maximize my return even though it is definitely not enjoyable. I do spend the time in those unpleasant situations as well.

What is your favorite part of being an angel now that you have been doing it for so long?

I like the high-growth period when the company is changing rapidly and you can see a small investment blossom into something bigger. That is kind of the exciting part. When you're starting to hear other people talking about the company before you've mentioned that you're an investor, that's pretty cool. You're around the bar and people are saying, "Hey, have you heard of blah, blah, blah, I hear they are hot, they are smoking, they are on fire," and I am thinking, "Oh yes, I am one of the angel investors." That is a pretty cool thing to do.

What is the thing that you like the least?

Sometimes I will see or deal with founders or CEOs who're making mistakes. The worst situation is when they're making the same mistakes that I myself have made in the past. I learned my lesson, I conveyed that lesson to the CEO, they didn't listen, and then the exact same bad outcome occurs to them that happened to me. It is the talking to the wall part that's probably the worst part of angel investing. Talking to the wall and then watching failure happen is no fun; saying "I told you so" after the fact isn't a pleasure. Having somebody listen to you and avoid the bad situation is better. I think the worst is giving advice, having it not taken, giving good advice based on sound experience, and having it rejected, and then watching the same train wreck occur. That has occurred in the past. That is the worst.

What advice would you give to other angel investors?

I will give you some advice that somebody gave me after I sold my company, advice from a wealthy guy who had also come into money: "Go slow." He also told me, "Stick to what you know." So he told me, "Go slow, and stick to what you know." Those are the two superb pieces of advice that he gave me. I took the first one, and the second one, "Stick to what you know," I mostly took. I violate that one on occasion, and I learned my lesson. I would say those are my two bottom line pieces of advice.

* * *

Warren and I had a great conversation, and I was again surprised that I continued to learn so much. Warren's insights into the mentorship's role in being a true value-added investor make a lot of sense.

GrabCad, one of the companies Warren discusses, was acquired by Stratasys a few months after the interview for $100 million after only taking $13.6 million in funding in three rounds between June 2011 and October 2012. The other company Warren discusses, Harmonix, continues to make games, building on their early success.

FIND YOUR ALPHA WITH VC MARK SUSTER

"If you want to be truly successful, invest in yourself to get the knowledge you need to find your unique factor. When you find it and focus on it and persevere your success will blossom. "

—SYDNEY MADWED

"What's your unique advantage? If you don't have one, you're literally in Vegas sitting at the table just hoping that you get dealt the royal flush."

—MARK SUSTER

MARK SUSTER IS A PARTNER at Upfront Ventures, the largest venture capital firm in Southern California. Mark previously built and sold two companies and is an avid voice in the startup community. He blogs regularly at http://www.bothsidesofthetable.com/ on the topics of building and investing in great companies. Much of my research leading up to my interview with Mark involved poring over the great insights and advice he makes available on his blog. I reference a few of the articles below, but I highly recommend you read all of them at http://bit.ly/1jlKAjK.

Mark talks a lot about his journey from developer to venture capitalist. After reading his articles, though, I never got the sense about what really triggered the move from operator to investor, so I wanted to understand this a little more. Of course, Mark, an LA-based investor, used basketball analogies instead of baseball analogies like his Northeastern counterparts.

How did you decide to make the move from operator to investor?

I often use a basketball analogy. I use this with a lot of young people who're trying to decide if they want to be VCs or entrepreneurs. If you're talented enough to be on the court, if you're fast enough, if your dribbling skills are good enough and if you can hit a three-point shot. When the game is down, with 10 seconds left, you have the ball and you're down by two, you want the ball and you want to be on the court. There is no better feeling than being on the court. There is no better feeling than being the guy who's trusted to make that shot. And then at a certain point in your career where you've been the guy on the court, you realize that there's younger, faster, leaner, more aware players than you and what they lack maybe is a bit of experience and wisdom and maturity to play the game, and you become a better coach. I just reached that point in my career where I felt like my experiences were better applied as a coach than being on the court. If I were good enough to still be on the court, I would be.

How should new investors go about figuring out how to get at the right table?

If you don't know who the sucker at the table is, you are. Every deal I see from anybody where they're already an existing investor, my starting position is, why am I so lucky that you're calling me? It's not that I'm not self-confident, I am. It's not that I don't have friends who'll send me interesting stuff, I do. But I just want to know what's the angle. You know, what am I being played for? I try to say this to a lot of new angels.

If you worked at YouTube in YouTube's early days, and you know how the systems inside YouTube work and you quit to go create a company, or if you know all the guys who were there because you were there with them and they quit to create a company, you're an insider. You know the industry better than anyone else. You know what works and what doesn't. You know who the decision makers are and you know whether this kid named George Strompolos, who quit, is liked and respected and likely to get deals done that favor him over everybody else in the YouTube ecosystem. If you're that insider, awesome! That's why people refer to the PayPal mafia. It really *was* a mafia. Or Salesforce mafia or Facebook mafia. And if you're not part of the mafia, somebody else is.

What's your unique advantage? If you don't have one, you're literally in Vegas sitting at the table just hoping that you get dealt the royal flush. The odds are that eventually even the people without good poker skills will get one. That's just statistics. But that doesn't mean that you sitting at the table are likely to get it.

How do you balance being diversified with having an edge?

I think the two can be related. The best investors I know aren't trying to fund the next social network. The best consumer games guys I know aren't trying to fund alternative energy companies. The problem is the market between 2009 to 2015 has only gone in one direction. As a result, everybody thinks they're the world's best investor. Sometimes that's because they get huge markups on deals that they did and they confuse a markup with a return. Sometimes that's because a company got acquired really young for $40 million and after putting in $50,000 they made $200,000. In a bull market there's a lot of M&A and you can confuse being a great investor with timing the market really well.

Let me give you the perfect analogy. In 1999, 2000, and maybe early 2001, my brother was a young kid, earning small money in his job, but he started day trading. His profits were so big from day trading that it dwarfed anything he was earning in his job. He thought, "Why are people so stupid as to work for a salary when you can be a trader and make money?" He thought he was the smartest guy until the market corrected and he lost everything. This is human history, and today's angel market is no different.

Everybody's up at the blackjack table, everybody's winning so they're betting more and more. You know that eventually the night will be over. At the end of the night when your Jack Daniels and Coke are done and you finally leave at 3:30 in the morning, you know most people are going to have lost money. Despite that you keep betting. Your greed builds because you won so much throughout the night. Right now, I don't know if it's 11 pm or 1:30 am but it's not 3:00 am yet.

At what point do you know that you're in a party round?

In 2004 I was really loud at cocktail parties and dinners about how overvalued the real estate market was. In 2005 I was loud about it. In 2006 I was loud about it. In 2007 I was loud about it. And every year I had these self-righteous, young punks who were buying property in Miami, Palm Beach, and Las Vegas who were making tons of money saying that I didn't understand that things were different because there was a limited supply of real estate in South Florida, and therefore it was a good deal. I said to them the fundamentals of real estate haven't changed. The thing that drives real estate valuations. There are only two things. Maybe a third, but two things.

One is the price of the people's salaries in a region. If people earn $100,000 in one region and in another region they earn $50,000, property prices will be about 2x in the place where people earn $100,000.

Two is the rental prices versus the price of property, and there's a fixed ratio between rental markets and property markets. So when the price of property goes up, the price of rental markets should go up commensurate with that. If they get out of balance, you know that either the price of owning a property is too expensive or the price of renting a property is too cheap. From 2004 to 2007 those two factors were at historical imbalances. Like, the highest in human history. No matter how many times I said that to people they wouldn't believe me. I said just because you're in Vegas and just because they've rolled red four times in a row and you've made a ton of money doesn't mean you're right. The same is true in angel investing right now.

There are some factors in startups that have fundamentally changed the value of companies, but the fact that red has been rolled four times in a row doesn't mean every company is valuable, and that's what people are confusing. They're confusing four reds in a row with assuming that the next four rolls are going to be red and probability says they're not.

The things that have changed that make tech companies more valuable than they were 15 years ago is 15 years ago there were 200 million people online. Now there's two and a half *billion*. Fifteen years ago we were on 56k dialup. Now we're on average 4mb. Fifteen years ago, no one had social networks so the idea work, that took time to propagate. Fifteen years ago, no one had their credit cards online so I couldn't do one-click purchase. All of that has changed and now we're carrying computers in our pockets.

As a result, startup companies are infinitely more valuable than they were 15 years ago, but that doesn't change the fundamental dynamic that the underlying value of a company is only determined by its current and future free cash flow. Unless these companies eventually generate free cash flow, they're not going to be valuable. Just because there are dumber investors willing to pay higher prices doesn't mean that your asset is necessarily worth what you think it's worth. Everyone has assumed that everything in their portfolio is valuable because there's so much money that most everything is getting funded or acqui-hired.

My belief is that the most stable situation of funding a company is when somebody has their proverbial head on the chopping block if it doesn't work. Because most companies aren't immediately up and to the right. Like the Pottery Barn rule, when the shit hits the fan who's the person who has to fix it because they broke it? Who owns it? If I have six investors around a table, and each of them put in $200,000 and these are big funds that usually write $2 million or $3 million or $5 million checks. If someone knocks over the plate at Pottery Barn, everyone else looks around and says it's not on me.

That's what happens. When a company goes immediately up and to the right, it's okay if you have a party round. When a company takes time to succeed and nobody's head is on the chopping block, the company gets stranded. The founder may still be able to work it out and it may not fall back on investors, and I know entrepreneurs love to just say investors never add value, they never do anything, but from my experience that couldn't be further from the truth. And by the way, I would say the same thing is true about CEOs. Most heads of marketing and sales and product I know say about CEOs, "Oh, he's okay, but I could do his job." Most engineers I know look up at their CTO and say, "Yeah, he's pretty good, but I'm better. I could do his job." The reality is that everyone plays a different role, and I think successful companies have large, interested investors.

Are online platforms like AngelList making party rounds too easy?

I'm willing to bet you serious amounts of money that AngelList syndicates don't dramatically change the structure of the industry. Let me tell you why. I know that I'm on the opposite side of that argument for most people, but most people are usually wrong. Let me give you my scenario. Let me say there's an AngelList syndicate led by Joe Bloggs, to avoid naming any real names.

If Joe Bloggs has a day job and a ton of other things to do, and he can get into some really interesting deals because he parties with the right people or is an insider - great, awesome. But at some point in time, companies have to choose between Joe Bloggs and Bill Gurley.

At some point they're going to decide whether Bill Gurley, who does this full time and who does work through good markets and bad and who has sustainable capital and who spends time building downstream relationships, is the guy. At some point they're going to decide between those two, and I'm betting that through bad markets more people will bet on Bill Gurley than Joe Bloggs. When capital is cheap and undifferentiated you might as well take it from Joe Bloggs 'cause he's a cool guy and he pays a higher price, but I don't think that builds good long-term companies. Joe Bloggs knows nothing about how to IPO a company. Joe Bloggs doesn't spend any time trying to figure out how to do mergers. Joe Bloggs won't sit with you while you're trying to hire your new head of operations who has five other offers but you're trying to persuade him this is a better offer.

I think active investors matter a lot and AngelList syndicates solve the problem of "How do I raise money quickly from a bunch of people?" It doesn't solve the problem of "How am I an active investor?" If Joe Bloggs does this as a career and doesn't have any distractions, all you're really saying is Joe Bloggs is a VC, and his capital comes from a lot of small people rather than institutional endowments and foundations and public pensions and whatever, but he's still a VC. I would rather have a VC with six partners and eight analysts and a team helping with recruiting and everything else than I would have a VC who has a syndicate.

What are the three things early-stage investors should do to be successful?

If you really want to understand angel investing, make sure the people you're interviewing about it have invested at least since the 1990s. If you're like my brother as a day trader who's been in the Internet market when it's only going one way, you won't get a realistic perspective. You will get people telling you, "Venture capital's being disrupted, the world is different now," "You just have to back the right company," "Angels are changing the world," "Would you rather have a bunch of entrepreneurs backing you or finance people backing you?" You'll hear every argument, but I don't think you'll get the right answer.

I'm not saying don't get that perspective, but if you really want to get a nuanced understanding, talking to people who've been through multiple cycles will give you a better understanding.

Number one, you need deal diversity. If you don't have the cash to do at least 10, 15, 20 deals, you shouldn't be an angel.

Number two, you need the ability to put more money behind your winners. If you don't have the money to put more behind the three, four, five best things in your portfolio, you shouldn't be an angel investor.

Number three, if you don't have an inside edge in terms of relationships, or information, or access to people or deals or exits or an industry more than other people, you shouldn't be an angel.

How can someone truly know if they have an edge?

Everyone thinks they have an edge.

Anyone who's ever played pickup basketball, maybe they played high school ball, maybe they played a little bit in college, thinks they could jump on the court against Kobe or LeBron and carry their own. They don't realize that Kobe has been playing all day, every day, religiously for hours against the best people in the industry. He wakes up earlier, he works out harder, he puts in the commitment. At that elite level people are so fucking good. What is it that makes Kobe better than everybody else? Absolute dedication and commitment. The thought that you could step on the court and compete against Kobe is fanciful.

Why do people think investing is any different? Do you think that it's different for Mike Moritz, John Doerr, or Bill Gurley? These guys spend all day, every day, as insiders in this industry. That you could be the guy who does a little programming on the side or runs his own startup company or used to work at Facebook and doesn't have the access to the research and the inside information and the ability to call Larry Page, do you really think that you can be a weekend warrior and step on the court with LeBron?

Everybody thinks that their pickup game is great. Everybody thinks it, but you're playing against people who have that absolute dedication and skill level. You know, Mike Moritz didn't become Mike Moritz by accident.

There are young people who have insane access that other people don't have. Just look at Josh Kushner at Thrive. He has relationships through his Harvard network, through his childhood, through being a startup entrepreneur and through hustling.

Most people I know don't work as hard as Josh. That guy is always on. So is it a surprise that in his late twenties or whatever he is, that he's become a superstar investor? No. It's no surprise. You can be young and do great things. I'm just saying that I don't believe you can be part time or casual about it. I don't believe I can just chuck money into a syndicate or start a syndicate myself or do 12 deals with my buddies and play at that level.

I know that we're in a bull market, and therefore everybody thinks they're great and the same is true of venture capitalists. A lot of VCs think they're great because of their paper markups these days, but the judge of a great investor is not how much money you make in good markets, but bad markets.

I know that's a counter-conventional view, and I'm not down on angels, I'm not down on the market, I'm just saying we have to be realistic about all this, and when the book is written in 2022 it'll be written very differently than a book written in 2015.

* * *

The insight here isn't too much different than the insights from Joanne Wilson. Early investors should strive to add a lot of value early on to the company but also establish a relationship with the founding team that will last throughout the future phases of the company.

You can see that early-stage venture capitalists act as highly sophisticated angel investors. This is their livelihood and the strategic approach they take is something every angel investor can learn from. Professional investors in public and private markets both focus on mitigating systemic risk and building strategies to avoid un-systemic risk. There are selection strategies, capital allocation strategies, and ecosystem management strategies that all play into their sophistication. Learning to behave in a similar fashion will help to improve the sophistication of an angel at any level.

INVESTING FOR THE LONG TERM WITH VC MICHAEL GREELEY

"Flaming enthusiasm, backed up by horse sense and persistence, is the quality that most frequently makes for success."

—DALE CARNEGIE

"First and foremost I figure in this market you're backing people. Invest in a world-class entrepreneur in the B market and they can still build a compelling company, but the opposite is not true."

—MICHAEL GREELEY

MICHAEL HAS BEEN A VENTURE CAPITALIST since the mid-1990s and continues to refine the way he invests. You may be surprised that I included Michael in the book, considering how long he has been a venture capitalist. Michael's venture investing focuses on the early-stage healthcare technology and often happens alongside other angel investors. Most of the angels who made it into the book have been investing for just as long as Michael, but not necessarily in a professional capacity. It is this mix of longevity, professional investor, and focus on the first two rounds of investment that makes Michael offer such a unique perspective in the context of the other investors included here.

Michael's perspective on investing and his process solidify many of the insights that other angels and venture capitalists have shared. I wanted to start at the beginning with Michael to offer some context on his perspective.

How did you get started with early-stage investing?

I'm a partner with an early-stage venture fund, and this is my third venture fund. The institutional angel phenomenon is a decade old; it hasn't been around forever. We love having angels in our deals; not all angels are created the same, but we do enjoy having them as co-investors.

My first firm was started in the mid-1990s; it was a $200 million fund. The second firm, my most recent firm, was Flybridge Capital Partners. I was the founder of that firm. We raised three funds totaling $560 million, but we invested in over 80 companies. Certainly the last fund, Flybridge, which is a 2008 fund, had angels as co-investors; my guess is a third of those companies had angels as co-investors. Now, I just raised a healthcare tech fund. It is mostly software investing, but dedicated to the transformation of healthcare. It will be between 20 to 25 core positions. My guess is more than 50% of those companies will have angels as co-investors.

What amount do you typically invest?

We are obsessively early-stage investors, we do seed and Series A investments. As early-stage investors we may see a couple of late-stage investments where we know the team or we have real conviction about the space, but certainly the bulk of what we do will be early stage, and the bulk of those will have angels as co-investors.

We will invest half a million to $3 to $4 million in an initial investment and then reserve, depending on the starting point, another 2-3x that. Over the life of the relationship with the entrepreneur we'll have invested $10-15 million. The art of managing a fund is how you really think through the reserves analysis because most of the dollars get invested after the initial investment. Where many angels are "one and done," we think very hard about our initial ownership position, how we protect it so we don't get unnecessarily diluted. That portfolio management piece of what we do is a big part of our investment strategy.

How do you decide which companies you do the follow-on for?

The tricky thing to avoid is the "sunk cost" trap, which is putting in good money after bad. Ideally you want each investment, to the best of your abilities, to stand on its own and to be insulated from the fact that you have already invested.

The worst thing you can do is invest multiple times in one company and then shut it down because it did not work out. We spend a lot of time thinking about the dynamic of that follow-on decision-making process.

My experience with a lot of the angels has been they are more focused on the initial bet and they're happy to let the company run. For us the initial investment is important, but how we invest over time is perhaps more important.

How do you make the decision to invest?

First and foremost I figure in this market you're backing people. Invest in a world-class entrepreneur in the B market and they can still build a compelling company, but the opposite is not true. A B team rarely builds a great company. We spend a lot of time thinking about teams; we actually have a score card with six to seven attributes that we rank our teams against.

How engaged do you get? It sounds like you're working quite a bit with the right executives on these things.

When you're on the board, you're very, very active. We take that honor as a board member very seriously. You're recruiting, you're focused on all of those company building activities. I don't know what the number is, but my guess is when a company raises capital, 70% or more of that round goes to new salaries so the initial task is recruiting.

I think angels are really effective at recruiting. My observation is they're much more effective with recruiting because they're in the middle of so many companies; if they're really active angels.

Do you have a preference for who you invest with?

Angels with great industry networks, relevant operating experience, a great sense of product development, or a good sense for the voice of the customer.

THE ALTERNATIVE INVESTORS

IMPACTFUL, NOT PHILANTHROPIC WITH DAVID BANGS

"You cannot tailor-make the situations in life but you can tailor-make the attitudes to fit those situations. "

—ZIG ZIGLAR

"Revenue redemption options actually lead to a higher level of engagement, because each investor has to decide annually whether to accept the redemption option or leave all their shares in the pool. "

—DAVID BANGS

I MET DAVID through the Seattle Angel Conference. David was one of the most interesting people I met through the conference, an incredibly bright person who's passionate about improving the world. David is a co-founder of the Seattle Impact Investor Group and a member of the board of the Element 8 angel group in Seattle. David extends a passion for promoting a resource-efficient world through investment and business development throughout everything he does.

I was lucky to know how great of an investor David really is so that I could include him in the interviews. Too often the concept of impact investing is pushed into the philanthropy corner, and I see many of the efforts that David Bangs is working on to pull impact investing out of that corner and place it right in the middle of the room alongside all the other highly profitable investments. David's goal is to turn a great investing profit while investing in companies that are innovating and improving the world. It isn't hard to look around and find companies and products that are using our natural resources more efficiently. David looks for the ones that are economically sustainable and have high growth optionality.

Here in Seattle there are a lot of angel investors thinking about how their investing activity can be directed at high-growth private companies who are also making our natural resources more efficient to use. I personally haven't made that a focus of mine, and after finishing the interview with David I began to think more seriously about how our everyday investment and consumption decisions can have a drastic impact on the world.

How did you start as an angel?

It is hard to say when you start being an angel investor. I made my first startup investment 15 years ago. It was in a relative's company that has always had revenue but still hasn't exited.

After leaving Microsoft, I became a frequent volunteer for environmental causes. But supporting nonprofits can only accomplish so much. Since it will require a lot of innovation to solve tough problems like climate change, I wanted to help as many businesses as possible get established.

I started calling myself an angel investor in 2007 when I joined Northwest Energy Angels and invested in a few clean-tech venture capital funds. Now I had a network of smart peers, deal flow, and even places to send companies raising more money than angels can raise.

You call yourself an "impact investor." What does that mean to you?

An angel investor is someone who allocates part of their money to investing in early-stage startup businesses. Every angel investor wants to make money, but some of them also want to make a difference. That difference is the impact. The kind of impact people want to make is very personal. For me, it is supporting innovative technology and business models that will lead to long-term sustainability.

I started calling myself an impact investor when I decided to invest all of my assets with the goal of making a difference. This has led to investments such as green building lending funds, commercial real estate, and even farmland. I'm still working on it, because finding opportunities with great impact stories and great financial returns takes time.

This quest led me to co-found the Seattle Impact Investor Group, which currently involves 15 like-minded individuals working together to figure out how each family can maximize both impact and returns. As we grow the group, we will grow the impact.

What structure do you prefer to invest with?

Traditional angel investing only pays off when companies have exits. This is fine if you're willing to make exit strategy your top consideration. But when you're trying to create impact, you may not want to pressure companies to sell out to whatever big-pocket buyer happens to come along. And admittedly, not all the companies that interest me have great exit prospects.

My personal breakthrough came when I learned about a new incubator in Seattle, founded by Luni Libes, called Fledge. Like most incubators, Fledge takes an equity stake in each company going through the program. However, it is unique in requiring each company to agree to repurchase half those shares back, over time, at a pre-agreed price out of a pre-agreed percentage of revenue. As long as the "fledglings" earn revenue, Fledge can make money and continue operating. This gives Fledge the unique ability to incubate viable companies that are built for impact rather than just those built for a quick exit.

My insight was that individual angels could scale this approach. Would companies make a redemption feature available to whole groups of angel investors?

Yes, it turns out. Many companies with predictable margins are willing to allocate a small percentage of revenue to repurchase shares as long as that percentage is small compared to their margins. A company with 40% margins may very well be willing to allocate 5% of revenue to repurchase shares, leaving an effective margin of

35%. This arrangement is beneficial to founders because repurchasing shares leaves them with more ownership and a bigger eventual exit. It is beneficial to impact investors because they can reinvest returned capital early to create more impact.

Angels aren't commonly doing partially structured exits. Are you changing that?

So far, Seattle Impact members have invested with me in four companies that agreed to offer revenue-based redemption options to angel investors: Moving Worlds, Earth Equity Farms, Community Sourced Capital, and Adaptive Symbiotic Technology. The SVP Fast Pitch Investor group and members of Element 8 have also invested and intend to participate in redemption.

This was made possible by some hard work and good help. I personally created some tools and delivered training to groups like Element 8 and the Seattle Angel Conference. Seattle attorneys like Carter Mackley and Joe Wallin have been invaluable in refining and analyzing terms and breaking through possible legal and tax barriers.

At this point, with tools and legal documents available, angel groups aware and Fledge continuing to use this structure with all participating companies, I think revenue-based redemption options will continue to increase in popularity.

How do entrepreneurs react to revenue redemption structures?

They all react differently. When I put the idea in front of an entrepreneur and they get it, it is a magical thing. It helps to understand that this person is a good listener who's willing to grapple with new and potentially confusing ideas.

I try to make it easy by providing a framework. One step is to ask, "Can you update your financials to see how your business could afford redemption payments and how the redemption would take?" If they send that back the next day, I know they really understand their business. If the entrepreneur says, "I couldn't possibly pay this, I need all the money to grow the business," that's also great, as long as they can defend that statement using the spreadsheet and business plan.

Above all, I want to make sure that the entrepreneur loves the approach and understands how it could benefit all parties mutually. If not, then this isn't the right structure.

Are the companies you invest in only interesting because of the revenue redemption?

No, they are all great companies with great stories. And they have all passed rigorous diligence. But I am still waiting for exits from about 20 companies that I invested in using standard terms. These companies all have revenues, but I don't receive any of it. I just don't want to invest any more money like that until the exits start flowing.

One of my investments, Adaptive Symbiotic Technologies, is particularly exciting. The founders are PhD scientists who did about $12 million worth of research on government grants before they started the company.

They were trying to figure out why plants grow in extreme environments when they're not adapted to those environments. There are tons of plants in the desert that they couldn't figure out why they were growing there. They expected to find some sort of genetic adaptation, but instead found there were symbiotic organisms present that gave the plants super powers. If the right fungus is present at germination, almost any plant can enter modes to better deal with stresses such as low water, extreme temperature, or even salty soil. Amazingly, this seems to be achieved by awakening the plant's own genetically coded ability to survive in such environments. Trials have shown that commercial corn yield can be increased up to 80% under drought conditions just by coating the seeds with AST's BioEnsure product.

Given the benefits, it is easy to guess which large companies might want to acquire AST. It is also easy to understand how the world might be better off if this technology is not controlled by a single large seed company. The founders of AST want their product to be available to as many seed distributors and farmers as possible. They want it available to local and organic farmers, as well as the big guys.

Most potential AST investors thought primarily about the potential for a quick exit. In contrast, The Seattle Impact Investor group thought about how we could spare the company from the need for a quick exit. The company committed to repurchase shares from investors at a generous multiple out of a generous percentage of revenue in order to maintain its independence and ensure the company could realize its mission. So far, the company has raised $3 million from investors, with all of the shares being redeemable under these terms.

How do you engage with companies after you invest?

I read all the reports they send and often take opportunities to do site visits and coffee with the entrepreneurs. We also have a member of our group join the board or serve as a board observer. We help find follow-on funding and make introductions to people who present new opportunities.

Revenue redemption options actually lead to a higher level of engagement, because each investor has to decide annually whether to accept the redemption option or leave all their shares in the pool. This naturally leads to reading the investment reports more carefully, attending more site visits and even making more introductions.

Simply put, having to make a decision every year leads to higher engagement. Since I'm not an expert in any of the industries I invest in, I usually recommend a different investor to represent our group on the board.

* * *

This concept of revenue or profit redemption is incredibly fascinating and one that we don't talk about much. Some investors talk about never doing follow-on rounds and working out deals to sell their angel shares to the Series A investors, but even that's generally unaccepted as a norm here in the US. The goal of both of these is to make angel investing something that has a more predictable or smooth return. David talks about doing this so that he can invest in more companies on a faster pace so that he can have a larger impact on the world. Any wealth manager or individual who understands risk, return, and profile management can get behind the concept for another reason. If you can reduce the risk on the asset class that can still have this size of return, the percentage allocation of the portfolio can also go up, and so can the overall portfolio returns as a result.

Investors who are just meeting the bar to be accredited should pay special attention to this concept because the reason most aren't investing is because the risk is too daunting, even though the return sounds great. If it comes down to investing 5% of your portfolio instead of 0% of your portfolio, that can turn out to be a meaningful thing for your overall wealth. Even if the returns on that 5% are going to be lower than the typical angel.

NICHES ARE PRODUCTIVE WITH KIRK COBURN

"Your team matters more than the big idea that you have."

—EUGENE KLEINER

"…there are four categories we look for: market, team, business model, alignment."

—KIRK COBURN

I WAS REALLY LUCKY to score an interview with Kirk. I reached out to him as one of the top investors in Houston and the founder of one of the top accelerator programs in the country. I was interested in learning what he was doing with these early-stage energy investments that were gaining so much attention. I reached out through a mutual connection and was thrilled to dig a little deeper on how Kirk approaches angel investing and building a startup ecosystem.

Let's start with how you got started angel investing.

I think it's from the success of my startups. It started out as success as an entrepreneur, and realizing that I wanted to put money to work, not in the stock market, but in things that I control, or at least have more visibility into. That was the genesis. You can't make great investment decisions when there's imperfect information, and the only way to truly get better returns than what the market produces is having more information than someone else, and you can do that in things that you have more control of.

How long ago did you start?

My first investment was six years ago, so I'm still relatively new to the game. Now I'm currently at 45 companies today. I'm relatively new at it and I jumped straight into doing it.

Have you seen any exits of any kind?

I've had two exits and I have a few that are duds. I have another one that I'll see what happens. It's one of my oldest investments, and it's still in nowhere-land. Company's still around, and they're trying to figure out if they need to pivot, how to pivot, and what to do.

How long did it take for you to see the two positive exits?

One exit came within a year, so that was a great deal, and then the second exit came after three years. I don't expect exits to come that quickly.

Were the duds the same length of time?

The two duds were very quick. Part of it is I run an accelerator, and I'm also the largest investor in that, so we try to kill our companies quickly if they're not going to make it.

Are you only investing in companies that come through the accelerator?

No, not at all. My personal investment philosophy is I'm hedged. I don't speak about my real estate holdings, which is probably the majority of what I own. I own a lot of real estate, but in terms of just angel investments, 75% of my investments are energy related. The rest is based on stuff I'm interested in.

How do you go about finding the companies?

That's actually why I created SURGE in the first place. We're one of the top 10 accelerators now. Originally, I created it as a way for me to build a strategic way to find good deal flow. My grandfather ran the west Texas oil field in World War II; my father sold the company to the Carlisle Group—that was an IT company whose customers included energy, and so I had a lot of understanding of the industry. After a lot of research, I came to the conclusion that the market was right and this was the time to jump in and invest in early-stage companies in this space.

Are you working a lot with other angel groups, or mostly independent of those?

In our accelerator fund, we have investors that include institutional investors, guys like Mercury Fund, which is a VC based in Houston. We have some of the largest energy companies in the world that are investors. Then we have angels who are investors; we deal with the Houston Angel Network, the Central Texas Angel Network, and other angel groups in Texas. There are some groups outside like Queen Energy Venture Group, which is an angel group based in Boston. They don't all invest in our fund, but they do invest in our companies.

Are there terms that you care about or prefer to have?

We're in Houston and so there are a couple big trends that are unique in some ways to us. Our valuations are typically lower than you'll see on the East Coast or the West Coast. We focus on the other terms as well as how much control we actually walk away with. We tend to make decisions that are founder friendly.

That is true for me personally and for the SURGE accelerator. Anything we do through SURGE has people behind us who are going to come in and ask for the same terms, so we rarely take any board seats or things like that.

There are two terms that we care a lot about. One is the right of first refusal. I want to have the ability to reinvest my current amount into the next round. Two is information rights.

Do you always invest on the next rounds?

Almost every time, when companies are doing well. I'll always keep at least my percentage. Most of the time, I'm always going into the next round. Companies that aren't doing well, I won't go in. Companies that I think aren't actually hitting milestones, I'll just wait it out. I'm relatively a data-driven investor.

What are the data points that you're looking for?

We have milestones—they need to hit the milestones. They are almost always financial related and customer related. Since we're energy tech, our deals take longer. While we have mostly software companies in our portfolios, we're still penetrating into an enterprise industry. What I look for from our milestones is which customers we are gaining traction from. Our program focuses on leading pilots, so when do those pilots convert to the customer, and who are the referenceable customers?

What data are you looking for when you're first making an investment?

Really, there are four categories we look for: market, team, business model, alignment.

Market, do they have a value proposition? How big is the market? Are they solving a problem that the customer cares about?

Team is straightforward but harder to describe. Is there a good team there?

The business model is about scale. Is this a company that over time can scale and make money? What will the company need to scale in terms of capital and equipment? What are the equipment needs going to be for higher revenue sizes of the company? You can run an analysis, if you look at different industries, there are different profit margins made at different levels by the industry.

A good example is an investment I have in a supply chain company, not energy related. They earn between $50 million and $75 million in revenue, which is low for the industry. As a supply chain company, you have to choose whether to stay under $50 million, because the amount of investments you need to make the scale are expensive. You either have to scale and become a more than $100 million company to really make money there, or stay as a small niche player. Most investors don't understand that concept. Why would we look at scale? Because it's important. It is important to know when and where they are going to hit the hiccup, and how much is that going to cost them? First it comes in capital equipment, then in people, then sales and marketing.

The other component of the business model and scaling is capital. We really take a look at the capital efficiency of the business. We look at those two primarily. That's the business model. What are they going to need as a business model to make money here? We're dealing with a lot of new companies that are new technologies trying to do something that's unique, and we have to look at business models to see if it makes sense.

Finally, alignment is mostly around, "Can I actually help the company?" I rarely invest in things where I can't help. I look at money as being relatively stupid. If you have a good company, everyone wants to put money in. Raising money is not as hard as people tend to make it. It tends to be bad ideas or bad teams that have a hard time raising money, but if you have a good team, you're going to be fine. The question is, who should you take that money from? That's something that I tend to look at. "Hey, can I help this company? Do I have relationships that they could benefit from to help?"

You were saying a "good team," but you didn't really go into that. What are the metrics there that you're looking for?

The team is by far the most important decision here. We look for teams that are coachable. We look for teams where we can validate their background. We look for teams that get what it takes to build a company, who wants it, and they have the capacity to do it. Do they get it? That just doesn't apply to the number one CEO, but to the team itself. Do they get it? Did they want it? Are they hungry? Are they willing to do what it takes? One of the big metrics I look for is skin in the game. How much personal money do they have in the business? If they don't have a whole lot, I'm not as excited about the company.

I've had great ideas, good companies where the founders walked away because things got hard. They didn't have enough money in it to matter, so I look at money and the skin in the game as one of our core values at SURGE.

You have to be an expert in your field. I invest in really complicated, really science-heavy or quant-heavy ideas so the teams are mainly technical, or all technical.

They have to get it. They have to be really smart. They have to want it, and want it meaning they have skin in the game. I think that they're actually going to make it through hard times, and they have to have the capacity to do it, so they're willing to move to the right city to make it happen, or willing to work late hours. They have the capacity, both intellectual horsepower as well as desire to pull it off.

Once you make the investment, what kinds of things are you doing to stay engaged with the companies?

I'm the most hands-off investor of all time. I tell them, "Once I write a check, don't call me unless you need access to a customer, I can help you solve a problem, or you need more money." I have information rights, so we have asked them to give us updates, but that's for us to just continue to track data, but I don't really get involved in my companies very much.

How much time would you say you spend on the companies after you've invested?

I'll do 30 minutes every other week. An hour a month. It depends on what it is, usually it is just connections, and I'm the uber-connector in energy. I know everybody. We literally can touch just about anybody in the industry.

Can you talk a little more about one of the companies you saw an exit on?

Sure, I knew the founder for five years. Great idea, needed money, and it wasn't through any organized angel group, it was more of a personal relationship. I really liked his background and I was one of the first to write a check. I stayed relatively hands off and connected him to a lot of people, which was very helpful. Vector, probably one of their most referenceable companies, came from me, in terms of one of their big customers, and then they raised private equity money and recapped the company, bought my equity out.

Sounds like already knowing and trusting them made it a lot easier?

That's right, and that something I didn't consider for one of the exit opportunities was private equity recaps, which was cool.

Can you talk more about one of the duds you had?

I think it comes down to just the team. Companies always fail and usually fail from within. They don't fail because of external forces, it's usually a team dynamic issue. Both of my duds, I didn't do a strong-enough job of doing due diligence on the team. Sometimes I invest in teams that are unproven, or they've never worked together, and I think that's been the biggest learning. The odds are hard and that's why I've added skin in the game as a top metric. If someone doesn't have money in, I really just get sketchy about investing.

What three things should angel investors do to be successful?

There is a great venture capitalist named Kevin Lalande. He runs Sante Ventures in Austin. His advice to me was to become an expert in something and don't deviate. We've learned from this at SURGE, when we've seen 20 deals exactly like this one and this one is far superior to the other 19 we have an investable edge with. When I know the customers they're trying to work with and I know the actual people making the buying decision at those customers, that's when I feel like, "Man, I've got a superior understanding of whether this is a good company or not."

The next thing is to invest in people you're willing to lose your money with and ask yourself, "If I lose all my money, would I reinvest in this guy and these people?"

I think the final one is, can you add value to the company?

Are there ways that are more preferential to add value?

No, everyone brings something different to the table. There are all kinds of value-add investors. There's one I know in Houston who's an expert in financing. He studies what other angel groups do, and angel investors do, and he helps the entrepreneur understand how to raise the funding. I think that's interesting and valuable. What I can do is connect you with a customer, to help grow your top line. That's my sweet spot, it's what I'm good at.

What relationships do you think are the most important for an angel investor to have?

I think it's going to be different based on who it is. For me, I'm about entrepreneurs first. I put entrepreneurs ahead of everyone else. I was an entrepreneur and I think that really matters. In energy, the money that funnels to most early-stage companies is from private equity. Those guys are generally not entrepreneurs themselves, and so they have a hard time approaching entrepreneurs. They would rather get rid of an entrepreneur, because they don't know how to tell them that they're the wrong guy or are hiring a bunch of bozos, but I can. One of the things I've been able to do is just talk to them and give them real feedback.

You need to build a team. Where are you going to find those people? You need customers. Where are you going to get them? You need more money. Who are good sources for that money? We have to know people with all those relationships. All of them are important.

How do you think angels should go about making some of those connections if they don't already have them?

Get involved. Angels in Houston with energy interests usually get involved with us, and we hold a lot of events for them to connect with others. We have a big demo day next week, and our demo day is unlike others. We don't have just investors. We have 200 investors. Andreessen Horowitz will be there because they are starting to look at the space. We have 600 people attending, 200 of those are executives from most of the large energy companies and decision makers, so that's a great place to meet. But we have 200 investors showing up too.

That's what I recommend. It's an ecosystem you're trying to build. I think in other cities, you should find accelerators or incubators and get involved with what's happening. I think that's a good way to get to be known and to show off the skills you can bring to the table.

Do you have any last thoughts that you think would be valuable for newer early-stage investors?

Don't forget the J-curve. When you start investing, don't spend all your money in the beginning. Failed companies are going to be first and your winners are going to be later, so just surviving is important. Successes come in five to seven years or longer. Failures come in the first three years.

Don't spend more than 10% of your net worth on risky investments. I tend to tell a lot of investors, "Look, investing's not for everyone, and if you can't go in expecting to lose this money, then you have the wrong perspective." Don't look at an entrepreneur as the guy who lost your net worth because if that's what you're betting on, you're a fool. I'm not sure the stock market has turned out any better, but the point is, this is more of a passion and a calling than it is a diversification strategy. If you're smart and you have expertise, I think you can actually leverage that into making good returns.

* * *

Kirk's investing style isn't too terribly different than the style of any other early-stage investor who's focused on investing in B2B companies. Investing in areas where he can add real value and focusing a lot on the development of customer connections is the same approach I use looking at enterprise IT software. I've never invested in any energy startups and probably never will, but the approach and rigor that Kirk builds into his process is something that resonated for me.

COPY WHAT WORKS WITH NICHOLAS WYMAN

"All great achievements require time."

—MAYA ANGELOU

"Somebody who's interested in angel investing as an ongoing activity should understand that it is an ongoing activity and it's not investing in one company."

—NICHOLAS WYMAN

SHORTLY AFTER MEETING NICHOLAS, I was hooked on his enthusiasm. He is continuously setting new goals for himself and achieving those goals. One of the goals he set for himself, after a successful career in real estate in New York, was to become a successful early-stage investor. Some may think that an MBA is the furthest thing from necessary to understand early-stage finance and how to evaluate the best companies in existence, but when Nicholas tells his story, anyone thinking about getting into early-stage investing would easily consider moving to Boulder, getting into the MBA program, and doing just about everything else that Nicholas did to get started.

His education wasn't just an MBA; he spent his summers as an associate with Techstars and immediately began investing in companies coming through the accelerator. I've even interviewed some of the founders of the companies he invested in and I get what he saw in guys like Bart Lorang, whose profile is online. Nicholas tells it much better than I can, though, and he clearly learned enough during that time working with Techstars and investing to start working at Foundry Group and then on to lead the Galvanize Fund.

Out of all the investors in the book, Nicholas has been investing for the least amount of time. I've included his profile, despite having a huge stack of investors with a decade more experience, for one reason. His enthusiasm and goal-oriented approach to becoming an angel is something that every angel can learn from. Nicholas continuously surrounds himself with brilliant investors as role models and learns what makes those role models tick, not too different than what any reader can do by starting with the profiles in this book and online. Nicholas follows that up with setting goals for himself and practicing what he learns, internalizing the lessons, and making it second nature. I hope that you can be inspired and motivated to do the same in your own angel investing journey.

How did you get started with early-stage investing?

My first career was in real estate. My father was a single-family home developer in Westchester, New York, which is where I'm from. I moved out to Boulder for my undergraduate degree and in the summer of my freshman year in college I got my real estate broker's license and began selling out-of-state students and their friends on the virtues of buying a house as opposed to paying their landlords. They got to be a kind of slumlord in the college market, collect rent, build equity, and learn about real estate while going to college.

Then I moved to New York after college and worked in large-scale commercial construction management, for a company called Cauldwell Wingate in New York. I was doing projects for them like the New York Public Library and the Thurgood Marshall US Courthouse in downtown Manhattan. While I really loved a physical manifestation of my everyday work, I was right out of college and was really into technology, mostly in the consumer space. My whole life was working in an age-old industry in a hundred-year-old company and didn't really feel like there was enough information and interest around what I was doing. The people I went to work with every day were fantastic, but they weren't really excited and passionate about what they were doing. They were just going through the motions and working really hard but not really thrilled about being in the office every day. I kind of had this come-to-Jesus moment when I decided this wasn't what I was interested in doing for the rest of my life and decided to leave and apply my project management skill set that I had been building to help a bunch of my friends in New York who were building early-stage technology companies and help them wrap some method around the madness that was their product vision, or pinpoint the solution they were trying to bring to market. While a lot of the thought process was very similar, I found out very quickly that the inputs were different and there was a lot I needed to learn and understand to better support these companies.

I came to a few realizations very quickly. The first and probably most important was that these were the people I wanted to work with in my career. They were incredibly passionate about what they were doing. They went to sleep thinking about their company and their business and they woke up early thinking about it. They'd work on it all day, they were enthusiastic. While it was a roller coaster, they were doing what they wanted to do. My goal was to figure out how I could best support them. The second thing I realized was, while a lot of the thought process was the same, I didn't necessarily understand how to translate building a building into building a company, and the foundation of a startup is a whole lot less concrete than the foundation of a building.

There are a lot of different things happening—customer dynamics, raising capital, and figuring out how to effectively deploy it to make sure that you've got the best chance of success. They couldn't really pay themselves or their employees, let alone pay me to be a consultant. So it was the culmination of all those things that helped me fall into venture capital as what I wanted to do. It helped me support the people, products, and markets that I believed in get access to the resources that they need, financial and otherwise.

It wasn't me looking at venture capital as the riskiest asset class possible. It was that my appetite for risk wasn't quite the same as the folks building these companies. I loved what they were doing. I wanted to support them and my passion wasn't one of these products; it was helping them get a leg up and building their company. I decided upgrading my skill sets with an MBA was a good way for me to learn about what I wanted to be doing. Having done college in Colorado and then living in New York reading about what was going on at Techstars, I decided that Colorado was where I wanted to be in five years and I didn't need to wait five years to get there.

I elected to apply to the MBA program here and in that application process, I wrote an essay about wanting to work for Techstars and how it was really the re-creation of what I thought was fascinating about building early-stage businesses. I was fortunate to realize my goal and not only get into business school but parlaying my first year to get an associate role at Techstars that summer between my first and second years. That experience blew my mind, watching all these companies go through this process and meet with all these incredibly talented and giving mentors who had seen some success in whatever their business was and we were meeting with these companies to help them understand their business and direct how they should think about the foundation of their startup.

Through that experience, I interacted with a bunch of angel investors and a bunch of companies. I knew what I wanted to do, had a modest amount of money, and was able to take my own leap of faith. Knowing that I didn’t want to be in venture, that I wanted to be an angel investor, and coming to the realization that I was never going to have the opportunity to live with 12 companies for three months and watch them execute in that way, but even if I didn't know what I was doing, if there ever was a time to start placing bets and investing in early-stage companies, it was then. So I got some skin in the game and started learning by doing.

I invested in two companies out of that Techstars cohort. The first was Full Contact. Full Contact's CEO, Bart Lorang, and I sat down. He was probably the front-runner in that Techstars class, if you could call him that. There was a really strong class overall, but Bart had raised money coming into Techstars and had a number of successful wins, not necessarily home runs but meaningful wins, under his belt. I watched him day in and day out and his team execute all of the goals that they set for themselves, really ambitious goals, and then deliver; he had effectively an oversubscribed round.

To me this was a totally new concept - you had to pitch your money to the company and explain why they should take your capital over somebody else's. I was incredibly naïve at this point, but I sat down with Bart after the whole program and it took me a while to realize that I was going to invest in a few companies. I had never told anybody I was going to do this. But I sat down with him and knew that he was oversubscribed and told him, "This is what I want to do as my career. This is what I've gone back to school for. This is why I came to Techstars. I know your round is oversubscribed and that my experience and what I've done doesn't necessarily warrant you taking my $25,000 investment over somebody else's, but this is what I want to do with my future and I want you to be my first investment. As much as this is me investing with you with my money, it's also you investing in me, in what I want to do moving forward."

It was a really fun conversation over beers in his backyard. He understood where I was coming from, what I wanted to do, and was very supportive. He was kind enough to take my money. That was kind of my foray into angel investing. One other thing about Full Contact that's important is, I was passionate about the problem they were trying to solve and I had tried a number of different services that flirted with it over time and knew this had massive potential to touch everybody in the world in some way, so I was really interested in that.

The other company I invested in, Mocavo, was trying to be the open version of what Ancestry.com is around genealogical information and I was interested in solving this problem for myself.

I made those two investments and then went back to school and studied venture capital. Took a class taught by Jason Mendelson. Jason is one of the partners at Foundry Group. I had this ridiculous idea that I wanted to be in venture and to live in Boulder, a pretty limiting option set, especially given that the only name-brand venture group was pretty vocal about never hiring anybody. I listened to David Cohen, Jason Mendelson, Brad, Ryan, and Seth at Foundry talk about this idea of give before you get.

That's important in the ecosystem and community, so I worked hard to help support the community by selling events and connecting people. I worked to understand the needs of the companies in the ecosystem and what I could do to drive value, not just for the companies but for the individuals who work in the ecosystem. I threw all my efforts there in between taking different classes and competing in a venture capital investor competition, which is a global competition of business schools that have effectively reversed the business plan competition where, instead of business school students coming up with a business plan and have investors come in and vet and select the best business plan, it's a team of B-school students who interview and go to a number of real entrepreneurs who are in that community trying to raise capital to gain the best out of the set of five and then negotiating investment terms with that company in front of a panel of investors.

That was a fantastic experience. Probably that and Techstars were the highlight of the MBA program for me. We were lucky and worked hard enough to win the international competition. Through all those activities, my partner Dane and I were able to secure a position working at Foundry, where I spent about two years helping them and learning from the inside what makes them so special. When I think about venture capital, growing up in the school of Foundry, seeing how they align themselves with entrepreneurs, the way they structure their investments, the way they have conversations, and the way they interact with the community and companies was a wonderful and humbling experience. I couldn't think of a better way to get a frame of reference in terms of what I would like to emulate in the industry moving forward.

I realized that it is more fun and interesting to talk about investing with other people who're like-minded, have a similar approach, have similar motivations, and objectives. So I and four colleagues I met through Foundry and Techstars teamed up to put together an investment entity that would effectively diversify our investments, diversify our deal flow, and cut checks for what we like in industries, markets, competition. The entity writes the same-size checks that we were all writing individually so we could get into more companies without actually having to ask these companies to take smaller amounts and get their cap table dirty.

We've been doing that for almost a year now and we're approaching 20 investments. It's been really fun because we've played with the model and seen a lot of innovation in the angel investing and venture investing landscape since starting. I don't know that I can say we were one of the first, but we were certainly very early on in terms of deploying our funds on AngelList. Instead of just taking our $500,000 fund and investing it in $25,000 chunks in a number of companies, we also took a portion of our portfolio and decided to allocate that to investing directly in companies on AngelList.

We first started making thousand-dollar investments and then we realized that $250 investments from each of us didn't quite carry enough weight, so we kicked that up to $4,000 investments on AngelList so we could again increase what we had exposure to in our investing activities. We could invest in more companies, learn more from our network, and get access to deals that were beyond our reach, despite the fact that I live in Boulder and Benny lives in San Francisco and Brett lives in New York. We started doing that and shortly after that, AngelList opened their syndicates, so we started to incorporate investing in some syndicates on AngelList through that entity.

We've been doing that since about August. I left Foundry Group in January 2014 and it was bittersweet because I felt like I could have spent five lifetimes there and continued to learn. Given the way they had envisioned Foundry Group, and the way it was structured, it was always meant to be those four guys and never really conceived as a legacy company. So I had the opportunity to join my current company, Galvanize, and help start their new venture fund. I left Foundry in January and started here in February and it's been exciting.

For the first time I've started to realize what was my goal back in 2011 as an associate at Techstars, investing not only my money, but other people's money in these early-stage companies with entrepreneurs I believe in and are building meaningful and impactful companies. That's my life in a nutshell.

Do you invest in the same type of companies between your personal account and the Galvanize account?

The Galvanize entity is newer than my own, but we have a number of overlapping investments, a small number because we've only made four out of the Galvanize fund. It will be five after the meeting I just had before this one. Yes, I think my angel investing activities are very complementary to what I'm doing at Galvanize right now. The reason that I'm able to do this for now, and probably not forever, is that they brought me on as a partner. They already had the LP documents and already raised the capital without me on the scene.

I am not beholden to the traditional venture partner requirement to not invest alongside the fund as I was not in that initial agreement. Right now I think it's open and clear about what I invest in. Everything I invest in I bring to Galvanize and there's not really an element of cherry picking.

Do you find companies for your personal investments and the Galvanize investments in different ways?

No. Kind of everything I do is trying to generate deal flow for both, and since I invest in very similar types of companies, it's very much the same process. I think about them. I parse them in different ways and this is kind of an interesting dynamic that's playing out, investing personally and that's different than investing other people's money. Is there a degree of risk I'm okay taking by myself that I might not necessarily feel comfortable doing on behalf of others and what's right, I guess, both for myself and for the fund.

The return expectations and the responsibility that I have to the LPs and the motivations behind investing are different personally. They are very similar in terms of when I think about companies, but the motivations and expectations aren't in conflict - but certainly I'm going to try and figure out what the difference is, if there's one.

How do you go about finding companies to invest in?

I'm fortunate to have entered this ecosystem by working in Techstars, which is probably one of the best deal flow engines in the market right now. The exposure I got through that entity, interacting with the companies, interacting with the mentors and investors, has been incredibly powerful. Additionally, Boulder has a high-density entrepreneurial ecosystem, which is small enough that if you put yourself out there and make yourself accessible to meet with companies and individuals not just to invest, but to support them in any way that you can, you start to build a brand.

Providing them with candid feedback and information, with the caveat that your insight is only a data point that they have to incorporate into their decision-making schematic, was something I learned in Techstars and thought was fascinating, this concept of mentor whiplash. All these intelligent people have varying experience and expertise and perspectives and their take on what a company is doing and should be doing despite being very credible and valuable sources of information can be vastly different.

I'm giving my advice openly and candidly, but making sure that the entrepreneur understands that's just my opinion and they have to incorporate that into the collection of other data points and opinions that they've been able to amass. Through Techstars, through partnering with other folks who're very active, with another active entrepreneurial market or entrepreneurs themselves, has been a fun way to expand both my deal flow and then my review process. Now I'm excited about what we're doing at Galvanize as it relates to generating a fascinating proprietary entrepreneurial network and deal flow.

During the due diligence process, what are you looking for?

I'm early on in this and a big part of what I'm hoping to do is learn as much about markets and companies as I can. Getting an education through investing is a big part of what I do at this point in my career. While I don't have too much deep expertise, I'm starting to generate a lot more around technology companies. The basis has to be one of a real connection and belief in the CEO and the founding team. Then resonating with the problem that they're trying to solve, believing that there's a sufficiently interesting market for them to go after and capture, and correct marketing expertise for them to be successful.

Another element I look for is the ability to execute and a track record of past successes and relevant experience in an industry or a startup or early-stage company. Another thing I'd like to do at this stage in my angel investing and investing in general, which probably hearkens back to my appetite for risk and appetite for learning while investing in these companies, is also investing alongside funds and/or active angels whom I respect and want to learn from as well.

Is that mostly through syndicates or are you investing in other funds as well?

I'm an LP in two other venture funds and also just starting to get a sense of the landscape and who the active angel investors are in my sphere and sharing deals with them and vice versa. It makes me, at this stage in my investing career, more comfortable if I can find somebody else with an expertise in a different area and get them on board with an investment that I think is a good one, but I don't necessarily have their experience in a relevant component to that company.

Do you end up learning a lot from being an LP?

I wanted to be a VC, so I learned how they think about markets. How they report to their LPs. How they all have their own take on deal flow, diligence, and deal sharing. Just by watching which companies they invest in or try to. Calling them up and having a conversation about the companies they are investing in or discussions about potential companies and founders.

Even just reading about and trying to understand the investments of funds that you respect is easier once you have the framework of being an LP. If you're not an LP, you can still learn a lot from watching and reading. It just takes a little more creativity and imagination when you're observing things from the outside.

When you invest directly, do you have a preferred structure and terms?

I prefer equity whenever possible. I like to know what small percentage of company, my small check, is used for. I learned this through having worked with and observed hundreds of companies going through this to understand the virtues of convertible debt instruments and helping facilitate the execution of a round for them. Although I prefer equity, I understand and am comfortable with convertible debt.

How do you balance your preferences with the AngelList structure?

Given the size of the checks that I write and that I come in evaluating terms, I'm not negotiating them. In that respect, AngelList is similar to what I do anyway, and AngelList has been a really interesting instrument to understand how terms, even just on AngelList, differ by market and by location and what's hot and who the investors are.

On AngelList, even more so than personally when I have a relationship with the entrepreneur, I look for an adult, hopefully an institutional investor, whom I know will be a good steward of the investment.

How many investments have you done on AngelList?

I think it's probably around 25.

How do you analyze deals on AngelList?

I follow a bunch of people I respect and admire, both investors and entrepreneurs. I spend time there looking at what they are watching. One of the reasons I found myself in this industry was I was always looking at the stuff anyway and I find it fascinating, so I get some geeky pleasure out of reading about these companies and the problems they're trying to solve and the approach to the technology and the team they put together to do it.

If something interests me and I see a lot of companies I think have a good eye for that kind of baseline, interesting checkmarks that make it a potentially good investment, and if you compare that with a top-tier partner at a top-tier firm, it helps me get comfortable or as comfortable as one can be investing in a company that they've never met.

Do you talk to them on the phone or—?

It depends. Sometimes we'll just make small investments and not talk to them, and we'll do that through AngelList, but other times we use AngelList to identify deals that we will then reach out to and contact and discuss direct investment.

What do you look for in those deal leads?

A track record of success, thought leadership around venture in general and around industries. Often, some of the lead investors are more super angels than venture capitalists. There are plenty of lead investors who are institutional firms on AngelList. It has to do with their performance historically and their reputation in the industry.

For what reasons do you invest more?

Part of it's allocation. Part of it's interest. A lot of these deals on AngelList are, for better or worse, oversubscribed on the syndicate. So sometimes you can only get a certain allocation and sometimes you have to invest above a certain threshold in order to get an allocation. It's an art, not a science, and it comes down to how passionate I am about the space, company, and lead investor. You put all that in the pot and mix it together and figure out if you want to invest and then you figure out what you need to invest to get in and then you figure out how much you want to invest and the appropriate stake given your level of interest and excitement.

How is your engagement with those companies post-investment?

Within our group, each of us will take leads on different investments. A lot like a venture fund where each partner has deep engagement with the companies on behalf of the company. Investing directly via AngelList is different, but we share investor updates that are sent out and the investor updates are largely dependent on how that company out there communicates with direct investors. Then there's this other subset of problems around how they deal with their AngelList investors. I'm not on the board of any of these companies and it's not my job to make their job harder by asking for additional information, but I review every update to the bottom and I love it when companies have a section that says where they need help.

When I get to that section and if there's a place where I can be of service, or somebody else whom I know might be able to help, then I do my best to facilitate something for them.

Do you find entrepreneur behavior drastically different on AngelList or in person?

Not vastly different. The companies where I invested in person, there's a variety of behaviors that entrepreneurs have with how they engage with their investors. Some are incredibly open and transparent and always asking for help and some don't tell you anything except when they need money. A lot of it is contingent on them, especially given that it's not my role. I try to be an active and supportive investor, but I'm not, as of yet, a board member.

What is the top thing new angel investors should avoid?

One thing an early investor should not do is invest in a vacuum, whether that vacuum is not understanding the larger ecosystem, terms, competitive landscape, and the market or simply not understanding the dynamics of angel investing. Somebody who's interested in angel investing as an ongoing activity should understand that it is an ongoing activity and it's not investing in one company.

What is the top thing new angel investors should do to be successful?

One thing that they should do is engage with and support the entrepreneur as much as they can. You want to invest in people you want to have a beer with to celebrate the good times and commiserate with during the bad ones.

* * *

As you can see, in a short period of time, Nicholas has invested in a large number of companies. He's embraced both online investing tools like AngelList as well as pooled capital to diversify his risks and engage in more thorough due diligence.

Full Contact formed in 2010 and has raised a total of $8.9 million from angels and venture capital firms. Full Contact is a great example of how small the world really is; I've interviewed Bart due to his angel investing activity and his profile is available online. I've also interviewed four of the investors in his firm (500 Startups, Social Leverage, Foundry Group, and Nicholas Wyman), who are all in this book. If you read the profile of all these investors (Dave McClure, Howard Lindzon, Brad Feld, and Nicholas Wyman), you'll notice that they don't all agree on the best approach to angel investing. Some care more about truly believing in the entrepreneur as Nicholas described, while others like Dave McClure express the view that you don't have enough time to truly understand the entrepreneur so you can't rely as much on that "gut feel" that's so often described as the basis for an investment.

Nicholas now runs the Galvanize Fund and I did profile Jim Deters, who started Galvanize. That interview is available online and I highly recommend you find it to learn more about what makes Galvanize special and why Nicholas would choose that as the next step after Foundry Group.

FROM GROUP TO FUND WITH VC CATHERINE MOTT

"The secret of business is to know something that nobody else knows."

—ARISTOTLE ONASSIS

"It's not just about if this is the right company. It's also about whether we add value."

—CATHERINE MOTT

WHEN I FIRST SPOKE WITH CATHERINE, the music of a good Pennsylvania accent graced my ears. Nearly all of my father's family is from the area, and it was great to learn about the advances in early-stage investing that Catherine has been driving there. I think you'll find that Catherine is incredibly inspirational and motivating for any angel investor or potential angel investor.

How did you get started with early-stage investing?

I became caught up in the dotcom boom when I was sitting at the bar at the country club hearing someone talk about a deal that was going to make millions overnight because everything was listing on the stock exchange with no revenue. That was my first foray into it. I lost all my money on three deals that I did during the dotcom years. I finally asked a VC friend of mine, "You've obviously been successful at this venture investing. What should I be doing?"

He said, "Why don't you start at Angel Network? You increase your probability of being more successful when you aggregate more money, and when you aggregate more knowledge." That made sense. I did 18 months of research and visited different angel networks in California, New York, Washington, DC, Boston. I looked at best practices to determine what would work in Pittsburgh.

At that time, I could only identify 90 groups. Today, there's over 400, maybe closer to 450, I think. The phenomenon has grown. I felt like I was riding this wave—a new premise on angel capital, creating market efficiencies and engaging in best practices. The idea of folks aggregating their knowledge and their money to manage risk and engage in sophisticated processes made sense to me. All the principles you apply to your public stock portfolio need to be applied to this part of your portfolio as well. It just made sense to me. I started a group here in Pittsburgh. We grew to 65 members, mostly men in this area. Seven of us are women. We've invested over $30 million in about 46 different companies so far.

We probably invest in three to five or six new deals a year. It depends. What I find now is that the quality of deals are getting so much better. When I look at 10 years ago, 11 years ago, when we started this, the entrepreneurial support was only mostly available in Silicon Valley and Boston, and today is now available in other parts of the country. The regional support efforts of on-profits, incubators, and research institutions tend to yield better deal flow.

It's an exciting time to be in this business, because now everybody wants to be an entrepreneur. Not only the rest of the country, but the rest of the world is sharing that enthusiasm. I don't know if you've had a chance to look at what's going on in Israel, but if you look at the investment per capita over there, it far outweighs what's happening in the United States. It's fascinating to think about VCs and angels in Israel. I have no connection to that country, not at all, except someone brought it to my attention because as former chair of the Angel Capital Association, I became much more aware of what was happening around the world.

Did you engage women as investors on purpose?

I went after who was interested in investing in this asset class. I didn't care about gender, and thus, our group composite resulted in mostly men. I know many people make it their mission to recruit women or minorities, which I think is very admirable. But I'm a realist. I've been in Pittsburgh and western Pennsylvania all my life. It's a tier 2 city, not a tier 1 city, so when it comes to women's initiatives in private equity, we don't have the critical mass of women to tap—and we are still 10 years behind other cities in developing on the diversity front.

I was more interested in aggregating significant investment dollars. I was not interested in attracting investors who wanted to write checks for $5,000. I knew we could have a greater impact on the deals if we focused on folks who would write a check for $20,000 per deal. I really had no mission other than I wanted us to have a successful group that had access to quality deal flow, were savvy about putting the deal terms together, could meaningfully co-invest with other investors, and be successful on executing on returns. I didn't care where the people come from, except that they would add value to what we were doing, and they wanted to participate in what we were doing.

How did you go about putting together that quality deal flow?

It takes time to develop that. In our region, at the time we started, there were only a few incubators. It requires regular meetings with them. It also requires meetings with my colleagues from nearby cities like Philadelphia or Washington, DC.

It's something that has to be nurtured and fostered, and you also have to build the relationships with attorneys and service providers who can be good sources of deal flow. I think our best deals come from these good relationships.

We're also very visible. We have a website. We have a backend software system that manages all of our applications. We probably receive on average 350 to 400 applications a year, but keep in mind, it all gets whittled down to approximately five new ones a year. These new deals also have to compete with our portfolio companies seeking follow-on investing. If our companies are doing well, we support them. It's not uncommon for us to be investing in 11 or 12 companies a year because we're supporting our current portfolio, and investing in new companies.

What are you looking for when you make investments?

When we do due diligence, we're focused on management, market, and model, but at the end of the day there's something about the technology and its place in the market that will attract us, if it's unique enough, if it's differentiated enough to have the probability of being a great success, not just a moderate success, not just a good success, but a great success.

What I like about angel groups is they keep you grounded. You can fall in love with a technology, but someone in the group will recognize an issue that requires attention, and that deal is no longer such a hot deal.

What qualities make it the right time to do that for the technologies?

It's really very difficult to assess the management team. Some VCs are using trait and personality assessments. During due diligence, what we try to assess is, "How does this person fit as a leader? What leadership components does he/she have?" To a great extent when angels are interfacing with the team during the due diligence process, we're trying to get a sense of the leadership and the team. A good leader will surround himself with strong, suitable players. We try to understand if this is the kind of person who feels comfortable with A players or if they are going to hire B players.

We also try to assess if the leader is coachable. Is he/she afraid of criticism or accepting assistance/guidance? We try to assess as much as possible through informal conversations with the team and with the founder.

Are we right a lot of times? No, not always, but we try to do the best we can at assessing if the team works well together. Is there a lot of dysfunction? How well do the team members play together in the sandbox? It takes several visits to figure it out. We break up the due diligence into five or six different buckets; it requires five or six different conversations and meetings with different parts of the team, and meeting with everybody together.

How long do you typically spend with a company before you get that feeling?

This can be a very frustrating thing for entrepreneurs because due diligence can take four weeks and sometimes six weeks, and on some occasions, even up to eight weeks. We try to keep it around four to six weeks. We're hearing a lot of pushback on the amount of time that we take for diligence. However, the reason we join an angel group is to mitigate our risks in a very risky asset class, and that calls for tapping the talent of our investment group for sophisticated due diligence that will require time and process.

Our process is not just focused on the PID—our pre-investment decisions—but it's also focused on our PIM, the post-investment management; that's equally important. It's not just about how much we can do upfront, but it's also about what value we can add after we invest. Can we help? Can we introduce them to customers? Can we introduce them to vendors and suppliers? Do they need a CFO for about 10 months before they can really afford to hire one? Can someone sit in and help with financial strategy until they get to a point where they've got enough cash, enough revenue, to support hiring one of their own? Those are the kinds of things we do. It's not just about if this is the right company. It's also about whether we add value.

Does a lot of that depend on where they're at and what qualities the people who're investing in the group have?

Yes, definitely. Most angel group portfolios are a direct reflection of their backyard. For example, our portfolio is approximately 50% life science deals. In our backyard, Pittsburgh is number four in the country for NIH dollars, and thus we will see a good many healthcare deals. But if you look at an angel group portfolio in Rochester, New York, you'll see a lot more material science deals.

When you do get involved, is it one person from the group who's investing who's involved more heavily than others, or is there a lot of shared involvement?

We try to put structure into what can be a chaotic process. We do things by committee. We have a due diligence committee. We have a growth and transaction committee, and we have a deal flow and screening committee. Even our deal flow and screening committee is broken into buckets. We have one for life sciences, a subcommittee for IT and hardware, and one for material science and energy-related offerings.

We have a due diligence chairman. He will build a committee around who has the expertise needed to perform comprehensive due diligence. He typically will tap those who expressed interest in investing. Then we also have interns, graduate students, from Carnegie Mellon University, University of Pittsburgh, and Duquesne University. We put them to work, most often to perform market research and to gather good data such as industry exit comparables. It's typically a well-rounded team, and they put together a written report and present it to the group. We call it the deal memo. It can be anywhere from 35 to 60 pages long, depending on the technical difficulty. They might have talked to three customers. They might have talked to six or eight. Or if the IP is extensive, it will require a very technical review. It just depends on the complexity of the company, the technology, and of the deal.

Finally, our growth and transaction committee. They review the portfolio on a regular basis and talk with the CEO, and try to find what resources they need to grow. Do they need help with sales growth? Do they need investment bankers? Are they struggling with strategy or do they need to pivot? Do they need distributor partners? The committee focuses on how we can tap the talent and rolodexes of our group to help our portfolio companies be successful.

We're just trying to make the best out of the resources we have and trying to put some structure around it. It's pretty hard because a group can be very chaotic. The larger the group, the harder it gets.

Does everyone pool in their money for the investments, or are just a couple of people making the investments for the company?

People in our group are empowered to make their own decisions to invest. We form limited liability partnerships (LLPs). They're single-purpose LLPs. We'll collect all the money, and then LP will make the investment on behalf of all those investors through the LPs. [*Author's note:* Some regions form LLCs; state tax structures will determine LLP or LLC.]

We aggregate into a single entity because it's a best practice in the angel group industry. It limits the names on the company cap table and makes the corporate decision process more efficient and effective. It also helps to avoid discouraging sophisticated follow-on funding sources like VCs. They don't want to deal with a messy cap table.

Do you care much about terms? Do you always use the same investment structure?

Yes, we use the best practices of the National Venture Capital Association. We use their checklist for due diligence. We use their term sheet for Series A funding and for seed funding.

If you watch the funding trends in the United States, angel groups have become more Series A investors. We're moving further up the food chain, but that's because we're syndicating. We can aggregate $1 million to $3 million amongst five angel groups.

We're looking at one company right now that we like, and it's going to be priced as a seed round. It will still be a preferred stock, but the terms will be less complicated. We're not going to try to interfere with the Series A. We want it to be attractive for follow-on investing. We'll probably also be the ones following on, so we'll definitely want to make it reasonable and work with the entrepreneur.

Do the investors always typically follow on?

If the companies are doing well and they have been transparent with regular updates, then we will continue to invest. This is a psychological thing. We will avoid supporting a company that hasn't been transparent. We expect them to make mistakes, but if a company has been non-communicative and is missing quarterly updates, it's challenging for investors to step up—it has become an issue of trust.

The smart entrepreneurs learn how to ask for help to overcome the obstacles before they come back and ask for more money. They are always transparent, and there's a level of trust when they've been very open about challenges or a strategic pivot.

How about the other investors? Do you do a lot of work to connect them?

We do. You get to know with whom you want to connect. To me this is no different than VCs. They have their partners that they prefer to co-invest with, and you'll see they're pretty much the same partners in multiple deals. As an investor, you also learn industry preferences of the various angel groups: who prefers life science, who likes IT, who understands pharmacology, who has a penchant for material science. You try to seek out those kinds of partners.

Why don't we walk through a deal that turned out great, from when you saw it to what happened?

One of our first deals was a company called MedSage. MedSage was a pure angel deal, never needed any VC money. It was led by us, and we brought in some other local investors, individual investors, with us. This was one of our earlier deals. I'm thinking we first invested in late 2005.

Then we doubled down a year and a half later. I think we invested around $1.2 million, $1.5 million, and then we doubled down the following year, for a total of over $3 million in the company. The company was sold in approximately four years. One of our investors was able to step in as CEO when the founding CEO was diagnosed with health issues. Our guy successfully drove it to a very profitable exit. That was the beauty of being totally engaged, helping the company from the beginning. It also was a short timeframe to exit, and we were thrilled because some of our companies were taking eight or nine years before achieving a profitable exit.

Let's look at one of the companies that you invested in that didn't turn out so well.

We lost everything in one investment that will remain nameless. This was a challenge; we did not have majority control because a regional VC led the deal with most of the investment dollars. We lost all our money. We put in, I think, $1.2 million in this deal, and we'd encouraged a few other angel groups to invest in this deal—we all erroneously believed the VC would be a good board rep. Unfortunately, the VC refused to control the CEO and rein in his consistent mistakes. That was an eye-opening experience. Today, we do more due diligence on VCs.

I value the relationships we have been able to build over the years. We are much more aligned with our partners today—we all are more value aligned and care most about the portfolio company's success.

What is the most important thing a newer angel investor should do to be successful?

Diversify. To add to that, I would say apply all the principles that you apply to your public stock portfolio to this asset class as well.

Should they diversify across different types of investments?

Yes, I would say that. Don't put all your eggs in one industry, and don't try to pick three. To be successful in this asset class, one must invest in a minimum of 10 companies over five years. Only one or two will drive the bulk of the return.

Beyond diversification, there's something similar to that familiar axiom of "location, location, location" that applies to real estate investments. The axiom in this business is "management, management, management." You can have a great idea, but if you don't have effective people executing, it doesn't matter how great the idea is, it won't be successful.

My final piece of advice for new investors is to put as much effort in the post-investment management as one would put in the pre-investment decision. As angel investors, we tend to put more effort in the front side of our activity because we like the thrill of the hunt for the next great deal. We need to be equally as savvy about how we help companies navigate and manage for a successful exit.

It is a challenge because sometimes we are just a minority shareholder. How can we influence things? We need to stay close to the founder and the management team. We need to be an advocate or ally for our portfolio companies so that we can be part of the company as it continues to grow.

Is there a point where you're done being able to support and help them grow?

There is, especially for capital-intensive companies. There comes a time when you no longer have influence. Here's an example. We introduced one of our portfolio companies to Bain Venture Capital. But once Bain invested, we were out of the picture. I think the company had $30 million in revenue when we brought in Bain. Now Bain needs it to grow to $300 million. It restarts the clock, doesn't it? Now Bain has their five years to pursue an exit, and that adds five years to our holding period.

The good news is that we're still very close to the founders of that company, all rounds have been up rounds, and we still get the quarterly updates. However, we're out of the picture for providing help with the decision-making processes.

SMALL AND FOCUSED WITH VC CHARLIE O'DONNELL

"Doing things that impress your peers is a good heuristic when you're old but a bad one when you're young. "

—PAUL GRAHAM

"One of the hardest things I have to do is find syndicate partners for some of these deals. A lot of times I'm willing to go earlier than a lot of other folks."

—CHARLIE O'DONNELL

I GOT IN CONTACT WITH CHARLIE O'DONNELL after we started conversing on Twitter. I was making an investment in a financial technology company out of NYC and I was trying to understand the NYC startup space along the way, and Charlie is a well-connected investor whom I recommend any tech startup investor reach out to.

Charlie is young and ambitious after a brief stint with GM looking at private investments. He jumped on board with Union Square Ventures, the best-known VC in New York City in my opinion, as an analyst. He moved quickly from there into a bunch of different opportunities as entrepreneur in residence, starting a company of his own, a stint at First Round Capital, and now runs his own micro-VC Brooklyn Bridge Ventures. You can find more about him on our website, and of course online.

How do you think about your early-stage fund?

It's interesting because when people ask me if I do angel investments, I feel like what they're really asking me is do I do smaller, early bets on companies. At the end of the day, I'm not sure if it really matters where the money is coming from, at least when an entrepreneur asks. I generally forget I do angel rounds, but it comes out of a fund.

I do a lot of investments with other angels. A lot of the reason why they're most useful to me is twofold. One, my fund is unique in the sense that it's a little bit like a fund and an angel group. I show my fund investors the deals that I'm working on. If you're a fund investor, you're already going to be in the deal. I give you an opportunity to double down if you want. I'll look at an opportunity and I'll say, "Okay, this is the first $750,000 into the company, I'll do approximately $250,000 of it or whatever. Let's see if anybody else around the table has an interest in doing more than that."

For example, in the seed round of Canary.is, the connected home security business, I did $200,000 but my fund investors did $325,000 on top of me. It's great for me because effectively I wound up doing more than half the round and I got the board seat. And I only wrote a $200,000 check.

Do you often fill the round with your LPs?

No, I would say it really depends on the company. It's a little inconsistent, actually. Sometimes they jump on stuff and sometimes not. I think the hardest thing for some of the investors doubling down is the deals that are real early. I think they realize that one of my best-performing companies is a company called Tinybop. They make kids' apps. When the first app came out, it totally blew the doors off and all the numbers. I invested at the stage where it was a guy and an idea.

Realistically, the LPs are risk averse to making big investments at that stage. They tried to get into the next round, but everybody wanted into the next round. That's why I think they realized, "Oh wait, we should pay a little more attention to these things." It didn't look like anything, but the point at which it actually looked like something, it was too late. I think they've been paying more attention to these deals going forward. Some of the deals also move very quickly.

The best individual investors are folks where they think about it like a portfolio. They say, "Hey, I'm going to try and make four or five bets of these a year." They may have a good sense of how much information they need and how much information they're just not going to find the answer to. Where are they going to take risks and just pull the trigger? Otherwise, they will fall behind and they're just not going to be able to keep up, frankly. An entrepreneur can't take four meetings with somebody who wants to write a $25,000 check.

Do you see entrepreneurs meeting with early-stage funds instead of individual investors as a trend in the early-stage market?

Yeah, that's one of the difficult things, I wonder where angel groups are going. If you have an angel group that can put together $200,000 or $300,000, you're comparing how you get money from them versus how you get money from me. In comparison, they're a very poor customer experience. You try to get a meeting with me and I can meet you sometime this week or next week.

You try and get a meeting with an angel group and you have to submit a whole form. The group meets on the first Thursday of every month, and that was yesterday. Now you have to wait a whole month. You go to the screening meeting. After the screening meeting, people are excited about it. You figure out who's excited about it. Then you go to the due diligence meeting. You deal with this meeting three weeks later.

I could literally write a check by the end of the week if I really needed to. It's one decision-maker for $300,000. The thing is that the more votes you need from the investing entity definitively, the less risk that investing entity takes. It is very difficult to substantiate the "guy and an idea" kind of startup. "Why do you like this?" "I don't know, I just kind of like the guy." If I had to justify that to a group of 20 other individuals, that's going to be really hard to do.

I only have to justify my ideas to myself. Every four years I have to justify the portfolio to my investors. I believe that will happen on an individual deal basis a little harder.

How many of the investments that you do are more along the lines of "A guy you like with an idea" versus some other form of deeper analysis?

Most of these deals are very, very early stage, so I've done things such as two people and a prototype; a few pre-product companies; early customer traction—you know, one customer kind of thing. It could be very, very early stuff. One of the hardest things I have to do is find syndicate partners for some of these deals. A lot of times I'm willing to go earlier than a lot of other folks.

How do your LPs respond to being so early? Is that essentially what you have optimized for in offering those LPs?

Yeah. One of the reasons they're investing is they know that they wouldn't be able to do what I do in terms of dealing with the fire hose of companies at that stage. This is what I do all the time. I have an angel investor who invested in my fund who was looking at the same deals I was. I said to him, "This is probably a dumb question - we're already working on the same deals here, why would you need to be a fund investor?"

He said, "Yeah, well, it just takes so much time." He was also a later-stage food investor. Those companies you're either really manufacturing stuff or you're not. There's so much less noise. It's not like two kids with an idea and they're pitching. It's like everyone here's a real company in this space. The opportunity versus the lead is just so much higher. He just felt like it was very low odds for him as a check investor to look at those opportunities if he's not going to be looking at them full time. That's one of the reasons why he's interested in fund investing.

When you look at these early companies that maybe your LPs aren't ready for or prepared to analyze, what're you mostly looking for or optimizing for?

One, it's got to be in New York. I want to be one of the first $50,000 angels who go into the deal. I can't need to be a scientist to understand what this thing is. It's got to be some of that basic stuff.

Outside of that it's a lot of things like, is this an opportunity where the size is a fit? What are your five year projections, can you afford $2 versus $350,000? Is the opportunity presenting itself a venture-style opportunity? That's a big one. Do you and your team have the capability to execute this? Does your skill set match what we're trying to do? If this is a sales execution–driven business, can you execute on sales or is it a couple of tech dudes who don't know how to make phone calls and don't know how to generate leads? That could be problematic.

Do the resources match the opportunity? If you're going to be a Microsoft Office competitor and are raising $200,000 to build it, that's not enough money. That's a red flag. I've seen plenty of those where it's not realistic that they're going to get done what they say they're going to do given the amount of time. That's an indicator of an entrepreneur who isn't ready.

We had somebody come in the other day and they were raising $550,000. They were doing something with an extremely long sales cycle. I asked, "Why wouldn't you just raise more money for this? I don't understand." The answers were not well thought out. I told them, "I just don't think your thinking is very sharp to be honest. It's not logical."

I think one of the other things is from a character perspective. Is this somebody great to work with?

Do you help these companies move to the next round of financing?

Oh, sure. I go out to the West Coast probably once a quarter to try and network with other VCs and people who might do the next round of various companies that I might be investing in; or help them lay out their pitch stuff; help them think about what milestones do we need so you can get a next-round funding. That's an important part of my process, especially since I don't want to just write the one check. I got to make sure that they get there.

You don't do any follow-on investing?

No. I think it's a bad bet, actually. It depends on what you want to do with the firm. I don't want to grow my firm, to be honest. I like being on my own. I think the most amount of money I could reasonably manage in a fund is probably about $15 million. I don't need to scale, or need money to work. I have the luxury of having all of my dollars, easy to achieve dollars. I think the two best places to invest are seeds and pre-revenue rounds, like $200 million into AirBNB. We know AirBNB is a company. We can stick a panel of analysts and debate as to how much more room they have to grow in each market. If they went public, what would the valuation be and all that other stuff. It's not going to be zero. You're not going to lose your money putting $200 million in there.

That's the kind of thing, in terms of getting a bang for your buck. It's in these rounds where you're coming in at valuations of three, four. When you're going in where you feel like it's a real business and you're relatively protected. The middle stages are really hard. Harry's is a great example. Canary/Khosla Ventures led a $10 million round for that startup. It's an absolutely terrific team, but they have yet to do the hard part, like deliver the product. They paid a big step up. People asked me, "Do you see the next round?" I'm happy where I am, given the risk is still in the company. I don't care about ownership percentage. I care about multiple on my investments. All my dollars are seed dollars. One 40 or 50 times makes up for a whole lot of mistakes.

Are you just not excited about companies at those later stages?

No. In fact, when I have entrepreneurs telling other people their company wouldn't exist had I not invested in the seed round, I don't think anyone would accuse me of not being excited about the company. It's not like I'm choosing which companies to invest in. I write one check and that's the deal. It's no knock on the company at all. It's no different than an angel investor who write $50,000 checks and somebody comes along and says, "What do you mean? You didn't write a $100,000 check?" They often answer, "No, that's not what I do. This is just what I do."

What would you say are three things that early-stage investors should be doing?

I think a recognition that you have to take some risk. Getting really comfortable about how your portfolio risk and return is going to work. I have to create three or four hundred million dollars of enterprise value across my companies to build a 4x returning fund. That's actually not a lot. It's not that much. I know how my economics work. I think there're a lot of people who don't quite understand that. You just have to be conscious of that in your decision-making.

If you're investing in one company a year, you have to be conscious of the fact that you're taking huge amounts of unsystematic risk. Most people don't even think about systematic and unsystematic risk. I think your investment decision-making would be different if you were more conscious of these factors.

I had a company ask me whether I did background checks on the entrepreneur for a seed round. Is it a higher likelihood that this guy has a criminal record that I don't know about or he just sucks at managing his startup company? You shake hands because there are lots of people you deal with in your life that you don't do background checks on but you trust them. It's a likelihood that somebody has a mysterious criminal record but also pulled one over on you because they elicited trust from you. They seemed like a good person. You talked to other people who know them and nobody knew about this record. It seems statistically low versus well, this startup has no revenues yet. That's where I'm taking risk.

I'm very conscious of that kind of thing. When you think a lot about where you take risk, I think investors would change a lot of how they do due diligence and open themselves up to a lot of ideas and think about things a little differently. I'm a big proponent of using portfolio theory. I'll do a deal that I can't prove to you is going to be one of the ones that works but it has an interesting trajectory. It's interesting enough for me to bring this to be one out of thirty investments.

The other thing is building discipline structure and oversight in the company. Any company that comes along and says, "I really need a board." Big-boy companies have boards. You want to be a real company one day, you'll have a board. We'll have some meetings. An entrepreneur who doesn't want to do that kind of thing or doesn't want to sit down and talk with you and doesn't act like a steward of your capital—that's not a great relationship that you should have.

What are the best ways for angels to work with early-stage funds like yourself?

I had an angel just send over the list of all the deals they were looking at. I thought, "That's awesome!" He's not doing all of these rounds. He's not competitive with me. I'm certainly not going to squeeze him out of a deal that he sends me. He needs other people to do these rounds. These are the types of things where I could look at a list and go through it, and the one that was at the top of his list I didn't like at all. But one of those that was about five down I thought was super interesting. He's getting feedback from me. I'm getting deal flow. It's a win-win. I'm happy to get the firehouse.

It's not like he's introducing me to all these founders. He's just sending me the list. I can do my own Googling and figure out what the company is and all sorts of stuff. It works out on both ends. I'm just happy to get regular updates, like what they're looking for. I always tell people don't worry about playing VC. If he's sending me a bunch of deals and I don't want to do any of them, I'm not going to automatically delete the emails he sends me, that'd be stupid. It's one email. If I automatically deleted all sources of bad deals, I would basically shut off my in-box. Most of the deals are bad.

Maybe a partner at Sequoia might feel differently. At the same time, are they really going to ignore it? They might miss your email. It's not like you had such a great relationship with that partner from Sequoia to begin with. What's the downside, right? I sent a note to 95 journalists who cover the New York tech scene and said, here's the stuff I'm interested in. I told them, "If you don't like any of this, if you want me to stop sending you this—it's a once a month mailer—let me know how I can be helpful. All the folks went, "Oh wow, this is awesome."

I repeatedly have to put together lists of the hot startup companies. I do it all from scratch. I'm creating a structured thing that they know they're going to get on a regular basis. They're going to look through those lists. If there's nothing in it, then they just move on. It's been great. It's led to some stories, some coverage. I think they're more than happy to get it and not like saying, "Oh, that guy's annoying, he keeps sending me stuff."

How do you find the 10 hot startups this month in New York?

Just trying to pay attention. I'll ask other investors if they have companies that they want to share. To be honest, that actually happens. It's a huge source. I don't think a lot of people relate to the media like this. They don't have a good sense of what's really interesting or the timing of it. They'll send me companies—"Oh yeah, this company's really big. They're under the radar." I'm like, "Not really that interesting." You can't send me guilt. Guilt is not under the radar. Everybody knows about them already.

I've actually found a number of under-the-radar companies. I ran a sales meet-up the other day with heads of sales for all these companies to give a presentation of sales leaders across organizations. There's this one guy from this company, Longtail Video, which is now called JW Player. That company is amazing. It's got a really talented sales leader who has great experience. He told us about the opportunity. I was like, "Wow, that's a serious startup."

This is a company that was making open-sourced flash video players that actually made the video player that YouTube used. You could pay them $35 for the site license to use the player. They thought that was the business—you know, "Hey, you want a player? Pay your $35." Somebody basically said, "Wait, maybe we should be charging these people a lot more money." If you go to Kickstarter and you look for one of their videos, you get a link to this JW Player site. The site itself has five million unique visits from people who've shown up saying, "What's this thing?"

They're converting to these enterprise site licenses and all sort of stuff onsite. It's crazy. That's the kind of deal that no one's talking about. No one cares about this company. That's a great under-the-radar type of story.

What is one thing that angel investors should avoid doing with early-stage investing?

I have one more thing they should do, actually, and it sounds completely self-serving. They should be investors in funds because you get diversification. If you say, "I'm going to be an angel investor and I'm going to put $10,000 to $25,000 to work in each company," unless you're building a portfolio of 20 companies, you don't get portfolio diversification. I'm making the assumption that these people are doing three, four deals a year. At least they should be.

If they're putting that kind of money to work, an investment in a fund that has a three-year life cycle, it's kind of like a $50,000 commitment to a fund or $100,000 to a fund is like $25,000 a year or $16,000 a year. That's like one deal. It's not really that much. For that money, a really bad fund probably would return half your money. That would be a disaster fund. If you invest in 30 companies, one of them is going to accidentally be a hit.

Being a fund investor is generally good. It gives you a very different kind of relationship. I pay attention to my LPs in a different way from the way I pay attention to others. They get insight. They get deal flow from me and I share deals with my LPs first. They can see these deals as they're coming through. I would suggest them picking a small fund. If you're an LP aiming to a venture and you put $50,000, they can't pay attention to every $50,000 investor. It's a time and effort thing. For me, my $100,000 guys are really meaningful actually.

Do you tell any of your LPs how much of their portfolio should be in this asset class?

It hasn't really come up. When I first started fund raising, I was willing to take any amount of money. Later on, when I had more momentum, I just set a certain bar. I was like, "Yeah, I know, I'm not taking investments of less than $100,000." I didn't go through the process where I said, "Oh, you have this amount of money, you should actually be doing…" Nobody really asked. They had numbers that they were comfortable with. I guess for a first time fund, a lot of people did the minimums; whatever I was willing to take. Somebody came along and said, "I'm thinking about doing $200,000, $250,000. He settled on $225,000. I honestly don't know where he got that number, but it worked for him.

HOW THE BEST ANGEL INVESTORS MAKE MONEY IN STARTUPS

WHILE YOU MAY FIND several of the investing styles in this book resonated with you, there are some insights that can be drawn from all of the investors. Angel investing isn't easy; in fact, it is a fairly difficult way to make money. Even a diversified portfolio can produce poor returns.

Here are your quotable, tweetable, and otherwise easier-to-digest insights:

Invest with Great People

From the Momentum Investors

Joanne Wilson: "You really have to trust your gut instincts—'Are these people or is this a person that I think has the ability to execute in scale?' I think those are the two words that make a really good entrepreneur..."

Jeffrey Carter: "...Go out and try and fail, be willing to lose money."

Geoff Entress: "...Know who you're getting in bed with, whether it's the entrepreneurs or your angels."

Rui Ma: "What I really focus on is the entrepreneur's commitment and understanding the market, because I don't."

From the Value Investors

Christopher Mirabile: "...The other main thing is really going to be about the CEO; get a lot of blind reference checks on the CEO and really figure out whether they're quality or not. We've all had a CEO flake out on us."

Michael Dornbrook: "...It's best to avoid friends. I invested in three early on and I don't avoid them just because they may go bad, if they don't go as expected it can hurt the friendship."

Tim Berry: "Due diligence."

Charles Porter: "I like founders who're coachable. You know, if they're not coachable, there's nothing a board can do to help them be successful. "

FROM THE ALTERNATIVE INVESTORS

Kirk Coburn: "...Invest in people that you're willing to lose your money with and ask yourself, 'If I lose all my money, would I reinvest in this guy and these people?' "

Nicholas Wyman: "...Engage with and support the entrepreneur as much as [you] can. You want to invest in people that you want to have a beer with to celebrate the good times and commiserate with during the bad ones."

Greg Neufeld: "Investing in a team and in their ability to pick good teams."

Understand Your Investment Strategy

FROM THE MOMENTUM INVESTORS

Brad Feld: "When I talk about not necessarily having an allocation of my net worth that was a deliberate decision. [...] I said I think I feel comfortable investing $25,000 a year in 10 companies, which is a quarter-million dollars a year. I'll reserve one-to-one for some of those companies I'll invest another $25,000, for others I won't."

Bob Bozeman: "It's not a get-rich scheme. [...] It's a lot easier to make money just in public stocks, because you don't have any liquidity issues."

Rudy Gadre: "Try to minimize the impact of mistakes. If you're worth $5 million, don't make your first check $1 million. Try $25,000 or something like that. Start learning about what can go wrong."

Geoff Entress: "Figure out how much your budget is, your investment that you're just going to go put forward, not in the next one or two years, but the next five years."

From the Value Investors

Andy Liu: "I'd be very thoughtful about the down rounds. Think about how comfortable you feel. Do you feel like they've made optimal decisions given the information they had? Do you feel you've been kept in the loop? I'd just spend a little bit more time figuring out if I would participate in a down round and be more selective there."

Christopher Mirabile: "...One mistake that you see a lot of times is people tend to write a little bit too big of a check in their first couple of deals. What I'm trying to say is 'Don't be impulsive. Being quick and decisive is necessary but be thorough too—don't be impulsive."

Mark Suster: "You need the ability to put more money behind your winners. If you don't have the money to put a little more bit behind the three, four, five best things in your portfolio, you shouldn't be an angel investor."

Chris Sheehan: "I would just be a little cautious about a really rapid pace of investment."

Matt Dunbar: "You got to be patient. You can't go into these things expecting to get your money out next year."

Will Herman: "Can you tie up that money for 10 years?"

Get To Know Yourself

From the Momentum Investors

Brad Feld: "...If you're going to be an angel investor, start writing checks. If it takes you 12 months to write your first $25,000, you're making a mistake. You're going to get better deal flow by making investments and getting known as somebody who actually writes checks."

Bob Bozeman: "...This idea of vision investing versus metrics investing, if you're really more comfortable with metrics investing then don't do angel investing. The early stage really isn't going to be good for you and you're going to be driving the entrepreneurs for all the wrong reasons. They don't have metrics until they're well into their business. A pure metrics investor should try to participate more in A rounds, or something like that, or syndicate behind people that are vision investors."

Rudy Gadre: "I think you've got to pay your dues. It's like that, you're going to make some mistakes, just like you would with anything new that you try."

From the Value Investors

Jim Connor: "...As an angel investor, you have to decide if you totally want to be a passive investor. Maybe you give advice, you help out, you do some mentoring but that's all you can do because you're in a lot of companies and you have limits on your time. You can easily get your time fully consumed."

Warren Katz: "...'Go slow, and stick to what you know.' Those are the two superb pieces of advice that [I received] and I took both."

John Ives: "I would make sure the person makes a conscious decision between is this a hobby or is this your career."

Chris Sheehan: "Find your own comfort zone of the style of angel investing that you want to do."

From the Alternative Investors

Kirk Coburn: "There is a great venture capitalist named Kevin Lalande. He runs Sante Ventures in Austin. His advice to me was to become an expert in something and don't deviate."

Diversify Your Portfolio

From the Momentum Investors

Brad Feld: "...Angel investors should be promiscuous. You should do more rather than less investments. You should do more that are smaller."

Gil Penchina: "I needed to make 25 investments to get one amazing company."

Bart Lorang: "...The three Ps [...] care about the people, products, and be promiscuous and do a lot of investments."

From the Value Investors

David Verrill: "...If you're a new angel, and you don't make a number of investments that gets to a portfolio effect, you're likely not going to be an angel for long, because losses happen before winners."

Mark Suster: "If you don't have the cash to do at least 10, 15, 20 deals you shouldn't be an angel."

Will Herman: "They decide they're going to make two or three or four deals and something's going to pop up. It's way too few. You have to drill a lot of holes."

From the Alternative Investors

Charlie O'Donnell: "I have one more thing they should do actually and it sounds completely self-serving. They should be investors in funds because you get diversification."

Catherine Mott: "Diversify. To add to that, I would say apply all the principles that you apply to your public stock portfolio, one should also apply to this asset class as well. "

Find The Best Companies And Markets Possible

From the Momentum Investors

Bob Bozeman: "Focus on quality. Then make sure the fit is good. If you try to wear a pair of shoes that don't fit, then you've got blisters on your foot."

Boris Wertz: "The deal flow is everything. For me, work on getting as much deal flow as possible."

From the Value Investors

David Verrill: "...You really need to figure out where the best deal flow is and make sure that you're seeing the better deals in your ecosystem."

Christopher Mirabile: "...Don't look for shortcuts. Don't invest in things that are too good to be true and look for shortcuts, because nothing, nothing is as good as it looks. Be a little bit more penetrating and don't be lazy."

Rui Ma: "...Focus on diligence. Somebody who just sold a company for $100 million feels funny saying, 'Hey, I don't know how to do diligence? Could someone teach me how to do this?' "

Study And Learn From Others

From the Momentum Investors

Manny Fernandez: "I would suggest if you're an individual investor you join a group. Learn from others. Don't rush into investing, just learn."

From the Value Investors

David Verrill: "I really think that a group offers a new angel the opportunity to see a rigorous process. To see screening. To see presentation. To see due diligence. To see term negotiation and governance. That's an educational process. I think groups do a very good job of educating people."

Rui Ma: "...Take one of the angel educational courses. The Angel Resource Institute offers some, other people offer some, but study angel investing. Let go of the pride that just because you're rich and successful or can operate a company that you know how to angel invest. There is a learning curve in investment just like there is in every other thing in life and so you need to understand that learning curve and things you can do to mitigate it."

Matt Dunbar: "I think investors serve themselves well by getting involved with the group."

Rob Tucci: "You need to really educate yourself about the process."

Don't Invest In A Vacuum

From the Momentum Investors

Brad Feld: "You should be very focused on building your network of other people that are angel investors to both bring them into deals and have them bring you into deals. I think if you just show up and are just making investments, that's a problem."

Geoff Entress: "Make sure that you get out to all the different events and are networking and use LinkedIn to its full extent and make sure that you have as broad a network as possible of people to call on."

From the Value Investors

Michael Dornbrook: "I think it's been underlined for me that somebody is going to need a lot of future investments. If I don't feel that I can continue to protect my share, I'll probably get screwed at some point in the future. I've kind of learned to stay clear of those companies that are going to need a ton of cash."

From the Alternative Investors

Nicholas Wyman: "...[Don't] invest in a vacuum, whether that vacuum is not understanding the larger ecosystem, terms, competitive landscape, and the market or simply not understanding the dynamics of angel investing."

Understand Your Role with the Company

From the Momentum Investors

Brad Feld: "...Don't ever lose sight of what your role in the process is, right? Here a $25,000 investor, a $50,000 investor in a company where you now own half a percent or 1% of the company, don't torture the entrepreneur. Your job is to help the entrepreneur be successful. "

Jim Deters: "...Make sure [you] understand the ethos of the entrepreneurs. Angels need to be angels and not assholes."

From the Value Investors

Chris Sheehan: "...Avoid being a pain in the butt to the entrepreneur."

From the Alternative Investors

Kirk Coburn: "...Can you add value to the company?"

Pay Attention To The Economics

FROM THE MOMENTUM INVESTORS

Gil Penchina: "Lean in on the winners. Angels rarely use pro rata. "

FROM THE VALUE INVESTORS

Rob Tucci: "Get a qualitative assessment of risk."

Charles Porter: "...Make sure that you're raising enough money to get to that next inflection point."

Don't Invest In Things You Don't Care About

FROM THE MOMENTUM INVESTORS

David Cohen: "It's specific to the investor so I, for example, generally avoid Adtech. I don't understand it well enough and I really don't care about it. I have no energy for it. So I think you avoid things that don't excite you personally because you just won't put any energy into it and you'll write it off sooner. You have to care about what you're investing in so just avoid investing in something that doesn't sound like a good business opportunity. If you don't care about it, don't do it."

FROM THE VALUE INVESTORS

Mark Suster: "If you don't have an inside edge in terms of relationships, or information, or access to people or deals or exits or an industry more than other people, you shouldn't be an angel."

Walk Away From Red Flags

FROM THE MOMENTUM INVESTORS

Joanne Wilson: "When you see a red flag you know it."

CONCLUSION

AS I WRAPPED UP the final interviews, I reflected on my angel investing over the year and thought about the things I had learned. The interviews here are a good representative set, but I encourage you to go online to http://startupwealth.com to read the others. As I read and re-read these during the transcription and reviews with each of the interviewees, I had a lot of time to reflect on the things that I'd learned from talking to so many investors who've been investing in early-stage companies profitably for the last couple of decades.

It became obvious that despite so many different views on investing and so many different types of investors in the group of interviewees, there were a few basic principles that everyone touches on in one way or another. Bijan Sabet, an excellent investor with a great track record, posted these four things on his blog recently as being the only four things in his investment thesis:

Are the founders extraordinary?

Do I love the product?

Is the vision compelling?

If I wasn't a VC, would I want to work for the founders at the startup?

Each of these are explained in much more depth here in this book by many other investors; you can see that these four things are generally important for momentum, value, and alternative investors. Each emphasize one of those four questions more or less depending on how they invest.

One thing that many of the value investors add is a fifth:

Do the terms and timing make sense to invest now?

Taking these one by one, we have team, product, market/vision, company, and deal.

Looking at the team, we've heard from angels who describe it as a gut feeling, a recognition of all sorts of traits or qualities a team could have—passion, intention, ability to push through walls, stamina, coachability, listening skills, past success, desire, charisma—yeah, I know the list is really long. This got me wondering a lot about what it is about the team that makes everyone describe a "good" team so differently. Why is it that everyone says that it is a gut feeling and they "know it when they see it"? Certainly all of these words used in the interviews aren't describing the same thing, so what is it?

One of the interviews I didn't include in the book but have made available online is with a gentleman by the name of Bill Warner. Bill is an angel investor from Boston and I met him through Brad Feld. He's been investing up in Boston for a couple of decades and is fairly involved in Techstars there. One of the interesting things about the interview is that Bill has been trying to figure out what it is that makes great founders successful. How can someone analyze a great founder? He's on to testing his second hypothesis now, and by testing, I mean develop a hypothesis, invest money in companies based on the hypothesis, see if the hypothesis correctly had higher results than the baseline (in this case, his baseline is no firm founder criteria). Bill's first hypothesis centered on passion and you'll recall there were many other investors in this book that used this term to describe a great team. Bill wasn't able to invest with better results if he focused on teams that had passion (you'll have to go to the website and read the interview to learn more about why). Bill is now investing based on a hypothesis centered on intention. It is too early to tell what the results of that will be.

Paul Graham says in his essay *Before the Startup* that "Startups are very counterintuitive. I'm not sure why. Maybe it's just because knowledge about them hasn't permeated our culture yet. But whatever the reason, starting a startup is a task where you can't always trust your instincts." This counterintuitive nature of startups makes it incredibly difficult to find founders who can run their company on instincts. Yet, after all the interviews it is clear that the best teams are instinctively suited to run their company. They react on instinct to run their business. Those instincts are developed over years of practice and learning. They are activated by a burning desire to succeed in that particular business. They reflect an ability to learn and implement those learnings into their daily practices. They encase the teams' entire being in a way that dangerously pushes each of them to an edge where they forgo personal needs in exchange for successfully running their business.

Their instinct can be described a lot of ways, but its nature is why investors often can only say that they will know it when they see it. It is also why many successful angel investors have past experience as successful company operators. Recognizing another person's instincts in and of itself is quite a feat and one that most people get wrong.

Some investors can focus on the entrepreneur but not be good at picking good entrepreneurs. Pay attention to how the momentum, value, or alternative investors focus on picking entrepreneurs to avoid this trap.

Bijan's number two is *product*. There is a lot of discussion about what makes a great product here in this book, in the interviews online, and basically anywhere you look (universities, blogs, books, and so on). Gil Penchina told me that he looks at the product as "...the manifestation of a highly skilled obsessive team that can focus." The focus on how to build great products is rightly deserved; a great team that can run a business will build a product that suits their business. You'll notice that some of the investors here in the book are okay if the product changes as the team learns. Some of the huge successes discussed in the interviews are a direct result of the products changing over time.

What is important to keep in mind is the process flow that Bob Bozeman talks about. Companies that succeed do so more often when they walk through the growth process that has already been well defined. They get some ideas that they want to try out and have some friends and family or a seed investor throw some money in to see what really works, and once they have some customer interest, they build some of the ideas and evolve it as customer interest increases and influences the direction. Then they raise a Series A and really try to run with what they've built. They raise enough capital to get the idea out there and they take much less influence from customers, but they may take a little. By the time they go for a Series B, they are ready to scale and grow. Maybe they need more money after that, but ideally they wouldn't.

Some of the alternative investors have other components of the product that matter to them, such as how does the product impact the world or how does the product align with a specific focus.

Bijan describes his third as *vision* and I add *market* to it. The reason I add the word is because a vision for a product is a vision about a market. Think about Bob Bozeman's bet on the "Internet." It is a description about the way things will work in the future. It describes human behaviors, product interaction, sociological norms, and marketplace influences. A vision is a very broad thing, and the definition is quite simplistic; the Oxford dictionary states it as "the faculty or state of being able to see."

For a vision to be compelling, it must also be clear. If you're going to get into their bus and put some money in the can for gas, having a clear vision is helpful. The vision may just be to go down this road for a few hours and we'll see if we can sell the remaining gas in the tank at a profit, but it sure as heck better be clear. Don't get on the bus if the team has the instincts to build the greatest four-wheel bus that ever existed if their vision is to drive it across the Atlantic. The vision doesn't clearly align with what they have the instincts to build or even the product they are building.

David Bangs talks about this a lot, this intersection of team, product, and vision. He talks about it as a compelling story, one that he can get excited about and one that he wants to brag to his friends about. He wants to be able to tell a friend at a dinner party that he invested in this team that figured out this innovative way to deliver on a new vision and that vision has a positive impact on the world and to David's pocketbook.

You can see how a momentum or alternative investor may get vision wrong because they're afraid of missing out on the next Internet investment. Many of the investors here outline their approach to vision that helps them to find success.

The *company* is Bijan's last area and one that he describes as would he work there if he wasn't a VC. That is an interesting way to describe it, because the reasons that people want to work at companies can be so different. Some people like to work for companies because they are good, well-run companies. Other people prefer to work for companies simply because a friend works there. Of course, there are plenty of other reasons in between.

When I think about company, though, and review all the interviews that I've conducted, I think a lot about the qualities of the companies that the interviewees talk about most. *Efficiencies, sales, culture, smart, honest, integrity, thoughtful,* and *customer focused* are all words that were used to describe good companies. This shows the most in the discussions where investors have talked about companies that failed, despite being good companies. When the interviewees talk about these companies, it is interesting to note that they are saying here is a company where they lost their money, but next time that team wants to build something they'll want to invest again in any case. Often it is associated with the company showing integrity by attempting to return as much of an investment as possible. It is also associated with companies that, despite failing, ran their business really well with low-capital requirements, lots of early testing, and a strong customer focus.

It doesn't stop there, though. Looking at the successful companies discussed in the interviews, the real rock star successes were efficient and more, but they also provided people who went to work there with a feeling of camaraderie and shared goals, a reason to be excited to go to work because they truly believed that the company was honestly doing its best to work together toward success and that everyone would share in the results.

I talked a little about my public market investing at the beginning of the book and this company culture, a company culture of success, where frugality, efficiency, and team participation in the results is one that spans good company culture at any stage. It is discussed a lot in Jim Collins's book *Good to Great* and is a key thing that I personally look for in any company that I invest in. This alignment and effort to work toward something that's bigger than they are is a natural human desire. Companies who embrace that desire and feed off of it are ones that people want to work for and are ones where culture is truly influenced by all the people in the company.

Bijan doesn't talk about the deal itself. I'm adding that as the fifth. Every interviewee I spoke with cares about terms and valuation on some level. Some value investors like Peter Weiss have an amazing depth of understanding of the terms and heavily optimizes his investments based on that understanding. You'll note that some of the areas he cares about most are areas that other value and momentum investors completely gloss over, yet having a good deal is an important thing for all of the investors.

If you're educated enough to have a good gut reaction about the team, product, market, vision, and so on, you're educated enough to understand the terms that you want to care about the most. There will always be debate, but you can see in the interviews that investments in companies with valuations that are too high were always in the negative category. None of the interviewees said, "I invested in this company at a really high valuation and still made out great." It may happen, but that's even more of a rarity than finding great companies at a great valuation.

David Bangs talks a lot about how he constructs deals differently than many other investors out there and he talks about why getting money back early is an advantage to both the companies he invests in and to himself as an investor. Understanding these alternative deal terms as well as the standard ones like pro-rata rights that Joanne Wilson goes into some depth on are important.

Most of the discussion in all of the interviews about investing in good deals centered on valuation. At the crux of all investing is investing at a good price. Every investor the world over understands that you have to buy low and sell high. If you thought investing early meant you were investing low, you're sorely mistaken. I encourage you to re-read the discussions on negotiating the right valuation and the different approaches to doing that negotiation. Most of the interviewees simply took the perspective of educating the entrepreneurs about the investment process that Bob Bozeman lays out so eloquently and then talked about what a fair valuation will be at each of those product milestones so that everyone makes money. If the entrepreneurs get too greedy, then perhaps this final filter caught something that should have been captured in one of the earlier filters but wasn't.

The other component of the deal is the timing. Is the timing right for you to be making an investment with the terms and conditions on the table? Some investors prefer terms that are less favorable in exchange for the ability to make an investment at a time that they prefer, when more risk is off the table for example. Similarly, is the timing right for this business? It could be a great deal, but if you can't answer the question, "Why now?" then there may be a problem.

Regardless of the type of investor you identify with the most, momentum, value, or alternative, there are a lot of ways you can optimize your investing style to be a better investor. If you're raising capital, it's good to identify the type of investor you're approaching as there will be different things that carry more weight depending on the investor type.

There are a lot of great resources out there to discover this stuff already. I've listed my favorites here. You'll find references to books, websites, and so on. All of the resources I have personally used or use on a regular basis. If it is a book that I am recommending, I've read it and a few others like it and have found the one that I am recommending the best of the ones I've read.

If it is an accelerator, I am mentioning it is because I have either engaged with the accelerator or you yourself have already read all about them and the investors there.

Accelerator Resources

Techstars — http://www.techstars.com/

Y Combinator — http://www.ycombinator.com/

SURGE — http://www.surgeaccelerator.com/

ValueStream Labs — http://www.valuestreamlabs.com/

Global Accelerator Network — http://gan.co/

AngelPad — http://angelpad.org/

9Mile Labs — http://www.9milelabs.com

Angel Resources

Angel Capital Association — http://www.angelcapitalassociation.org/

Angel Resource Institute — http://angelresourceinstitute.org/

Kauffman Foundation — http://www.kauffman.org/

CB Insights — https://www.cbinsights.com/

CrunchBase — http://www.crunchbase.com/

Mattermark — http://mattermark.com/

DataFox — http://www.datafox.co

Valleyball — http://valleyball.co/

Halo Report — http://www.angelresource.org/research/halo-report.aspx

VC Experts — https://vcexperts.com/

PitchBook — http://pitchbook.com/

StartupViz — http://startupviz.com

Angel Investing Research

Angel Investor Performance Project (AIPP) — http://sites.kauffman.org/aipp/

Center for Venture Research, Analysis Reports — https://paulcollege.unh.edu/research/center-venture-research/cvr-analysis-reports

Expected Returns to Stock Investments by Angel Investors in Groups — http://papers.ssrn.com/sol3/papers.cfm?abstract_id=1360817

Historical Size of the US Angel Market — http://www.rightsidecapital.com/assets/documents/HistoricalAngelSize.pdf

Note on Angel Investing — http://mba.tuck.dartmouth.edu/pdf/2002-5-0001.pdf

Returns to Angel Investors in Groups — http://papers.ssrn.com/sol3/papers.cfm?abstract_id=1028592

Review of Research on the Historical Returns of the US Angel Market — http://www.rightsidecapital.com/assets/documents/HistoricalAngelReturn.pdf

Siding with Angels — http://www.nesta.org.uk/publications/siding-angels

Startup Pre-money Valuation: The Keystone to Return on Investment — http://www.angelcapitalassociation.org/data/Documents/Resources/AngelCapitalEducation/ACEF_-_Valuing_Pre-revenue_Companies.pdf

Term Sheets and Financing

Techstars — http://www.techstars.com/docs/

YC Documents — http://www.ycombinator.com/resources/#documents

Angel Groups Discussed

Alliance of Angels — http://www.allianceofangels.com

Seattle Angel Conference — http://www.seattleangelconference.com

Launchpad Ventures Group — http://launchpadventuregroup.com

Central Texas Angel Network — http://centraltexasangelnetwork.com/

Element 8 — http://www.element8angels.com/

Tech Coast Angels — https://angel.co/tech-coast-angels

New York Angels — http://www.newyorkangels.com

Sand Hill Angels — http://www.sandhillangels.com/

Hub Angels — www.hubangels.com

Life Science Angels — http://lifescienceangels.com

Common Angels — http://commonangels.com

Venture Capital Groups Discussed

Union Square Ventures — http://www.usv.com

First Round Capital — http://firstround.com

Brooklyn Bridge Ventures — http://www.brooklynbridge.vc

Canary/Khosla Ventures — http://www.khoslaventures.com

Foundry Group — http://www.foundrygroup.com

500 Startups — http://500.co/

Founders' Co-op — http://www.founderscoop.com

Social Leverage — http://socialleveragellc.com

Blue Tree Applied Angels — http://www.bluetreealliedangels.com

Flybridge Capital Partners — http://flybridge.com

Techstars — http://www.techstars.com

What Areas Are Investors Trying To Invest In?

a16z — http://a16z.com/2015/01/22/16-things/

Homebrew — https://quip.com/rcLXASq4IbIj

Techstars — http://www.techstars.com/companies-techstars-wants-to-fund/

YC — http://www.ycombinator.com/rfs/

Online Early-Stage Investing

AngelList — https://angel.co/

SeedInvest — https://www.seedinvest.com/

OneVest — https://onevest.com/

DreamFunded — http://www.dreamfunded.com/

CircleUp — https://circleup.com/

SharesPost — http://sharespost.com/

MicroVentures — https://microventures.com/

FundersClub — https://fundersclub.com/

SeedUps — http://www.seedups.com/

WeFunder — https://wefunder.com/

FundRoom — https://www.fundroom.com/home?0

EarlyShares — http://www.earlyshares.com/

Crowdfunder — https://www.crowdfunder.com/

Fundable — https://www.fundable.com

Angel Group Software

Gust — http://gust.com/

Proseeder — http://proseeder.com/

Seraf — https://seraf-investor.com

Helpful Blogs

Fred Wilson — http://avc.com/

Brad Feld — http://www.feld.com

Mark Suster — http://www.bothsidesofthetable.com

A16z — http://a16z.com

Seraf Compass — https://seraf-investor.com/blog

Other Startup Resources

Startup America – http://s.co

Startup Weekend – http://startupweekend.org/

Global Entrepreneurship Program – http://www.state.gov/e/eb/cba/entrepreneurship/gep/programs/index.htm

Startup Next – http://www.startupnext.co/

Startup Genome – http://startupgenome.co/

World Startup Events – http://www.worldstartupevents.org/

Bijan's post on his four things – http://bijansabet.com/post/95169795918/four-things

Paul Graham post – http://paulgraham.com/before.html

GLOSSARY

A RECAP OR LONGER EXPLANATION for readers on a few of the terms mentioned in the book. I hope you can find the definitions and context useful in your learning.

409(a) valuation

Determining the valuation of the common stock so that more stock or other deferred compensation can be issued. The valuation can be set by the board, by the CEO or CFO, or by an independent third party.

Accelerators

Accelerators are programs that usually make a small capital investment along with a defined period of support and assistance with the business. Usually accelerators are three- to six-month programs and focus on driving customer-focused design and access to the top mentors and investors to develop a company that's investable.

Accredited

The Securities and Exchange Commission are the ones who define the accredited investor requirements. Currently, if you have $200,000 annually ($300,000 combined with your spouse) or have a net worth (excluding your primary residence) of over $1 million you're considered accredited by the SEC.

Acqui-Hire

The acquisition of a company for the purposes of hiring the people instead of for the purposes of accessing assets, technology, or customers.

Angel investor

The term *angel investing* comes from Broadway where passionate supporters of a show would rescue a production from financial doom and perhaps collect a healthy profit as a result. Investing in early-stage companies has been around since the first companies were created in the late 1800s. Jack Whitney was the first to formalize his angel investing activity into a venture fund and created what we know today as venture capital (a subset of private equity).

We've since married the term angel investing with the practice of investing in early-stage companies. Most angels in Europe take it a step further and refer to angel investing as "business angel investing" to differentiate it from "theater angel investing." In Asia, the term angel investing holds, though.

Angel investing is not inherently philanthropic, it is inherently capitalistic. The reason people get into angel investing may be because they are passionate about a particular idea; however, there's an expectation of a return on the investment for angel investors, regardless of whether they're investing in the next great Broadway show, a restaurant, sustainable farming, or wireless power.

Anti-dilution provisions

Anti-dilution provisions is a generic way to describe all of the provisions that could be included in an investment that would help to prevent dilution of the investor's ownership of the company. Usually, investors get diluted when new shares are added to the number of shares a company has issued and then sells those shares. The most common forms of these provisions are a full ratchet provision and a weighted average provision.

If an investor has a full ratchet provision, their shares are re-priced to the lower share price (regardless of how many new shares are issued). If an investor has a weighted average provision, the price per share as well as the number of shares are taken into account and the adjustments are made based on both of these factors.

Cap table

A cap table or capitalization table is really just a list of the shares in a company. All of the shares that people have purchased or been granted are listed there alongside all of the shares that have been set aside to grant later. Usually, there are a few different classes of shares listed (first there's common and preferred, and there are multiple types of preferred that are tied to the round of financing). Next to the shares that have been purchased are the dollar amounts paid. Next to the shares that have been granted are vesting schedules with how much has been vested and how much remains.

Often people discuss the problem of a messy cap table. This is the result of one of two problems.

The first is unaccredited investors who were allowed to finance the business early on. If any unaccredited investors are allowed into the business, the business is required to report on their business as though the business were a publicly traded entity, and even then, if the unaccredited investor loses his or her money there's a risk of real litigation being entertained by the courts.

The second is too many investors on the cap table. In reality, a business could accept hundreds of investors into the group of people financing the business. Imagine trying to figure out who owned what when the spreadsheet is hundreds of rows long.

Capitalization

The capitalization is the capital structure of the business, where the money came from and what was exchanged for that money. A business may have a capitalization that includes common and preferred stock as well as bonds or other debt instruments.

Carry (carried interest)

Carry is short for carried interest, which in itself makes no sense whatsoever. Unless you're familiar with the financial industry, carried interest makes no sense. It would be much better stated as management profits or share of profits, considering these two sentences mean the same thing: "Each of the general partners at the venture capital firm receive a portion of the management profits."

CBOE & CME Group

The Chicago Board Options Exchange is the public exchange where equity options are traded. Essentially all options for equities (stocks, ETFs, and so forth) are traded on the CBOE.

The Chicago Mercantile Exchange is the public exchange where options for everything else are traded. Essentially all options for everything not traded on the CBOE (Energy, commodities, and so forth) are traded on the CME.

Convertible equity

Convertible equity is preferred shares of company stock that convert on the next financing round to either preferred or common stock. The purpose of convertible equity is to reduce some of the problems with convertible notes, such as leaving a startup with too much debt on the balance sheet and making them technically insolvent.

Convertible equity carries many of the features of convertible notes, such as the ability to have a valuation cap, a discount, automatic conversation clauses, and optional conversion clauses. When you make an investment using convertible equity, you're buying preferred shares of the company. The trick is that regardless of what value you've placed on the company, you've also agreed to take the valuation at the next financing round, or if no future financing happens, your preferred shares persist or convert to common shares.

For some example documents that you can use, Y Combinator maintains a set of documents called SAFE (Simple Agreement for Future Equity) on their website ycombinator.com/documents. The original convertible equity documents are also available at convertibleequity.com.

Convertible note

With a convertible note you will be owed money for as long as you hold the note. The payment plan is written in the note and usually consists of interest payment accrual until the time that the note is converted into equity. In this way you get a small discount and are able to enter into a debt contract. The discount usually isn't enough to get excited about, so most convertible notes in 2014 also have a discount on the share price on conversion. This last part is based on the idea that because the money was invested early on it, it took more risk, and therefore should be compensated for that risk.

Crammed down

Being crammed down is just the natural result of a new investor buying new shares at a higher price/valuation. Essentially, if you own 10% of a company and the company takes on new investors with a new capital infusion at a higher valuation, your percentage ownership will be decreased because more equity is issued to those new investors.

This is different from what's colloquially referred to as dilution where new shares are being issued at a lower price so anti-dilution provisions won't really help here. The only way to combat being crammed down is to include pro-rata rights (pre-emptive rights) in your terms and then, most important, being willing to put up the cash to buy your pro-rata shares.

Crowdfunding

Crowdfunding is a poorly used term, often used to describe what's happening on websites like Kickstarter and Indiegogo. It is also used to describe what's happening on websites like AngelList and DreamFunded. Both are leveraging the capital of the crowd to fund an activity so in that regard they mean the same thing. Pre-sales campaigns like those on Kickstarter and Indiegogo are different from equity investments that take place on AngelList or SeedInvest.

The former is an example of a crowd who is pre-purchasing a product and then waiting a really long time and hoping that the company can actually develop and build the product. If they do build it, that's great, because the funders get the product; however, they don't participate in future growth.

The latter is an example of a crowd who is investing for equity and isn't purchasing any product. The crowd is waiting a really long time and perhaps making introductions, giving advice, and so on in the hopes that the company will grow and they can participate in the growth of that company.

Deal Lead

Angel groups will often refer to a deal lead as the person leading the due diligence on a possible deal.

Due Diligence

Due diligence is the art and science of figuring out if it makes sense to invest. There are all sorts of things that people include during due diligence, some have lists, some have their gut, some spend ten minutes, and some spend 20 to 40 hours. Rob Wiltbank and Warren Boeker's work on investor returns to groups http://papers.ssrn.com/sol3/papers.cfm?abstract_id=1028592 indicates that 20 to 40 hours of due diligence lead to a better return, but due diligence above 40 hours doesn't lead to better results.

Eats

Marc Andreesen and venture capital firm a16z coined this term, referring to software "eating the world"—basically, software that will change the way everything in the world works. An example would be "software eats bookstores," as in how Amazon, at its beginning, was "just" a company using software that would change the nature of bookstores.

Employee Stock Option Plan

Employee stock options plans are contracts between a company and its employees that give employees the right to buy a specific number of the company's shares at a fixed price within a certain period of time. The fixed price is often called the grant or exercise price. Employees who are granted stock options hope to profit by exercising their options to buy shares at the exercise price when the shares are trading at a price that's higher than the exercise price.

Exits

This is a reference to how angel investors bow out of a startup situation—as in exit strategy.

Finra

Finra is the Financial Industry Regulatory Authority, the main entity that creates and enforces disciplinary rules within the securities markets. If you're buying or selling securities (public or private) and there's a third party involved, you need to understand how they're regulated and if they're in good standing with their regulator. The tests that mean the most to angel investors today are the following:

Series 7 — General Securities Representatives. This is essentially a license to sell any securities (public or private).

Series 85 — Securities Representatives. This is very similar to Series 7, but only for private securities. People who are licensed with a Series 85 test under their belt can only sell private companies and not public ones (many employees of equity crowdfunding platforms are required to have this license).

Series 65 — Registered Investment Advisor

See NASAA.

Series 63 — broker/dealer

See NASAA.

Full Ratchet

See Anti-Dilution Provisions.

GP (General Partner)

The GP is generally a partner in a venture fund who is making the decisions about what companies to invest in and is collecting carried interest for this service. They are the owners of the partnership with unlimited liability. A general partner is also commonly a managing partner, which means that this person is active in the day-to-day operations of the business. Because any partner in a general partnership can act on behalf of the entire business without the knowledge or permission of the other partners, being a general partner offers poor asset protection.

Information Rights

Right to financial and other information relating to the company, such as quarterly and annual income statements, balance sheets, cash flow statements. Information could also include budgets and budget reconciliations, a dashboard of key metrics as well as notices of material litigation.

Intrastate Crowdfunding

This is just crowdfunding (meaning selling private securities to non-accredited investors) rules and regulations at the state level. States are allowed to implement their own crowdfunding rules so long as the company operates within the state and all of the investors reside in the state.

Interstate Crowdfunding

This is the crowdfunding (meaning selling private securities to non-accredited investors) that everyone is really excited about. Any company in any state selling securities to non-accredited investors in any state.

Liquidation Preference

When thinking about liquidation preference, it is important to also understand participation preference.

Liquidation preference is how much of a return the preferred shareholder receives before common shareholders receive anything.

This can be 1x (the current norm so that the preferred shareholder at least gets their money back before any common shareholders get anything) all the way up to any number the VC wants (could be 2x, 3x, 10x, and so on).

Participation preference is how much of the proceeds after all the debt and preferred shareholders are paid are shared by those preferred shareholders. This can be full participating (each preferred share gets just as much on pro-rata basis as each common share), capped participating (each preferred share gets just as much on a pro-rata basis as each common share up to a pre-defined multiple), or non-participating (each preferred share gets none of the profits after the liquidation preference is satisfied).

Some caution to understand here. If you're an early investor and are going to end up with a 2x liquidity preference and no participation preference, your $25,000 investment will only ever be worth $50,000, regardless of how great the company does. This may be great if you barely squeezed that extra $25,000 out before the proceeds from the liquidity event were used up. This may not be great if all the common shareholders wound up with 10x their investment because there was so much money left over after paying preferred shareholders.

LLC (Limited Liability Company)

This is the easiest corporate formation to use when pooling funds to make an investment. It is sometimes used by companies that take investment; however, that's less common for growth-oriented startups and more common for non-growth (flat cash flow generating) startups. It is technically a company whose owners and managers enjoy limited liability and some tax benefits, but avoid some restrictions associated with S corporations. The tax benefits are why it is bad for growth (an investor may report some pretty major losses on their taxes the first few years and then have to report their share of the huge upside) and good for flat (pass-through losses and profits are a non-issue).

LP (Limited Partner)

If you're investing in a venture fund of any kind and aren't the person calling the shots and getting the carried interest, you're likely a partner in a company or venture who receives limited profits from the business and whose liability toward its debts is legally limited to the extent of his or her investment. Basically, you aren't taking any risk (liability), but you're providing the cash.

NASAA (North American Securities Administrators Association)

NASAA is really the association of state securities regulators. They are designed to mirror what FINRA does, but at the state level. Each state has their own per-state rules. In most cases these are uniform across the country (as with most commercial laws), but there are a few cases where a state may vary from the standard. Any person giving investment advice for payment (regardless of who's paying for the advice, the issuer, the advice recipient, or a third party) must take and pass a test outlined by NASAA.

Series 65 — Registered Investment Advisor. This is an exam that qualifies the examinee to advise clients on the best investments to make. They have a fiduciary responsibility with their clients and must consider each client's situation in order to offer advice.

Series 63 — Broker/Dealer. This exam qualifies the examinee to sell securities. The exam itself is on state law and regulation surrounding selling securities.

NASDAQ

NASDAQ manages several exchanges, including being the first company to build a fully electronic exchange. The term "NASDAQ" came from their first exchange created in 1971 by the National Association of Securities Dealers (NASD), which named that first exchange "National Association of Securities Dealers Automated Quotation." Today, NASDAQ continues to list more than 3,400 companies and recently has been working with companies such as SharesPost to begin work to cross the access barrier between private and public investments.

Beyond these functions, NASDAQ operates a number of markets throughout the world.

Net Worth

Net worth is a simple term that's calculated by adding up all of your assets and subtracting all of your debts. For the purposes of the SEC's definition of Accredited Investor, this calculation excludes the value of your private residence. So if you have $500,000 in cash/stocks, $1 million in equity in your home, and $50,000 in debt, your net worth would be $1.45 million, yet you wouldn't qualify as an accredited investor based on your net worth because the SEC would exclude the $1 million equity in your home. Luckily, the SEC also has a provision for salary.

See Accredited for more information.

OTC markets

Over-the-counter markets are markets with no centralized physical location. Trades occur via the telephone, bulletin board systems, and so on. OTC Markets Group runs the main marketplaces in this space and don't operate as a stock exchange. OTC Markets Group runs OTCQX, OTCQB, and OTC Pink marketplaces. Most of the 10,000 securities traded here have smaller market caps than those listed on the major exchanges (such as NASDAQ) or they don't meet the listing requirements of the major exchanges. It is easier for a private company to go public and trade on the OTC marketplaces; however, the amount of capital that could be raised is generally much smaller, and often investors will question why a new high growth–oriented company would attempt to raise capital through an OTC marketplace and incur the overhead of SEC regulated reporting for public companies instead of simply continue funding via private means.

Participation Preference

See Liquidation Preference.

Portfolio

Most of the references in this book refer to portfolio as the portfolio of startup companies versus the overall portfolio of an individual's investments. Occasionally, we discussed what percentage of an overall portfolio is allocated to early stage. In most cases, this allocation was under 10%, but a few folks such as Mike Crill and Semyon Dukach (whose profile is online) have allocated 100% or more of their entire portfolio to early-stage investments.

Power Law

The concept of power law distributions really boils down to outsized impact by a small number of items in the group. Concepts that are usually discussed relating to the power law are things like the 80/20 rule and other Pareto distributions. When thinking about what in our lives follow power laws, we can think about wealth distribution (the richest make a lot more than the average), car exhaust (a few cars are the worst offenders), and of course returns to early-stage portfolios. In 1993, Warren Buffett described it as:

"…If significant risk exists in a single transaction, overall risk should be reduced by making that purchase one of many mutually independent commitments. Thus, you may consciously purchase a risky investment—one that indeed has a significant possibility of causing loss or injury—if you believe that your gain, weighted for probabilities, considerably exceeds your loss, comparably weighted, and if you can commit to a number of similar, but unrelated opportunities. Most venture capitalists employ this strategy. Should you choose to pursue this course, you should adopt the outlook of the casino that owns a roulette wheel, which will want to see lots of action because it is favored by probabilities, but will refuse to accept a single, huge bet."

PPM (Private Placement Memorandum)

This is really the document that outlines the investment of a private stock offering. It lays out for the prospective client almost all the details of an investment opportunity. The principal purpose of this document is to give the company the opportunity to present all potential risks to the investor. A Private Placement Memorandum is in fact a plan for the company. It plainly identifies the nature and purpose of the company.

Preemptive Rights (Pro rata)

In many of the interviews and conversations, this term is referred to as "pro rata" in the context of the right to invest more. More specifically, the term "pro-rata rights" is also short for what ends up in the contract as pre-emptive rights. So let's back up a little bit on the definition. *Pro rata* really just means proportional. The Oxford dictionary has the example "as the dollar has fallen, costs have risen on a pro-rata basis."

If an investor has pre-emptive rights, they have the right to purchase shares to maintain a pro-rata percentage of ownership on a future financing round. If you own 10% of the company as a Series A investor and you have pre-emptive rights, you're allowed to purchase up to 10% of the company at the Series B round. Granted, this could be incredibly expensive, but it could also mean a much bigger payday. You'll notice than many of the investors require this as a part of their investment strategy, even if they only invest more money on a pro-rata basis one or two times after their initial investment.

Protective Rights

Provisions that require the approval of a majority (or supermajority) of a series (or multiple series) of preferred shareholders before certain actions can be taken by the company. Some examples of protective provisions include amending the certificate of incorporation and bylaws, a repurchase or redemption of shares of stock, a material change in the nature of the company's business, a change in the size of the board of directors, the issuance of a superior class of securities, and the liquidation, dissolution, and winding up of the company. Typically, the preferred stock (or series) will approve separately and then may vote with the common stock as a single class on any matter requiring common stock vote except as otherwise specifically required by the certificate of incorporation or applicable law.

Put provision

Another way to refer to Redemption Rights.

Redemption Rights

The investor's right to require the company redeem its shares at a point in the future (that is, five years) normally at the greater of the purchase price or the FMV (which can be determined by a formula, the board, or an independent appraisal of the business).

Reg D (Regulation D)

Under the Securities Act of 1933, any offer to sell securities must either be registered with the SEC or meet an exemption. Regulation D (or Reg D) contains three rules providing exemptions from the registration requirements, allowing some companies to offer and sell their securities without having to register the securities with the SEC.

While companies using a Reg D exemption don't have to register their securities and usually don't have to file reports with the SEC, they must file what's known as a "Form D" after they first sell their securities. Form D is a brief notice that includes the names and addresses of the company's executive officers and stock promoters, but contains little other information about the company. If you're thinking about investing in a Reg D company, you should access the EDGAR database to determine whether the company has filed Form D.

Rule 504 of Regulation D provides an exemption from the registration requirements of the federal securities laws for some companies when they offer and sell up to $1 million of their securities in any 12-month period. This is not commonly used by startups. See http://www.sec.gov/answers/rule504.htm for more information.

Rule 505 of Regulation D allows companies offering their securities to have those securities exempted from the registration requirements of the federal securities laws. This is not commonly used by startups. See http://www.sec.gov/answers/rule505.htm for more information.

Rule 506 of Regulation D allows companies to raise without limit so long as they follow the guidelines for accepting investments from accredited investors, registrations, and solicitation. This is the most common exemption used by startups. See http://www.sec.gov/answers/rule506.htm for more information.

Registration Rights

This is simply the investor's right to force the company, after a period of time, to register the investor's shares and offer them publicly, or to include them as part of a registration and public offering made by the company or a management stockholder. In other words, getting the company to include the investor's shares for sale on the public market just as they have done with their own common shares. Each class of issued preferred shares would need to have its own registration rights. This may mean that some shares never get registered by the company. If the company doesn't handle the registration, it is usually too costly for the investors to register them by themselves.

Restricted Securities

"Restricted" securities are those acquired in an unregistered, private sale from the issuing company or from an affiliate of the issuer. They typically bear a "restrictive" legend clearly stating that you may not resell them in the public marketplace unless the sale is exempt from the SEC's registration requirements.

Rule 144 under the Securities Act of 1933 provides the most commonly used exemption for holders to sell restricted securities. See http://www.sec.gov/investor/pubs/rule144.htm for more information.

Rule 504, 505, and 506 of Regulation D

See Reg D.

SEC (Securities and Exchange Commission)

The SEC was formed in 1934 in response to the crash in 1929 to protect investors. This includes public and private investors.

Series A, B, C, and so on

This is just the way that financing has been organized since the early days of investing in new companies. Basically, each series represents some milestone or accomplishment that helps the company move to the next place on the board.

The terms "Series A," "Series B," and so on refer to the actual shares of the company that are being purchased. Each series of shares can be organized a little differently with different terms that all the investors in that round share. What can happen is that a later investor can set up terms that aren't favorable to an earlier investor and thus make it difficult for those earlier investors. For example, a Series D or E investor can really change the structure of the company (disproportionate board seats, for example) and if the capital raise is approved despite objections by a seed or Series A investor, there's nothing that can be done.

Some investors get particular about how much money a company should be raising at each of these and other metrics. This evolves over time; however, the principle of having a ladder of capital inflows that are tied to company milestones and growth stages remains the key goal.

Side letter

Some investors love side letters while others hate side letters. Basically, a side letter sits outside of the structure of the deal. It is a letter that outlines an agreement or clarifies some terms in the actual sales agreement that indicates additional parameters. Commonly, there are things like pro rata buried in these as well as a few other areas that would benefit an early investor and perhaps be wiped out by a later investor. The goal of the side letter is to not let an investor come into the company later on and take away some part of the pie that an earlier investor intended to have.

Supra Pro Rata

If an investor has supra pro-rata rights, they have the ability to purchase more than their pro-rata share on future financing rounds. Refer back to pro rata for what a pro-rata right is and you'll better understand supra pro rata. An example would be if I have pro-rata rights and I purchased 10% of the company in the

Series A, I could purchase enough shares to always maintain 10% ownership of the company (well as long as I could afford it). If you had supra pro-rata rights and you also purchased 10% of the company in the Series A, you would be allowed to purchase more than 10% of the company on future financing rounds. How much more? Depends on the deal, but it could be 1.5x or more. If you had 2x supra pro rata, you could purchase up to 20% of the company during the Series B.

Stock Purchase Agreement

Agreement between a company and its shareholders for regulating the sale and transfer of firm's shares. It covers items such as who has the right of first refusal and provides a mechanism for the purchase (redemption) of the shares of the shareholder who becomes bankrupt, is discharged, resigns, retires, becomes incapacitated, or dies.

Syndicate

Generally speaking, this is just a group of people who work together toward a common outcome. For the purposes of early-stage investing, it is really a collection of investors who work together to fund a company. If multiple investors invested but didn't work together to do so, it wouldn't be called a syndicate.

Term Sheet

Really, this is an offer of terms to invest in a company. It isn't binding so it is a useful point of discussion. Sometimes entrepreneurs have a term sheet they shop around to get investors to sign onto and other times the investors offer a term sheet and compete with each other on the best term sheet. The earlier the company is, the more likely they'll be raising from a few parties who don't know each other and that often leads to different term sheets being used or the entrepreneur shopping their term sheet around to multiple investors.

VC (Venture Capital)

This is really just the sub-set, a small sub-set, of the private equity industry that focuses on investing in private early-stage ventures. John Hay (Jock) Whitney started J. H. Whitney & Co in 1946 for the purpose of venture investing and proceeded to invest in all sorts of private companies and early-stage startups. He eventually got bored and hired Benno Schmidt to run the firm. All the stories of these rich guys starting funds ended up this way: they put in a bunch of money, had some friends put in money, invested in things they had an interest in, and then got bored and hired someone else to run it.

Venture Debt

Venture debt funding provides emerging, venture-backed companies with the additional capital needed for equipment and infrastructure build out, as well as expansion into new business markets. Traditionally, venture debt follows closely to a round of venture capital funding, lengthening the intervals an emerging company needs to raise additional venture capital investments.

See Fred Wilson's blog to learn more:
http://avc.com/2011/07/financings-options-venture-debt/

Warrants

A stock warrant is just like a stock option because it gives you the right to purchase a company's stock at a specific price and at a specific date. However, a stock warrant differs from an option in two key ways:

A stock warrant is issued by the company itself.

New shares are issued by the company for the transaction. Unlike a stock option, a stock warrant is issued directly by the company. When a stock option is exercised, the shares usually are received or given by one investor to another; when a stock warrant is exercised, the shares that fulfill the obligation aren't received from another investor, but directly from the company.

Companies issue stock warrants to raise money. When stock options are bought and sold, the company that owns the stocks doesn't receive any money from the transactions. However, a stock warrant is a way for a company to raise money through equity (stocks). A stock warrant is a smart way to own shares of a company because a warrant usually is offered at a price lower than that of a stock option. The longest term for an option is two to three years, while a stock warrant can last for up to 15 years. So, in many cases, a stock warrant can prove to be a better investment than a stock option if mid- to long-term investments are what you seek.

506(a), 506(b), 506(c)

See Reg D.

83b

Under Section 83 of the Internal Revenue Code, the founder/employee wouldn't recognize income (the difference between fair market value and the price paid) until the stock vests. However, if a founder/employee makes a voluntary Section 83(b) election, the founder/employee recognizes income upon the purchase of the stock.

APPENDIX: MICHAEL DE LA MAZA'S MENTORSHIP MANIFESTO

WHEN DAVID COHEN, the driving force behind Techstars, created the Mentor Manifesto—a document intended to break down the mentoring process and communicate the Techstars mentoring philosophy—he not only set down the basic ideas in ways that are easily understood, but he created a standard for all Techstars mentors and is applicable to anyone interested in mentoring startups. The manifesto has had such a profound effect on me that I wanted to break down the 18 points and expand a bit on what each one means to me in the context of my own experiences and related endeavors in leadership, coaching, motivation, and mentorship.

01. Be Socratic.

"Be Socratic" comes first in the manifesto. Without it, everything else in the manifesto doesn't have the proper base needed for the mentor/mentee relationship. According to Wikipedia, the Socratic method is "a form of inquiry and discussion between individuals, based on asking and answering questions to stimulate critical thinking and to illuminate ideas."

The give and take of being Socratic allows ideas and plans to grow organically into the best solution, goal, or product possible and with the best possible foundation supporting it. An organically created idea is also the most supported idea in the long run.

Two of my favorite questions to ask entrepreneurs are, "What success would make everything else easy?" and "What evidence do you have that supports your opinion?" These questions help unravel the underlying logic of the startup and increase the entrepreneur's understanding of the strengths and weaknesses of their current course of action.

02. Expect nothing in return (you'll be delighted with what you get back).

Horace Mann wrote: "Doing nothing for others is the undoing of ourselves." When mentoring, expecting something in return is a business transaction, not mentorship.

A mentor gives freely of their time and skill. You give and don't expect anything in return.

Being a mentor is not a paid position. Mentors should not attempt to sell services to companies they are mentoring and they should not expect to receive stock in return for being a mentor.

I have heard of situations in which mentors have effectively asked for stock or an advisory position in exchange for continued mentoring. This behavior is inconsistent with the ethics of mentorship.

03. Be authentic and practice what you preach.

On a fundamental level, if a mentee doesn't see a mentor "walk the walk," when they "talk the talk" then whatever advice, skills, or knowledge the mentor is offering will fall on deaf ears.

A capable mentor is the real thing. One of the hallmarks of authenticity is a proven record of substance and results. An engaged mentee is more than willing to be led by example; if the mentor is acting un-authentically, the risk is that the mentee will lose trust. A mentor should genuinely share life experiences, warts and all. A mentor shouldn't paper over their own failings.

04. Be direct. Tell the truth, however hard.

Effective mentors fight the temptation to be nice. In the end, the entrepreneur and the company are harmed when the mentor sugarcoats the truth.

If the mentee, for whatever reason, doesn't understand basic facts about startups or has unrealistic expectations, the mentee is unlikely to improve if the mentor is not completely truthful and direct about the mistakes the mentee is making.

Over time, the mentor should seek to improve the way that the mentee thinks so that the mentee can discover the truth on their own. As the novelist E.M. Forster says, "Spoon feeding in the long run teaches us nothing but the shape of the spoon."

Telling the truth also means being completely open about your own failings and shortcomings. If you don't know something, say you don't know. If you failed at something, admit it. If you aren't an expert in an area, say so.

05. Listen too.

You have two ears and one mouth for a reason. In Johnny Hart's comic strip *B.C.*, there's a running gag that involves an advice booth. One such strip says, "Never ask a question to a person who knows all the answers." In other words, don't ask a know-it-all.

If the mentor isn't listening for what the problem is, how can they help solve the problem, and if they aren't listening, how are they really a mentor?

I find that listening for the "problem under the problem" can be extremely helpful.

Your experience may guide a mentee to a better solution. But without listening to the mentee's perspectives, tin-eared experience can sour the mentee's enthusiasm, and as a result, the relationship suffers.

Again, the Socratic method is defined as "a form of inquiry and discussion between individuals, based on asking and answering questions to stimulate critical thinking and to illuminate ideas."

06. The best mentor relationships eventually become two-way.

Every time a mentor relationship has lasted more than a year, I have learned an enormous amount from my mentee. Indeed, since my experience as an entrepreneur occurred in the late 1990s and early 2000s, I depend on mentees to help me better understand what's going on today when it comes to both technology and investing.

My wish is that every mentee relationship will eventually become a two-way relationship of equals.

07. Be responsive.

Assuming a person is clearly committed to the mentor/mentee relationship, being responsive is straightforward but often difficult to implement. Being responsive also encapsulates many of the other 18 manifesto points, but unlike the ethics of being a mentor, being responsive is in part about taking action with urgency.

For example, it's okay not to know something, but if you're going to follow up on getting an answer, the person must actually do so and in an appropriate amount of time. This demonstrates a person's commitment to the relationship and the agreed-upon goals, and demonstrates there is actual listening going on between parties.

Although it may seem trivial, getting the process set around this is enormously important. Is your phone programmed to interrupt you only when there's an emergency? Is your email sorted so that critical messages from key people are highlighted? Do all of the people around you know what's important to you and what isn't?

I have never canceled a meeting with a mentee and when a mentee is working through a significant issue, such as funding, I make sure that my systems and my schedule help me be responsive.

08. Adopt at least one company every single year. Experience counts.

I've mentored during two Techstars Boston batches and I've done the same thing each time: I sign up to meet companies for 30 minutes during mentor madness and then I continue speaking to one or two companies who want me as a mentor during and after the three-month session. During mentor madness I interact with most of the companies in the batch and learn about which ones are a good fit. Mentor madness occurs during the first two weeks of the batch, and Techstars helps to set up the 30-minute meetings.

If I find a good fit during mentor madness, the entrepreneurs and I set up regular meetings. Typically, I meet with entrepreneurs from once a week to once a quarter. Working regularly with entrepreneurs serves to build up my mentoring skills over time. I also speak with other Techstars mentors with the goal of improving my mentoring skills.

09. Clearly separate opinion from fact.

It is far too easy for a mentor to speak ex cathedra and blur the line between opinion and fact. And it is even easier to turn a fact (for example, "Series A funding is down 10% from last year") into an opinion ("Series A funding is harder to get now").

As I mentor, I've had to school myself on being explicit about the difference between opinions and facts. As a mentor, one of my goals is to support entrepreneurs in finding the critical facts that drive their business. I do that best by making sure that I don't turn my opinions into facts, which I then try to sell to the entrepreneur.

10. Hold information in confidence.

Mentees often share private company and personal information with mentors that must be kept in complete confidence. Even indirect statements that don't divulge confidential information, such as "That company is not making as much progress as I would like" can be extremely harmful.

Gossip betrays confidence and, therefore, breaks trust. There's also a practical side to holding information in confidence: It keeps you out of trouble personally, professionally, and financially.

You're treated as you act, so if you don't want to be gossiped about, don't gossip.

11. Clearly commit to mentor or don't. Either is fine.

Entrepreneurs are awash in ambiguity. Don't add to it by being unclear about whether you're a mentor.

I address this potential issue by simply pointing to this item in the manifesto and asking, “Do you want me to mentor you?” If an entrepreneur doesn’t want to be mentored by you, don’t force them to give you an explanation. Let them go. Anything besides that will often cause ambiguity to creep into the relationship. The entrepreneur might say, for example, that they would enjoy chatting with you occasionally, which then makes your level of commitment and responsibility unclear.

12. Know what you don't know. Say you don't know when you don't know. "I don't know" is preferable to bravado.

I don’t trust people who never say, “I don’t know.” I doubt that entrepreneurs do either.

Your mentee will respect you more and trust your answers if you’re willing to admit you don't know something. Not knowing something but willing to do due diligence to find the correct answer and follow up with the person is a sign of respect and willingness to collaborate to a mutually beneficial solution.

The mentee may not know as much as the experienced mentor, but that doesn't mean the mentor has all the answers either. Experience doesn’t equal having all the answers, given the vastness of the startup world.

13. Guide, don't control. Teams must make their own decisions. Guide but never tell them what to do. Understand that it's their company, not yours.

I don’t control because I genuinely believe that I don’t know what’s best for the entrepreneur or the company. Even if I somehow knew what was best for me in the entrepreneur’s situation, the entrepreneur is a different person and what works best for me may not work best for them.

What I can do is to give my best guidance and then support the entrepreneur in making that guidance their own. And I can hope that in making my guidance their own, the entrepreneur will improve upon it and achieve things that I can’t imagine.

14. Accept and communicate with other mentors that get involved.

A mentor should never impart to their mentee that their way is the only way of thinking about things or accomplishing goals. The mentor must not try to set the precedent or lock the mentee into a paradigm in which the mentor's way is the only way. The better mentors are lifelong students of entrepreneurship and accept the ideas and strategies of other mentors that get involved in their process. The mentoring arrangement depends on the mentee's willingness toward being open to new or different ideas; if the mentor accepts and communicates with other mentors in this setting, it will reinforce to the mentee that you as a mentor are authentic.

I have found my relationships with other mentors to be absolutely invaluable. And I work on growing and nourishing these relationships.

15. Be optimistic.

The relationship between mentor and mentee begins on a positive note: they've both chosen each other. The mentee comes into the arrangement with the understanding that the individual who's to impart their own unique mixture of knowledge and wisdom is there to do so for both the mentee's individual benefit and for the success of the overall company.

The mentee is already in the state of mind where they are halfway there and are ready and willing to accelerate their company's progress.

Startups can be crushingly depressing. The variance encountered in a startup greatly exceeds that encountered by an employee at any large company. Being optimistic is essential to overcoming the inevitable downturns.

16. Provide specific actionable advice. Don't be vague.

If a mentee walks out of a conversation confused about what the mentor said, that's a huge miss. Startups are hard enough without falling prey to misunderstandings and misinterpretations.

Mentors can coach entrepreneurs to ask, "Just to make sure, what exactly are you proposing?" whenever they are confused.

I have found that writing clear, actionable statements on a whiteboard and following up with an email works wonders. I often ask, "What do you plan to do?" followed by, "How will I know you have done it?" These questions set up a feedback loop that quickly identifies issues when they occur.

17. Be challenging/robust but never destructive.

There's a difference between being honest and being brutal. There's a difference between having high standards and being unkind.

When a mentee is having difficulty, one of the least productive things a mentor can do is to enhance that difficulty by accentuating the negatives. It is imperative that the mentor break down the issue with the mentee, see what's not working, and work together to fix the issue. Once the solution is found, reinforce the correction so that the mentee will perform to the best of their abilities as a result.

18. Have empathy. Remember that startups are hard.

It's the grandchild who claims the grandparent doesn't know what it's like to be their age, and the grandparent responds, "I've been your age. Times have changed, but people don't."

Startups are hard and plenty of mistakes are going to be made. The best thing about a mentee is that they're as fearless as they are ignorant.

Entrepreneurs are ready to make their mark in their chosen endeavor because they're not bound by the past.

A good mentor will guide, not control. An experienced mentor won't nitpick, but will be able to see a direction the mentee appears to be heading in, and if that direction is a perilous one, the mentor will help steer them to a better path.

In the mentor/mentee relationship, there isn't anything more encouraging and helpful to a mentee than a mentor saying, "You've got a great idea, you're making great progress, but before you make a mistake, you may want to…"

The mentor knows what the entrepreneur is going through during the startup period. No one person can foresee every pitfall and problem that may arise, but a mentor is there to help the entrepreneur succeed and has the experience and wisdom to help startups better avoid typical problems.

The overall idea of the mentor and mentee relationship is simple and if adhered to the dynamic should both be straightforward and produce the desired result. The mentor manifesto serves to give us guidelines for the mentor/mentee relationship in general and how it applies to entrepreneurship in particular. It enhance the capabilities of the experienced mentor through insights and application. As David Cohen shows us in theory and in practice, these tenets aren't only time-tested but fresh; steadfast with room for flexibility; and geared toward enriching the arc of the mentoring process that will yield spiritual, intellectual, emotional, and material results. Keep it simple and straightforward; be open to other ideas and improvement; be patient, optimistic, direct and truthful but nurturing and with an eye toward greatness; if one gives all as well as commits to the mentor relationship and expects nothing in return as the manifesto states, "relationships blossom and companies flourish."